MAKE THESE MOVIES NOW!

I would like to thank all my friends and family that inspired me throughout the years. The list is too large to mention everyone, but I would like to point out a few key figures in my life.

To my immediate family: Marge, James, Mark, Steve, Eric, Karen, Raven, Maureen and Dave—thank you.

I would also like to thank all that inspired my writing in these four screenplays: Dave Mixx, Uncle Sean Cullinane, Skipper (Nick Macadam), Mark Brown, Sophie Urbain, Ben Magic, Kate (The Stone Lady), Verdun Grey, Pepe Loco, Kenyon Alveres, Marc van Herpen, Ester Hann, Radio Active Rob, Jochem, Chrissy Ray, Mary (Poppins), Wilson Bezerra, Christine Kim, Jose Nunez, Uncle Jack, Jose (Joseph Wick), Paul Ferrio, JoJo, Chucky Tulum, Kai, Meghan, Mary, Wanda, Sam, Darren, Jennifer, Georgina, Robert, Sandy, Tom Prentice, Raven Idd, Rick, Kathleen, Paula, Stripes, Greg Pastor, Lucero, Karen, Lilly, Peg, Rene, Renzo, Steve Parento, The Hudson Valley Bee Co, Tommy, Bob, Billy, Cheryl, Patty, Lenny, Bo, Keith, Lorri, Dreeg, Antonio, Yukari, Carl, Ronnie Wood, Neil, Michael, Alison, John, Kelly, Laura, Jennifer, Kay, Sabina, David Bowie, Stacey, Glenn, Gaby, Daren, Iggy Pop, Fritz, Jill, Karin, Robert, Rocco, Julian, Terry, Matt, Jenny, Anna, Dylan, Buzz, Penny, Joe Pesci, Shelly, Scott, Mike. If you're not in the list it only means you inspired me in other writings, but not these four screenplays.

A special thanks Michelle Cheripka with the production and realization of this book: www.michellecheripka.com

Glenn Tripp
973-390-5797

Glenn Tripp contact: artistjetboy@yahoo.com
trippmixxtv@gmail.com
www.trippmixxtv.com

Book Design: David Clark Perry

ISBN 979-8-755-17953-9
Registered with the Library of Congress:
1-10567294021
Registered with the Writers Guild of America West:
2126610-2126611-2126612-2126616

Printed in the United Staes of America.

Limited First Edition 2021

Glowing with excitement while rubbing the sacred "Tree of Hope" at the Apollo Theater.

ABOUT THE AUTHOR

Glenn Tripp was born one of eight children in Paterson, New Jersey. His older siblings introduced him to theatre, film, television, music and the fine arts. Fresh out of high school, Glenn dove straight into the theatre world building sets and props with his brother, Eric.

After many years working off-Broadway and on summer stock, dinner theatre, and regional theatre, Glenn gravitated towards the art department in the film and television industries. Feeling quite blessed to have gotten the opportunity to experience these theatre, film, and tv in a short period of time, Glenn delved into studying these different script formats to keep his creative juices flowing.

In between gigs, Glenn studied Mime and guitar while doing stand up comedy to prepare himself for his unknown journey into the entertainment world.

While gaining confidence as he established himself in the entertainment industry, he grew bored with his living situation in Williamsburg, Brooklyn. After a brief stint in Los Angeles, Glenn relocated to Europe.

While living in Holland, Glenn created a lucrative business making, designing, and selling women's hats. In Glenn's spare time, he jammed with local musicians and became a radio personality for a local pirate radio station.

Feeling like the pieces of his life were falling in place, Glenn called his brother Raven to join him in Europe. Upon Raven's arrival, Glenn was awe-inspired by his musical and creative talents. With Raven's creative influence driving Glenn, they both brainstormed a musical act to create Glenn's first band experience, aptly named the Exploding Bedroom. Busking and booking venues throughout Europe opened Glenn's eyes to a plethora of experiences and stories that enhanced his versatile writings and creative inner being.

While enjoying the busking-gypsy lifestyle at the time, Glenn and Raven put their heads together again to create musical playing marionettes. This new artistic medium made traveling Europe a whole new experience which further enhanced the creative juices flowing through Glenn's veins.

Doug Moore interviewing me for the Public Access New Jersey show *Freak TV*.

In addition to writing poetry, comedy and assorted stories, Glenn added songwriting to his arsenal of tricks. After a handful of years living in Europe, Glenn left Raven behind and decided to move back to New York. There, he created a variety of musical acts that he performed at a multitude of venues including CBGB, Apollo Theatre, Apple Rock Music Festival, and Woodstock '98.

At this time, Glenn joined forces with his brother, Dave, to create the event production company, Tripp Mixx Productions. Twenty-five years in the making, Tripp Mixx became a lucrative and reputable event production company servicing the New York fashion, art and event industries.

With Tripp Mixx in full swing, it gave Glenn the financial opportunity to pursue his passion for gypsy-travel which created more content for his creative writings.

With nearly 40 years to date, Glenn has been exploring his artistic world of free expression without holding back.

This book of 4 raw, unedited screenplays sets the current stage for Glenn's creative thinking and generates 11 more established sequel screenplays from the content of these pages.

So grab a cup of tea, start reading, and enjoy the experience.

Left to right: Orlando, Raven, Brown, and me. While busking our handmade marionettes in Tilburg, Holland, Brown broke a string on the bass player's right hand, Raven tells him to get off the stage and take his broken puppet with him.

Marionette operator shows he's no Idiot

Despite monicker puppeteer proves quite successful

By JENNIFER L. WHITNEY

PARAMUS — Adhering to the old "sticks and stones" adage, one Paramus resident prefers to be called by a name most would find objectionable.

But for reasons known only to himself, Raven Idiot refuses to go by any other name. While he admits "Raven Idiot" is not his given name, he won't reveal what his parents first called him. He's used to stringing people along. It's his profession.

Well, he doesn't exactly string along *real* people.

He plays with marionettes.

Idiot, 33, has been working at every aspect of his craft for the past five years. He designs and constructs his own marionettes, writes scripts for his shows, and oversees the entire production.

Marionette, a word that was

allow their use in the church, these shows became a popular form of street entertainment.

Raven's interest in the art of marionette performance became piqued while he was living in Europe performing in an acoustical act. He said he was impressed with the live street acts because "anything a human can do, a marionette can do." Unlike the United States, streets shows are commonplace in European countries.

"It's a lot more art oriented there," explained Idiot. "New York City is supposed to be a city for the arts, but when you try to do the same thing (as in Europe) there, officials chase you away. Why make it difficult for people who want to break into this type of trade?"

The marionettes, controlled by a small wooden frame with strings attached to the base and various body parts, is comprised of assorted materials: wood, plastics, oil paints, fabric, and string. According to Idiot, marionettes are often con-

Raven Idiot, second from left, with fellow puppeteers Glenn Tripp, Dave Mixx, and Mark Brown.

Shoppers strung along by pavement artistes

Musical maestros: Shoppers in Ann Street, Belfast, received some surprise entertainment from three musical marionettes. The highly-strung buskers were under the direction of a group of New York arts students.

EOSTAR

From left: My brother Eric, Jeff Robbins, and me relaxing after building the set for the off-Broadway show "The Pretender" at the ATA Theater on 54th Street NYC.

THE TABLE

BY

GLENN TRIPP

EXT. BARN - AFTERNOON - 1930S

BRODY, a young carpenter, works on a king sized table in his
barn. His wife, MARTHA, watches him through the window.

                    MARTHA
               (yelling)
          Brody, lunch is ready.

                    BRODY
               (yelling)
          I'll be in in a minute.

Martha walks towards the barn with a plate of food.

                    MARTHA
          My dear, you keep saying you'll be
          in in a minute, but that was twenty
          minutes ago. You need to get some
          nourishment in that thin body of
          yours.

                    BRODY
          Ahhh honey, I was coming in, I just
          wanted to finish up this last side.

                    MARTHA
          You'll have plenty of time for that
          table after lunch.

Brody grabs a sandwich and a glass of milk.

                    BRODY
          That's the problem, I feel I'm
          loosing time, besides this is
          exciting.

                    MARTHA
          Slow down, you're gonna get heartburn.

                    BRODY
          This is not just any table. This is
          the table of all tables. This is the
          King's table. The Knights of the Round
          Table's, table.

                    MARTHA
               (interrupting)
          The table is rectangle, not round.

                    BRODY
I know, I know, okay! Whatever! I
mean, I mean its powerful, magical,
whimsical. This table will bring
everyone together at all times.
The family will break bread, have
great conversations, kids growing
up, holidays, birthdays. I just
can't believe I'm part of
generations and good family times
to come. Nothing but good will
happen around this table. I can
assure you, I can feel it. This is
probably the happiest day of my
life.
          (stuttering)
Uhh, except of course, when I met
you.

                    MARTHA
Yes dear, I know what you mean.

                    BRODY
Imagine that, out of all the
carpenters in the state of New York
and perhaps the whole East Coast, I
was chosen to build a family table for
the wealthiest shipping giant in
Italy. Me! Me! Me!
          (a beat)
I still can't believe it. This
truly is a turning point in my
career.

                    MARTHA
Don't get too big a head on your
shoulders, my dear. He was probably in
town to get some bootleg from the
Dutch, drove by our house, and saw
your sign. He was probably too drunk
to think straight.

                    BRODY
You may be right. But still... a
thousand dollars to build a family
table is nothing to sneeze about. I
would have made the darn thing for a
hundred dollars and shipped it to
Italy for free. Heck, I own the tools
and the wood is free. It's only my
time.

                    MARTHA
Like I said, my dear, he was probably
to drunk too think straight.

                    BRODY
Maybe so, but wow. Just wow. You know,
I was thinking, he probably wanted a
huge table because he has a big family
and wishes to bring everyone together
for the Holidays and good cheer. You
know those Italians, they're very
family-oriented, love a good family
gathering.

                    MARTHA
Yeah and they love their wine as well!
Maybe a bit too much.

                    BRODY
That they do. That they do. I heard
they let their kids drink wine at the
dinner table at the age of five.

                    MARTHA
          (interrupting)
Yeah, by the time they reach forty,
they purchase over-sized tables for
which they pay ten times the price.

                    BRODY
          (sternly)
Martha, easy now.

                    MARTHA
I know, honey I'm sorry. I'll let you
get back to work. This is a huge
table. How much does it weigh?

                    BRODY
I don't know, probably a few hundred
pounds. I think I need to do something
to make it lighter. Maybe I'll
concentrate on the legs. Somehow they
need to be lighter yet strong. I think
I may need an extra support in the
middle. There's a lot more to do and I
only have a few weeks before the
moving truck picks it up. I still have
to make the shipping crate, as well.

                    MARTHA
Ok, do what you need to do, I'm going
to town to the butcher.
                    (MORE)

                              MARTHA (CONT'D)
             You need to be done by five o'clock -
             we have the Rogers coming over for
             dinner at six. No late night
             tonight.

                              BRODY
             Ok honey. That said, I'll only work on
             the extra support leg today. Now go
             and let me get on with it.

                              MARTHA
             Love you.

                              BRODY
                  (mumbling)
             Love you more.

Brody talks to himself while examining a few logs.

                              BRODY (CONT'D)
             This will work just fine. I don't
             know if he'll know the difference,
             but this wood is a rare Maple only
             found in the Catskills. Only the
             best to be shipped to Europe, I
             say. I shall put my seal of
             approval on this one. Brody
             Galleger made in Phoenicia, NY,
             USA. That's right, USA! Let
             everyone know where real craftsmen
             and exotic wood comes from.

                                             FADE OUT.

INT. BARN - MORNING

Brody stares at the table. Martha enters the barn in her
nightgown.

                              MARTHA
             My dear?

                              BRODY
                  (startled)
             Shoot! You scared me! What are you
             doing up so early?

                              MARTHA
             What are you doing up so early? I
             turned over in bed and you were gone.

> BRODY
> Oh, I'm sorry honey. I had a great
> idea how to curve the edges to give it
> a beveled look. I was trying to get a
> visual to see how deep a curve I
> should give it.

Martha rubs Brody's shoulders.

> MARTHA
> This table can wait till later.
> Come back to bed honey, I want to
> feel your warm body next to mine.

Martha starts kissing Brody's neck and rubbing his chest. Brody
turns around, and they start passionately kissing. He unties her
nightgown and lays her on top of the table.

> FADE TO BLACK.

INT. BARN - AFTERNOON

Brody sands the table. KURT, an older man, enters the barn.

> KURT
> Hello Brody, whatcha doing?

Brody rolls his eyes.

> BRODY
> Hey Kurt, how's everything?

> KURT
> What are you sanding? That looks like
> a mighty big piece of wood.

> BRODY
> (excitedly)
> I'm building a table for a very
> important man from Italy.

> KURT
> Who? Tony?

> BRODY
> Tony? No, for a man name Sal. Why?

Kurt flings his hands in the air.

> KURT
> I thought you were making it for
> Tony. You know all guys from Italy
> are Tony. You heard?
> (MORE)

KURT (CONT'D)
When they came to Ellis Island they
put on their papers TO NY. The
passport controller would say Tony?
And they would say, "Yes, To New
York, TONY." And of course they
would be flailing their hands in
the air because Italians can't talk
unless they use their hands.

Kurt continues flailing his hands in the air.

                    BRODY
          (annoyed)
     Stop doing that. This table is for
     an important man named Sal. Not
     Tony. Kurt, did you come over to
     aggravate me or to borrow a tool? I
     have a lot of work to do and I
     don't have time for nonsense today.

                    KURT
     Well actually I was hoping I could
     borrow your wheelbarrow.

                    BRODY
     You know the rules. You have to return
     the last thing you borrowed before you
     can borrow something else.

                    KURT
     I knew you were gonna say that, right
     here in my back pocket is the
     screwdriver I borrowed.

Kurt pulls out a screwdriver.

                    BRODY
     What about the wrench you borrowed the
     other day?

                    KURT
     I knew you were gonna say that, and
     that, is in my other back pocket.

Kurt pulls out a wrench.

                    BRODY
     And the pliers? I suppose that's in
     your front pocket?

Kurt pulls out a pair of pliers.

                    KURT
          Whoah, do you have x-ray eyes or
          something?

                    BRODY
          Kurt, why didn't you just give me back
          all my tools at once, instead of
          playing the guessing game?

                    KURT
          Well, you see Brody, I still needed
          the pliers and if you lent me your
          wheelbarrow and I broke it I would
          still have the wrench right here in my
          pocket to fix it. I was really only
          thinking of you, Brody. That's the
          truth.

Brody snatches the tools.

                    BRODY
          Now, go, take the wheelbarrow and
          bring it back by sundown. I have
          too much work to do to go back and
          forth with you.

Kurt flails his hands in the air.

                    KURT
          Thanks Brody, I really appreciate
          it. Good luck with that table for
          TONY. Ohh, by the way Brody you
          know why Italy is shaped like a
          boot?

                    BRODY
          No Kurt, why is Italy shaped like a
          boot?

Kurt points to his feet.

                    KURT
          Because you can't fit all that crap
          in a shoe.
               (laughing hysterically)
          I gotta go, you crack me up.

Brody smirks.

                                        FADE OUT.

EXT. YARD - DAY

A truck pulls up with two MOVERS. Martha is in the living room, while Brody is upstairs.

> MARTHA
> Honey, the movers are here. Looks like there's only two of them. How the heck are two of them gonna move that great big crate? I'll call the Stanley twins to help. At least they're bigger than these two guys.

Brody looks out the window.

> BRODY
> Whoah there *are* only two of them!!!!

Brody runs downstairs.

> BRODY (CONT'D)
> Hello gentlemen, you must be here for the table. I've been waiting three days for you guys.

> MOVER
> (in a Brooklyn accent)
> You don't know how hard it is to find this place. Whoever heard of Phony-see New York?

> BRODY
> (angrily)
> That's Phoenicia, Pho-ne-chia. Established nineteen ten. Where's the rest of your crew?

> MOVER
> What crew? This is it! Me and Larry. So what are we moving?

> BRODY
> The crate under the tarp.

> MOVER
> Well wet my whistle, how the heck we gonna move that?

Martha runs out of the house.

                    MARTHA
          I talked to the Stanley twins.
          They're coming over to give you
          boys a hand.

                    MOVER
          Thank goodness for that, this thing's
          a monster.

                    BRODY
               (whispering to Martha)
          Wow, these two aren't the sharpest
          tools in the shed. Here comes
          reinforcements.

The STANLEY TWINS walk across the yard.

                    MOVER
          Look at these two body builders, they
          could probably pick up the crate
          themselves!

                    STANLEY TWIN
          Come on, let's get this in the truck.
          We have wood to cut.

Everyone struggles to put the crate in the truck. The moving
truck pulls away. Brody hands the twins money.

                    BRODY
          Thanks for the hand, boys. When you
          get a chance, drop off a load of
          wood by the barn, please.

                    STANLEY TWIN
          No problem, will get to you by the
          weekend.

Brody turns to Martha and gives her a hug.

                    BRODY
          Honey, I'm finally finished with
          that project. That turned out to be
          one beautiful table. I am sure the
          Italian is gonna love it. We should
          celebrate.

                    MARTHA
               (nervously)
          Yes, we should celebrate, my dear.
          But... Brody, I have something to
          tell you. I saw the doctor this
          morning. He said I'm pregnant.

Brody trips on a piece of wood.

>   BRODY
>   (stuttering)
>   You what? You what? That is
>   wonderful news. That is brilliant
>   news.

>   MARTHA
>   You're happy?

Brody picks up Martha.

>   BRODY
>   Of course I'm happy! Now we have a
>   very good reason to celebrate. When
>   did this happen? How did this
>   happen? Well I think I know how it
>   happened. Wooooow.

>   MARTHA
>   It must have happened on that magic
>   morning in the barn.

>   BRODY
>   Yes, that was a very special morning.
>   I told you that table was magical.

>   MARTHA
>   (rolling her eyes)
>   Yes, my dear, that was one magical
>   table.

>   BRODY
>   (frantically)
>   So what do we do next? We have to
>   buy clothes. Oh my goodness, I have
>   to start making a cradle, today! I
>   need to start now. I don't even
>   know where to start!

>   MARTHA
>   Start by calming down. We have almost
>   nine months before the precious
>   package arrives. We have plenty of
>   time to build a cradle and buy cloths.

>   BRODY
>   (talking fast)
>   I'm gonna teach him my carpentry
>   skills and then some. I'm gonna
>   learn new tricks and teach them all
>   to my new son. I'm so excited I can
>   hardly stand.
>   **(MORE)**

                    BRODY (CONT'D)
What are we going to name him? How
about Peter or Louie? Or Francis,
like the saint. You like the name
Francis? Francis Gallager. That's
nice, it has a nice ring to it.
Francis Gallager. I'm liking that.

                    MARTHA
        (calmly)
Slow down Brody, slow down. What if
it's a girl? You know it could be a
girl. We shouldn't get our hopes up
until we are absolutely sure.

                    BRODY
Wow. I didn't think of that. What if
it's a girl? Then I will teach her my
carpentry skills and then some. I can
teach a girl how to do carpentry,
right?

                    MARTHA
I guess so. Sure. Why not? A girl can
do anything a man can do and better
cause they put more love into it.

Brody looks out of the corner of his eyes.

                    BRODY
        (agreeing)
You're right. A girl can do
carpentry, too. I'm gonna teach her
- or him - everything I know. What
do we name her if she's a girl?
Peaches, maybe?

                    MARTHA
No. You do not name your daughter
Peaches. You give her a pretty name
like Christine, Sabrina, Cara or
Kayla.

                    BRODY
        (excitedly)
Maybe Francine. Francine Gallager.
That sounds nice too.

                    MARTHA
We're not gonna name our daughter
Francine. That would remind me of the
woman who used to live in town.
Remember, she moved to Las Vegas to be
a showgirl? I will not name our little
girl after a Las Vegas showgirl.

                    BRODY
Oh yeah, you're right. I forgot about
Francine. Everyone said she was a lot
of fun, though. Ok, ok. We'll think
about the name thing later. I have to
get to work building a crib. Oh no, I
don't have any wood, I used it all on
the table and crate. I better talk to
the Stanley twins. Wow my job is never
done! It's not easy raising kids.

                    MARTHA
Brody, calm down you've only been a
father for five minutes. You're not
raising kids just yet.

                    BRODY
We should celebrate. Do you want me to
go to the Dutch on Muddybrook and get
some shine? I heard he made a really
nice Honey Wine.

                    MARTHA
Ok, I know you like that. Remember, I
can't drink because I'm pregnant. I'll
have just a little though to
celebrate. But, please be careful and
don't get caught. The Stanley twins
said the feds were snooping around
town lately.

                    BRODY
I heard that, as well. Ok then, I'll
see if the twins will run up for me.
They know the back way and they're
quick on their horses.

                    MARTHA
        (staring at Brody)
I love you.

                    BRODY
Why did you look at me that way?

                    MARTHA
That was the look of love. You're
gonna make a very good father. I'm
glad you chose me to be your soulmate.
Come here, give me a hug and a kiss.

                                FADE TO BLACK.

EXT. FRONT LAWN - ITALY - MORNING

SAL, a funny, sarcastic, well dressed, older Italian man walks out of his villa to the sound of GIOVANNI arguing with his mover helpers at the back of the truck.

> SAL
> Yo, Giovanni, what's all the hen
> squabbling about? Careful with that
> crate, that was made in New York.
> Where've you been? I was expecting you
> yesterday.

The moving guys freeze and look at Sal. Then, they look at the crate. Then they look at Sal. Then they look at the crate.

> GIOVANNI
> (in broken English)
> I am so sorry, Big Sal, we couldn't
> get the crate in the truck. Now
> we're not to sure how to get this
> crate out of the truck.

> SAL
> (sarcastically)
> Why don't you knuckleheads open the
> crate with your stupidity and slide
> the table out with your
> personality?

Giovanni holds his hands in the air and gives a big smile.

> GIOVANNI
> Ok big Sal, we'll open the crate
> first, then we'll bring out the
> crate later.

Sal walks towards the house, shaking his head.

> SAL
> Why don't you honk your horn when
> you have it on the porch? Then,
> I'll show you where it goes. Oh
> yes, be careful, I don't have any
> insurance, and I bet you don't
> either. Also, watch out, there's a
> lot of old people running around
> inside the house. I don't want you
> dropping that thing on their
> shriveled up heads. One more thing.
> Hurry up. The shriveled up people
> are tired of eating on the floor.

                         GIOVANNI
                    Ok, Big Sal.

                                        FADE OUT.

INT. DINING ROOM - EVENING

SAL, with his FAMILY, sitting at the table holding up glasses of
wine.

                         SAL
                    This is a toast to our beautiful
                    family, may we always have a happy and
                    healthy life sitting around this
                    beautiful table for many years to
                    come. And, might I add, this table was
                    custom made in the good old U. S. of
                    A.

                         FAMILY
                    Cheers! Salute! Chin chin!

ANGLE THROUGH WINDOW ON SAL AND FAMILY PASSING AROUND PLATES
OF FOOD, TALKING, AND LAUGHING.

                         SAL
                    Hey Dad, pass the prosciutto, please.
                    Who wants more wine? Now this is a
                    party!

Sal picks up a bottle and drops it. Everyone laughs.

                                        FADE TO BLACK.

INT. DINING ROOM - LATER

Sal, kneeling over his father laying in the middle of the table.
Family gathered around. GRANDPA in-law still eating at the other
end of the table.

                         SAL
                    Dad, you ok? I thought we lost you for
                    a minute there.

                         GRANDPA
                    Tables are for eating, not sleeping.

                         SAL
                    Grandpa, my father was choking, he was
                    unconscious. He's not sleeping.

                        GRANDPA
           Well if he doesn't make it, can I have
           his dinner?

Sal looks at Grandpa, then looks at his father. He looks back
and forth a few times.

                        SAL
           No. If my father doesn't make it
           I'm gonna have his dinner. After
           all, he's my father.

                        GRANDPA
           Can we share his dessert?

                        SAL
           No one is gonna eat my father's food.
           He's gonna make it, he's just resting.

                        GRANDPA
           Isn't resting and sleeping almost the
           same thing? When I'm resting, I always
           fall asleep. But not on a table.

                                    FADE TO BLACK.

INT. SAL ON THE PHONE WITH SYE - DAY

Sal calls SYE, an old Jewish friend who looks like a younger
Einstein.

                        SAL
           Hello, Sye Sterling! How's everyhting?
           How's the weather in Paris?

                        SYE
           Well, hello Salvatore. This is a nice
           surprise! I haven't heard from you in
           almost two years. How's the little
           lady of the family? Does she need a
           new brooch? A ring? A necklace?

                        SAL
             (embarrassed)
           No Sye, actually the little lady
           and I are going our separate ways.

                        SYE
           Oy vey, Sal, I'm sorry to hear that.
           You two have been together for a very
           long time.

                    SAL
I know, I know. Not only did I lose
her, I lost my shipping company to the
feds. I'm filing for bankruptcy next
week. Everything's a mess.

                    SYE
Wow Sal this is very bad news. But of
course you didn't call me after two
long years to bring such bad news to
my doorstep. Do you need some money? A
place to stay? Sal we've been friends
for over twenty years. Anytime you
needed a fine piece of jewelry you
always called me. Im here to repay the
favor. Whatever you need.

                    SAL
Thanks Sye. Actually Sye, I could use
some money and I was wondering if I
could sell you back some of those fine
pieces you made for me and my family.
I know I can't get what I paid for
them but I need some money to get
back to New York to start my life
over. Please Sye, you know I'd
never look for a handout or reach
out to you unless I was in a bit of
a bind. I have no one else to turn
to right now.

                    SYE
Ok, ok, oy vey. Like I said Sal, I'm
there for you. What do you have?

                    SAL
          (thrilled)
Thanks Sye, I knew you wouldn't let
me down. I have five of those
custom, diamond-encrusted gold
watches you made for me. My wife's
second wedding ring.

                    SYE
          (interrupting, worried)
Does your wife know you have that
piece? I mean, that is a real
looker. That took me two months to
design.

                    SAL
No, no she has so much jewelry she
won't miss this one.
               (MORE)

SAL (CONT'D)
I also have a few men's and women's
bracelets, some brooches, necklaces,
some old gold earrings, and a bunch of
other stuff.

SYE
Ok, I know a few of these pieces quite
well. When can you come to Paris so I
can see my beautiful craftsmanship in
the flesh?

SAL
That's the hard part Sye. See, I can't
come to Paris, you would have to come
to Italy. Because not only do I have
jewelry, but I also have a few
antiques and some Renoirs, Van Goghs,
and a Rodin. I even have this table
that was custom-made for me in New
York. I wanted to do everything as a
package.

SYE
I'm very interested in the jewelry,
the art and maybe the antiques. But
sorry, I'm not in the market for a New
York table.

SAL
Sye, you have to see this table to
believe it. This thing is enormous -
all hand-carved, made of a the finest
wood. A really beautiful piece. I
don't want the ex to get it. It's one
of a kind. My first child was born on
this table. It has some sentimental
value to me.

SYE
Sorry Sal, but your wife's after-birth
on a table is not a real selling point
for me.

SAL
I know Sye, I just want to see this
table go to a good family instead of
my wife chopping it up and throwing it
into the fireplace. I'll tell you
what, you take the jewelry as well as
the antiques and art and I'll throw in
the table as a token of our
friendship.

                    SYE
          Oy vey, oy vey. Ok Sal. It sounds like
          the table is worth more than the
          jewelry, antiques, and art combined.
          I'll look at the table when I'm
          there. In two days, I'll be on a
          train to Italy. I'll invite my good
          friend Michael. He's a buyer of art
          and antiques, maybe between the two
          of us we can take the whole
          package. Will you pick us up at the
          train station?

                    SAL
          Yeah, sure Sye. But two days is the
          max. My ex will be back from Sardinia
          on Monday, I need to have everything
          out by the weekend.

                    SYE
          Ok Sal, see you soon.

                                        FADE TO BLACK.

EXT. TRAIN STATION - AFTERNOON

As the train pulls up, Sye steps out, dressed like a business
man. His friend, MICHAEL, is dressed in Orthodox clothing. Sal
and his CHAUFFEUR wait by their car.

                    SAL
               (jokingly)
          Look at these two. They're
          definitely not Italian. Maybe
          they're from the mountains, the
          Alps.
               (laughing)
          Maybe they lost their jobs and
          that's all they can afford to wear.
          They look like a bunch of circus
          freaks.

Sal begins laughing even harder.

                    CHAUFFEUR
               (seriously)
          Should I get them, Sir, or would
          you like to?

                    SAL
          Calm down, calm down, I'll get them.
          You're no fun.

Sal exits the car while wiping his tears. He stands with open arms.

                    SAL (CONT'D)
          Hey Sye, over here.

                    SYE
          Sal, it's so good to see you. It's
          been a very long time.

                    SAL
          It's always good to see you, as well,
          my friend. You look good with your
          fancy suit on.

                    SYE
          Thank you, Sal. I'd like to introduce
          you to my friend, Michael.

                    MICHAEL
          Very pleased to meet you, Sal. I heard
          so much about you. Have you been
          crying? Or are you so happy to see us?

Sal wipes his face.

                    SAL
          No, no. Just the wind I guess. And of
          course I am happy to see you. You came
          to buy all my stuff! Well boys, why
          don't we get a move on? We have a bit
          of a distance to travel.

They walk towards the car.

                                        FADE OUT.

INT. LIVING ROOM - LATER

Sal, Sye, and Michael walk into the living room. Sye heads
straight for the table with the jewelry spread out. Michael
heads to the corner where paintings are propped against the
walls.

                    SAL
               (surprised)
          Wow, you two move fast, you don't
          mess around. Guess I don't have to
          tell you two where everything is.

                    MICHAEL
          Very interesting place.

Sal goes in the kitchen and comes back with champagne.

                    SAL
          Yes, now it's time to celebrate.
          Let's have a drink, boys.

Sye and Michael turn to Sal.

                    SYE
          No thanks, Sal, not for me.

                    MICHAEL
          Not for me either, thank you. I don't
          drink while I'm working.

                    SAL
          What, no champagne? I thought we'd
          celebrate with a drink.

                    MICHAEL
          Ok, if we are celebrating, I'll take a
          tea please.

                    SYE
          Me as well, Sal.

                    SAL
          Tea? Tea? You're gonna celebrate with
          tea?

                    MICHAEL
          Ok, since we are celebrating, I'll
          take honey with my tea.

                    SAL
          Honey? Honey? I don't have fucking
          honey.

                    MICHAEL
          Ok, I'll take sugar then. And since
          we're celebrating, I'll take two
          cubes, please.

                    SYE
          Make that a double.

                    SAL
          Maybe you two lollipops would like to
          really celebrate and have a little
          milk with your tea?

Sye and Micheal look at each other and shrug their heads.

                         MICHAEL
          We can do that. Milk it is.

Sal looks at Michael, then looks at Sye, then looks at Michael,
then looks at Sye. He shakes his head and goes to the kitchen.
Sal comes back out with a tray of tea, cups, etc.

                         SAL
          Well, here is your celebratory tea,
          boys. I even brought out some extra
          sugar being that you two guys really
          like to party.

Michael and Sye hold up their tea cups.

                         MICHAEL
          Cheers, asante, prost.

                         SAL
               (disgusted)
          Really? I mean, really? You can
          cheer with tea?

                         MICHAEL
          We're celebrating, right?

                         SAL
          Yeah, we're celebrating but-

                         MICHAEL
               (interrupting)
          By the way, what are we
          celebrating?

                         SAL
          Me divorcing my wife, me moving back
          to New York, and you two guys buying
          all my possessions for a very handsome
          price before my ex-wife gets home.
          What do you think we were celebrating,
          your cute curls?

                         MICHAEL
               (dryly)
          No, I thought we were celebrating
          because we were going to pay very
          little for your worldly possessions
          and we might have a crack at
          meeting your ex-wife.

Michael stares with a stone face.

                         MICHAEL (CONT'D)
          Just kidding!

Sal, Sye, and Michael start laughing.

> SAL
> Wow, Sye, I really like this one. He
> has a good sense of humor.

Sye and Michael go back to business. Sal continues drinking more champagne.

> SAL (CONT'D)
> (buzzed)
> You know Michael, you should make
> your own tea. Yeah. You can call it
> He-Brew. Get it? He-Brew. Or even
> Tea-Brew, That's a good one, right?

Sal laughs hysterically. Michael sits on the floor with a deadpan stare.

> MICHAEL
> You know, Sal, you might be onto
> something. I'll give that some
> consideration.

Sal stops laughing and stares at Michael. Michael goes back to looking at the antiques.

> SAL
> Yeah, you do that Michael, you do
> that. Matter of fact, you can have
> that one. Yeah that one's on me. I'm
> getting another bottle of bubbly.
> Would you girls like another spot of
> tea?

> SYE
> No, not for me Sal.

> MICHAEL
> Me neither, thanks.

> SAL
> (sarcastically)
> And you two said you know how to
> party.

Sal goes to the kitchen, comes back, and pops the cork of champagne. Michael and Sye are startled.

> SAL (CONT'D)
> Now *this* is partying.

Sal looks at Michael staring at a picture of his wife.

                    SAL (CONT'D)
          Yep, thats the ex. She looks like a
          gargoyle, doesn't she?

                    MICHAEL
                  (seriously)
          No, not really. I never found her
          face to be on the side of any
          building that I know of. I've seen
          angels in the architecture, but
          none of them looked like her. Wow
          she is like a living angel.

                    SAL
          Yeah, what do you really call a living
          angel that takes all your money and
          half your life away?

Michael stares Sal up and down in disgust.

                    MICHAEL
          Funny?

                    SAL
                  (sarcastically)
          Yeah, real funny.

Sal shakes his head and walks towards Sye.

                    SAL (CONT'D)
          And what are you doing, my old friend?

Sye opens his briefcase, pulls out a jewelry eyeglass, scale,
eyedropper, and testing stone.

                    SAL (CONT'D)
                  (drunk)
          What are you testing it for? To see
          if it's real? What do you think you
          sold me? Junk?!!

Sal starts hysterically laughing. Sye turns around and stares at
him.

                    SAL (CONT'D)
          Ok, ok I'm sorry.

                    SYE
          I'm just doing my job, this is what I
          do. I appraise jewels and precious
          metals. I want to give you the right
          price for the cut, weight, and purity.

                    SAL
     I'm good. Do your thing. Make me an
     offer. Don't lowball me. I know what
     this stuff's worth. By the way, Sye,
     this is the table I was telling you
     about. It's a real beauty, huh?

Sye looks up from his jeweler's glass down the length of the
table.

                    SYE
     Wow, you were right. This is an
     amazing table. Very large, as well.

                    SAL
     Yeah, my father passed away on this
     table. He was eating some of the
     neighbor's old prosciutto and he
     chocked so hard he had a heart attack
     right at this very table. We tried
     everything but we couldn't save him.
     We got the prosciutto out though.

                    SYE
               (shocked)
     That's horrible. I thought your
     daughter was born on this very
     table?

                    SAL
     Yeah that too. You see, my wife's
     water broke in the living room right
     over there.

Sal points to where Michael is sitting. Michael jumps up in
disgust.

                    SAL (CONT'D)
     Calm down sissy pants, I had the floor
     cleaned. We knew we couldn't make it
     to the hospital in time so we cleared
     the table and she gave birth right
     there. The only real disturbing part
     about it was, while my wife was giving
     birth, my wife's grandfather was still
     eating his dinner watching everything
     like he was at a Saturday matinee.

Michael and Sye look at Sal with eyes wide open.

                    SYE
               (seriously)
     That is disturbing.

                    SAL
          You're telling me? Jeez that was
          something else.

Sal waves around his crotch.

                    SAL (CONT'D)
          Grandpa watching my wife's - his
          granddaughter's - you know, you
          know, you know?

                    SYE
          Yes Sal, I think we know.

Sal shakes his head.

                    SAL
          Wow, like wow! So you see, this
          table has sentimental value, a
          little bit of life, and a little
          bit of death. And of course some
          great entertainment for Grandpa.

Sal starts laughing then looks across the table.

                    SAL (CONT'D)
          Come to think of it, Grandpa was still
          eating when my father was lying on the
          table, as well. Grandpa, he was a
          hoot. He always did love a good meal.

                    MICHAEL
               (interrupting with dry
                humor)
          Maybe you should've cut up the
          table and made a box and put
          grandpa in.

                    SAL
          No, Grandpa's still alive. He's with
          my ex on Holiday. Now that would be a
          good idea to make a box for my ex. But
          I wouldn't waste such a good table. So
          what do you think about the table Sye?
          I'll throw in the table if you make a
          good offer on the jewelry.

                    SYE
          You see Sal, you have a lot of great
          pieces here and a lot of weight. But I
          could never give you what it's worth.
          There's no market right now with all
          the things that are happening in the
          world today.

                    SAL
          Ok, ok. Just make me an offer.

                         SYE
          I can give you sixty grand for all the
          jewelry.

                         SAL
               (shouting)
          Sixty? I think I paid two hundred
          or better just for the rose ring!

                         SYE
               (calmly)
          Sal, what you paid and what the
          market can bear these days are two
          different things.

                         SAL
               (calming down)
          I know Sye, but sixty? I was hoping
          for a quarter of what I paid and
          you're giving me a quarter of a
          quarter.

Sal looks up in the air.

                         SAL (CONT'D)
          Is that even an equation? Let's see if
          I have a quarter and I break that up
          into a quarter. That's six and a
          quarter cents. All you're giving me is
          six cents for all my jewelry?

Sye stares at Sal like he's stupid.

                         SAL (CONT'D)
          Ok, ok. You know what I mean. Aww Sye,
          I was hoping for a bit more. Actually
          quite a bit more.

                         SYE
          I'm sorry, Sal. This is all I can
          afford to pay for everything. If you
          tried selling it yourself piece-by-
          piece you could make at least twenty-
          five to fifty percent more.

                         SAL
          There you go with the percentages
          again. Alright Sye, you got me I'll
          take it.

Sye takes a checkbook out of his briefcase.

                    SAL (CONT'D)
Wait, wait, wait. Sye, this is
supposed to be a cash deal. I'm filing
for banckruptcy, going through a
divorce. I cant take a check for sixty
grand. I can't take a check for sixty
cents!

                    SYE
Sal, I don't carry that kind of money
around. Here is a check in good faith.
You come up to Paris in a few weeks
and I'll trade that check for US
currency. How long have we known each
other?

                    SAL
You're right, you're right. Okay then,
in a few weeks I'll meet you in Paris.

                    SYE
Yes, very good. And I want you to come
to my home for a nice, Jewish, home-
cooked meal.

Sal and Sye both shake hands and give each other a hug. Sye
loads all the jewelry in his briefcase. Sal turns to Michael.

                    SAL
So what about you, curly? You like the
art and the antiques? Or you just
gonna bust my fucking balls?

                    MICHAEL
          (seriously)
If I thought busting your balls
would make things better for you, I
would gladly help you out, but I
see you have enough problems.

Michael pulls out a pen and paper and starts hitting it really
hard.

                    SAL
Here we go, he's banging that thing
like he's playing a Mozart song.

                    MICHAEL
          (interrupting)
All kidding aside Sal.
                    (MORE)

MICHAEL (CONT'D)
For the three pieces of art, the
clock, the antiques on the table,
the antiques on the left wall of
the living room, and the first two
steps of antiques on the staircase,
minus my round trip train fare, and
minus my meal on the train, I will
offer you seventy-two thousand,
three hundred and sixty-two
dollars, and fifteen cents. And
consider that my final offer.

                SAL
        (in shock)
That's your final offer? That's
your first offer! Where the hell
did you come up with that crazy
number? Fifteen fucking cents?
You're charging me for going to
work and your fucking meal?

                MICHAEL
        (deadpan)
I guess it's the price of doing
business, Sal.

                SAL
        (ticked off)
Well then, I'm gonna charge you for
picking you up at the train
station.

                MICHAEL
Ok, so I'll add twenty dollars.

                SAL
And I'm gonna bring you back to the
train station.

                MICHAEL
Ok, I'll add another twenty dollars.

                SAL
What about the tea? Add another five
dollars.

                MICHAEL
Your tea is too expensive, I'll give
you three dollars.

Sal turns to Sye and points at Michael.

                SAL
Where did you get this circus freak?

                    MICHAEL
          So, do we have a deal?

                    SAL
          Yeah sure, do I have a choice? Take
          it, take it. I'll even throw in the
          picture of the gargoyle seeing that
          you two have a lot in common, like
          taking my money!

Michael reaches into his trench coat and pulls out a checkbook.

                    SAL (CONT'D)
          No, no I don't know you Abraham
          Lincoln. No checks, cash only.

                    SYE
               (interrupting)
          Sal, he's my friend. Let him give
          you a check for the full amount and
          I'll give you a check for the same
          amount as a good faith check and
          when you come to Paris, we'll work
          out the cash arrangements. Do we
          have a deal?

Sal looks at the ceiling, then looks at Sye, then looks at
Michael, then back at Sye, and back at Michael.

                    SAL
          Yeah yeah! Only cause it's you, Sye.
          Only cause it's you.

Both men write the checks, hand them to Sal, and shake hands.

                    MICHAEL
          May I use your phone Sal?

                    SAL
          Wise guy. Yeah, what are you calling
          the circus? You're afraid they're
          gonna give away your cage if you're
          not in by nightfall?

Michael talks on the phone in another language. Sal yells at
Michael in the background.

                    SAL (CONT'D)
          This better be collect. Who are you
          calling, Israel? I don't want to get a
          big bill. Oh fuck this, what am I
          saying? My ex is paying the bill. Stay
          on the phone. Call whoever you want,
          nature freak!

Michael hangs up the phone and turns to Sal.

>   MICHAEL
>   I just called my movers. They'll send
>   a rep here in fifteen minutes to
>   catalog everything.

>   SAL
>   Wow that's quick, I hope it's not the
>   same bozos I had. By the way, Sye, did
>   you want the table? No charge.

>   SYE
>   Well I guess it would look good in the
>   new house. Michael can I throw it on
>   the moving truck with your purchase?

>   MICHAEL
>   No problem, there's plenty of room.

>   SAL
>   Very nice. I'm glad to see it go to a
>   good home. I have the crate it came in
>   in the back of the property. I was
>   meaning to chop it up as firewood, but
>   I never got around to it.

>   SYE
>   Being that Michael has some extra room
>   on his moving truck, maybe I'll look
>   around. I might be interested in
>   purchasing a few more things for my
>   new home.

>   SAL
>   Sure, Sye. Look around. The more you
>   take, the better the deal. Maybe you
>   might be interested in my ex-wife's
>   negligees and maybe even buying one
>   for Michael.

Sal starts winking at Sye.

>   FADE OUT.

EXT. SYE'S FRONT LAWN - PARIS - MORNING

A moving truck with squeaky breaks pulls up to the front of
Sye's house. Sye walks out in his bathrobe.

>   SYE
>   (excited)
>   What's all the racket out here?
>   (MORE)

>SYE (CONT'D)
Where have you people been? I've
been waiting two days for this
delivery.

The movers look at each other, then look at Sye, then look at
each other, then look at Sye. They shrug their shoulders and
step out of the truck. Not a word is spoken by the movers.

>SYE (CONT'D)
Yes, I am talking to you! Ohh never
mind, just unload the truck.
Everything goes in the living room
except the big table, which goes in
the dining room.

Sye turns to walk away, then turns around to stare at the movers
opening up the truck, and shakes his head.

>SYE (CONT'D)
Never mind I'll point to where you
should put everything.

Sye walks up the steps and opens the door.

>SYE (CONT'D)
Iris baby, come take a look and bring
your mother. We have a lot of boxes to
open - maybe you should call your Aunt
and Uncle as well.
>(under his breath)
Maybe we have too many boxes to
open. What was I thinking?

>FADE OUT.

EXT. TRAIN STATION

Sye is waiting for Sal in his car with his chauffeur at the
wheel. Sal exits the station.

>SYE
There he is. He doesn't look very
Parisian. Matter of fact, he doesn't
even look French. He looks like a
Paris crossing guard. Looks like he
was in a Charlie Chaplin movie. He was
probably the tramp. I bet you he never
missed a meal. What's Sal thinking,
he's a secret agent? Or just a secret?

Sye starts laughing and elbows the chauffeur. Then he jumps out
of his car.

                         SYE (CONT'D)
                    Sal over here!

Sal walks over to Sye and the two men hug.

                         SAL
                    (happily)
                    Yes Sye, you are a man of your
                    word. I knew you wouldn't let me
                    down. Wow, it is so good to see
                    you.

                         SYE
                    Likewise my friend. Likewise. How was
                    your train ride?

                         SAL
                    Not bad at all, very comfortable. A
                    little long. They hit a few stops but
                    nothing terrible. Very nice scenic
                    view throughout the Alps. Wow, that
                    was majestic.

                         SYE
                    Good, I am glad you enjoyed your
                    journey. Did everything work out with
                    your wife?

                         SAL
                    Ex-wife that is. Yes everything worked
                    out as good as it could have. It took
                    a week more than I thought, but
                    everything's all settled, I think. I
                    told her I was going to the cafe to
                    meet a friend, I threw my suitcase out
                    the back window, and here I am.

                         SYE
                    Wow, you're very smooth, Sal. Let's
                    go, I'll take you to your hotel so you
                    can freshen up. I booked you a really
                    nice hotel overlooking the river in
                    the old part of town. I'll send my
                    driver around six to pick you up and
                    take you to my house for dinner with
                    my family. By the way, first thing
                    tomorrow morning, we'll take care of
                    business.

                         SAL
                    Sounds like a game plan and a good one
                    at that.

                                        FADE OUT.

EXT. IN FRONT OF SYE'S HOME - EVENING

MAID opens the door. Sal gets out of the car and walks up the front lawn.

                    MAID
          Bonjour, welcome.

                    SAL
               (nervously)
          Yeah, hi there. It's me, Sal. I'm
          here to see Sye.

Maid opens the door wider and gestures for Sal to enter.

                                        FADE OUT.

INT. FOYER - LATER

Maid escorts Sal.

                    MAID
          Please come in sir, may I take your
          hat and your jacket?

Sal, checking out Maid, takes off his hat and coat.

                    SAL
          Yeah sure, no problem. But don't
          bother looking in the pockets I
          cleaned out all the good stuff
          already. You might find a dirty
          handkerchief. Maybe, be careful.

Sal laughs. The Maid rolls her eyes, and takes his hat and coat.

                    MAID
          Follow me, please.

Sal follows real close behind her checking out her bum. The maid feels the closeness of Sal and steps up the pace while glancing behind her. Sal starts walking faster, as well. Out of nowhere Sye appears around the corner.

                    SYE
          Well, hello Sal I thought I heard
          someone at the door.

Sal extends his arm with a bottle of Manischewitz.

                    SAL
          This is for you: a bottle of
          Manischewitz. Manischewitz, it's
          Jewish.

                    SYE
          I know what it is. Thank you Sal.
          Please come into the study.

Sye, ERMA, and IRIS enter the room.

                    SYE (CONT'D)
          Good timing Sal, dinner is almost
          ready. I want you to meet my wife Erma
          and my daughter Iris.

                    ERMA
          It is a pleasure to meet you, Sal.
          I've heard so much about you
          throughout the years.

                    IRIS
               (shyly)
          Bonjour.

Sal nods his head and bends down to talk to Iris.

                    SAL
          You are a big little girl. How old are
          you?

Iris gets scared and runs into the other room. Sal looks at Sye.

                    SAL (CONT'D)
          I told you I have a way with women.

                    SYE
          I can see that. You're just the
          charmer. Let's go into the dining
          room, dinner is being served.

Sye, Sal, and Erma enter the dining room. Iris is already at the
table with the Aunt and Uncle.

                    SAL
          Hello, bonjour.

The Aunt and Uncle just stare a Sal and nod their heads.

                    SAL (CONT'D)
          Wise crack. Do you know those people?

                    SYE
          Yes, they are my aunt and uncle.

                    SAL
          What are they, mutes?

                    SYE
          No. They got into a fight with each
          other and they're not talking. This
          happens all the time. Their rule is
          when they aren't speaking with each
          other they can't speak with anybody
          else.

                    SAL
          They look kind of creepy in their
          silent movie mode. Anyway, wow, look
          at this table. This table looks really
          nice in this room. It looks like it
          was made for this palace of yours,
          Sye.

                    ERMA
          You know Sal, Sye really loves this
          table. He does everything here. I
          almost can't pry him apart from this
          table. Its like his King's table. He
          even customized some chairs. They just
          came this morning.

                    SAL
          I can see that. Looks great, Sye.
          Maybe I should have charged you for
          the table. Only kidding.

Sal holds his glass of wine in the air.

                    SAL (CONT'D)
          A toast to your wonderful table and
          your new chairs. May this table
          bring you happiness and good cheer
          forever, and make the two zombies
          want to talk to each other again.

Everyone around the table holds up their glasses then takes a
sip. Sal chugs his glass really quick.

                    SAL (CONT'D)
          Yeah, that is good. It's Jewish wine,
          you know.

The maid walks over and pours Sal another glass. Sal grabs the
maid by the skirt.

                    SAL (CONT'D)
          Hey toots, you can leave the bottle
          here, close. I hate for you to keep
          walking back and forth on my account.

The maid looks at Sal then looks at Sye. Sye nods his head in
approval. Everyone starts eating. Sal starts talking with food
in his mouth.

                    SAL (CONT'D)
          You know this Jewish food isn't half
          bad. I was expecting slimy pigs' feet
          or something.

Sye clears his throat.

                    SYE
          You know Sal, Jewish people do not eat
          pig.

Sal slugs down more wine with his mouth full of food.

                    SAL
          I knew that. I knew that. I just
          thought your food would have been, you
          know, tasteless and bland.

Sal looks around the table and everyone is staring at him. Sal
tries changing the subject.

                    SAL (CONT'D)
               (stumbling)
          So, this table is a real beaut. You
          know this table was made in New
          York? Yep, that's right. Upstate
          New York, in... in...

Sal looks around trying to remember the town.

                    SAL (CONT'D)
          Close to New York City, but in the
          mountains.

                    SYE
          You know, Sal, I don't think I ever
          told you, but my father lives in New
          York. In Scarsdale. When Iris gets
          older we're going to send her there so
          she can finish up her studies at
          boarding school.

                        SAL
          Ok, that makes sense. I should look up
          your Father when I get back to New
          York. You know, share a bottle of wine
          together like Manaschewitz maybe?

                        SYE
          I don't think thats a great idea. My
          father is a hard person to get to
          know. But I'll let him know you'll be
          in town.

                        SAL
          That would be great.

Sal looks around the room, then looks down at the table and
takes a slug of wine.

                        SAL (CONT'D)
          That's right this table is a real
          beaut. I had some really good times at
          this table. And some bad times, as
          well.

                        ERMA
          Oh my, bad times as well?

                        SAL
          Yeah, my father died on this table.

Sye spits his food across the table in disbelief.

                        SAL (CONT'D)
          Control it Sye, everyone's looking.

Sye wipes his chin.

                        SAL (CONT'D)
          Yeah the poor old goat had a heart
          attack while-

                        SYE
             (interrupting)
          Uh, that's enough Sal. That's
          enough. It's a very lovely table.

                        SAL
             (winking)
          Yeah Sye, I get it.

Sal turns to Erma, talking with his hands.

                    SAL (CONT'D)
               (a little drunk)
          There were a lot of good memories
          at this table, as well.

Erma stares at Sal as he spills wine on the table.

                    ERMA
               (uncomfortably)
          Really? That's nice.

                    SAL
          Yeah, like my wife - well, ex-wife -
          gave birth on this table.

Sye spits his wine back into his glass. Everyone looks at Sye.

                    SAL (CONT'D)
          You need to control that at the dinner
          table, Sye. That's not promoting good
          manners in front of the kid.

Sal picks up the bottle of wine, shakes it back and forth, and
turns to the maid.

                    SAL (CONT'D)
          Hey toots, could you bring another
          bottle to these good people please?

Sal turns to Erma.

                    SAL (CONT'D)
          I know good help is hard to find. But
          she's a real looker. I'd keep an eye
          on her around Sye.

Sye spits his food accross the table again. Sal with his hands
in the air looks at Sye.

                    SAL (CONT'D)
          What did I say this time?
               (then, to Erma)
          Does he always do this?

                    ERMA
          No, I think Sye's just a little
          excited about you being here. You know
          he's not seen you in some time except
          for his short trip to Italy a few
          weeks ago.

                    SAL
               (shouting)
          Hey Sye, that excited behavior
          needs to be toned down a bit.

Maid enters the room with a bottle of wine.

                    MAID
          Would anyone like dessert?

                    IRIS
          Chocolate.

                    SAL
          Just wine for me, toots.

                    SYE
          Well if everyone is done with dinner,
          we can go to the study and have an
          apéritif before you leave, Sal.

                                        FADE OUT.

INT. STUDY - LATER

Sal, Sye, Erma, Iris, and the Maid enter the study. Sal waves to
the Maid.

                    SAL
               (whispering loudly)
          Hey toots, bring out another bottle
          of that Manascheverwitz or whatever
          they call it. I'll drink this one
          now, and I'll take one to go. I
          don't know what's open in this
          town.

                    ERMA
               (whispering)
          Sye, that will be his third bottle
          and he wants to take one to go,
          don't you think we should say
          something?

                    SYE
          You know those Italians, they love
          their wine. It's ok, he's not driving.
          Besides, he's leaving tomorrow night.
          He's harmless.

Sal drops the bottle of wine on the carpet.

                    SAL
          Whoops, sorry about that folks.

                    MAID
          I'll get some towels and salt.

                    SYE
          Sal, we'd better call it a night. My
          wife's getting tired, and you and I
          have a big business day tomorrow.

                    SAL
               (drunk)
          Maybe you're right. I love you
          people.

                    SYE
          We love you as well, Sal.

Iris walks into the study with chocolates and stands next to
Sal. He startles.

                    SAL
          Now, where did this midget come
          from?

Erma turns to Sye.

                    ERMA
          I'll have the driver bring the car
          around.

                    SAL
               (yellsing)
          Don't go out of your way for me.

                                        FADE TO BLACK.

INT. AMSTERDAM - COFFEE SHOP - EVENING - MODERN DAY

IVAN, a middle aged man, sits on his laptop at a large table. A
few new age hippies sit at the other end of the table smoking.
STEVE, the middle age coffee shop owner, enters.

                    STEVE
               (in an English accent)
          Well, hello Ivan, mate. How the
          hell are ya?

                    IVAN
          Hey, Steve, where've you been? Haven't
          seen you in a few days.

                    STEVE
In court again! This thing is dragging
out for days upon days. Did you know
they're taking my coffee shop away?

                    IVAN
No way! Who is? Why?

                    STEVE
Landlord issues. Back taxes. Just a
whole mess of things.

                    IVAN
So what are you gonna do?

                    STEVE
Nothing. There's nothing I can do.
They got me by the old Royals and
they're squeezing tight.

Steve squeezes his crotch and makes a pirate face.

                    STEVE (CONT'D)
I'm just gonna look for a new
location, carry on, business as
usual.

                    IVAN
I hope you're gonna to stay in the
Centrum.

                    STEVE
Not sure if I can still afford the
Centrum. This place was affordable
back in the day. You know... rent
stable, kind landlords. The places
I've been looking at are almost triple
the price with half the space. I think
I might have to move to a quieter
neighborhood, just enjoy the locals
instead of the crazy tourists and the
now and then partying rock star. Most
of all, I'll really miss the
celebrities stopping by.
        (reminiscing)
Did you know that The Stones sat at
this very table? Also, Aerosmith,
ZZ Top, Leonard Skinner, The
Pretenders and even The Monkees.
The list goes on and on, this
table's famous.

                    IVAN
Now I'm really impressed.

                    STEVE
          Izzy, my buddy from Guns and Roses,
          still comes to my shop to this day.
          After he gets a smoke in, him and I go
          to the Slaughtered Lamb and pound a
          few pints till we close the place.
          He's a really good laugh, one of my
          best American friends. I'm not that
          crazy about the loud Americans, but
          Izzy is really cool. Did you happen to
          know I was one of the first Coffee
          Shops in Amsterdam back in the day?

                    IVAN
          Yeah, I heard something like that.
          You're showing your age.

                    STEVE
          I know, I know. I've been doing this
          since the early seventies. It was just
          the three of us back then. Rusland,
          The Bulldog, and me, the Crystal
          Palace. So you see I stood the test of
          time. I'm not getting any younger, but
          my girlfriends are.

Steve laughs like a pirate as he rolls a cigarette.

                    STEVE (CONT'D)
          Now I need to start enjoying a bit
          of life, as well, instead of
          running around like I'm still
          twenty years old.

                    IVAN
          Yeah, you're right. You need to start
          relaxing a little. Are you going to
          take everything with you? What about
          this table?

                    STEVE
          Well I can take everything I brought
          into the place which isn't much. But
          unfortunately the table was here when
          I got here so the table stays. Why?
          Are you interested?

                    IVAN
          What? Really? This can't be true.
          You're not taking the table? This
          table has been my life, my inspiration
          for the last ten years.
                         (MORE)

                    IVAN (CONT'D)
     I wrote three children's books and
     then some at this table. I can't live
     without this table. Where it goes I
     go!

                    STEVE
     I didn't know this table meant that
     much to you. They're having a public
     auction in a few weeks and this table
     will probably be on the block. I don't
     know what they can get for it with all
     the grafitti carved in it. I don't
     even know how the landlord got it in
     this tiny place or even how he'll get
     it out without chopping it up.

                    IVAN
     Wow, a public auction? When and
     where's the auction? To be honest with
     you, I really need this table, Steve.
     I need to do more writing on this very
     table. It seems like whenever I'm
     trying to create a story I draw a
     blank. But once I sit down at this
     table my creative juices come alive
     and magic starts flowing.

                    STEVE
     You sure it's the table? Or is it the
     Purple Haze Hash that make those
     creative juices come alive.

Ivan stares at Steve.

                    IVAN
     Maybe a bit of both.

Both men laugh.

                    IVAN (CONT'D)
     All kidding aside Steve, when is this
     auction?

                    STEVE
     I think in a few weeks. I'll speak to
     the landlord in a couple of days, he
     knows the scoop.

                    IVAN
     Cool. Thanks for the heads up. I'll
     definitely be attending that auction!
     I'd love to have this table in my
     place. This table has so many
     memories.
                    (MORE)

IVAN (CONT'D)

Like I said, I wrote so many good stories at this table. I also like the fact that all those cool people partied at this table - especially the Stones. This table brings nothing but good cheer to all who sit around it.

STEVE

It's brought me a lot of good cheer. I slept on this table many a night with a few birds, as well. You want to know something?
     (pauses, reminiscing)
You've been a very loyal client, as well as good friend, for years. You would sit there for hours smoking, typing away on your laptop in your own little world. You truly deserve this table if anyone does. You probably spent more time at this table than I have. If I have it my way, you'll get this table. You want to know something? I bet if you scraped the top surface of this table you would probably get a hundred euros worth of hash to smoke. Thank god this table wasn't in the Red Light District, you'd be scraping something else off the surface. That would be the true meaning of table love.

Both men laugh.

IVAN

You're crazy! Do you know anything about this table? How old it is? Where it was made? I really don't recognize this species of wood, and I've been working with wood my whole life. It's a very unique table.

STEVE

No, not really. I asked the landlord once and I think he said it was made in America. He's a Frenchman who acquired it in Paris many years ago. I thought he said it was a hundred years old or so, and judging by the looks of it, it looks its age.

Steve looks over Ivan's shoulder.

                    STEVE (CONT'D)
What are you working on now?

          IVAN
It's a cool story about Sylvan, the
creator of Art Decay. You know Sylvan?
He used to stop in the Palace now and
again.

          STEVE
Yeah the American-Dutch bloke that did
crazy dead art and loved those smart
shops. I met him a few times, he was a
nice chap. Didn't really know him
though. Seems like all you artists are
more into your art than poor little
Steve.

          IVAN
Poor little Steve is never around long
enough to have a quality conversation.

          STEVE
That's true! So what's the Decaying
artist story about?

          IVAN
Yeah, the story's about his life, a
biography if you will. He comes to
Holland, creates this new sensational
art called Art Decay. As his art gets
older, it starts decaying, taking on a
new appearance. As his art goes
global, he becomes a hot commodity in
the art community. He also changes his
name to Verdun Grey to confuse the Art
World. He then does something crazy,
unthinkable in the art world.

          STEVE
What's that?

          IVAN
I can't ruin the ending, it's an
artistic, bohemian, love story. I
think this is the big one.

          STEVE
I thought you had a big one already!
"The Honey Cure," where this scientist
creates a new super honey which
becomes the new excitement and cure-
all.
          (MORE)

STEVE (CONT"D)
Didn't you win all sorts of awards for
that one? Cannes, the Russian Film
Festival...

                    IVAN
Indeed, that was a good one. I think
the scientist in "Honey Cure" is
related to Sylvan from Art Decay in
some sort of way. My wife was so proud
of me on that one.

                    STEVE
I bet she was. That was a kick ass
story. Where did you meet your wife?

                    IVAN
Ester? I met her when I was at the
University in Tilburg. I'd seen her
around campus a few times then I saw
her on the streets during Carnival
stuffing her face with chocolate. I
walked over to her and said "you're my
soul mate." She burst out laughing,
gave me a big kiss, and got chocolate
all over me. Real romantic, huh? So we
started dating for a year or so until
we graduated. We lost touch for a few
years. When I was traveling through
Belgium, I looked her up and it was
like I saw her yesterday. After a few
months, I convinced her to move back
to Holland with me, and two kids
later, here we are.

                    STEVE
Were you with Ester at the time you
won those awards for the honey story?

                    IVAN
Yes, we were already married. She was
pregnant with our son at the time, so
I went to the Award Ceremony solo. Did
you know that when I was a young lad,
I worked for this French Event Company
setting up tables, chairs, red
carpets, sound systems, and so forth.
When I found out that my movie -
actually, it wasn't my movie, but my
story was winning awards in Cannes, I
was on the first flight to France. And
there they were backstage: the same
French Company, the same French guys I
used to work with setting up the
shows.

                    STEVE
          I bet they never expected that!

                    IVAN
          I just couldn't believe that I - Me! -
          would be walking the red carpet. That
          I would have my ass on one of those
          chairs that my colleagues set up.
          That's the first time I felt proud
          about what I was doing. A real
          achievement. A real sense of pride. A
          real artist. I was really hoping that
          the honey movie would have sold
          mainstream in the States, though. Then
          I would be a real big shot. Instead
          it's still the plain old simple me
          with a little more respect for my art
          and a lot more money in my bank.

                    STEVE
          I know what you mean, mate, about the
          money in your pocket thing. I used to
          have loads of money. I just kept
          spending and spending like there was
          no tomorrow. You know the ladies love
          it when you throw money around.

                    IVAN
          Especially at the Red Light District,
          right, Steve?

Both men laugh.

                    STEVE
          You know, if I could take all the
          money I ever spent on hash and girls
          and put it in my hands right now...
               (pause)
          I could buy a lot of hash and girls.

Ivan stares at Steve.

                    IVAN
          Ha, ha, that was good, took me a
          minute.

                    STEVE
          You know, your next story should be
          about me. I'm exciting, I'm
          interesting. You know what I mean?

Both men keep laughing.

                                        FADE OUT.

EXT. IVAN'S HOUSE - NOON

Ivan walks out the front door to greet movers, while his wife
ESTER follows.

                    IVAN
          Hi guys, weren't you supposed to be
          here yesterday?

The movers don't say anything, just shrug.

                    IVAN (CONT'D)
          Never mind. Easy does it guys, I don't
          want to fix more than I have to.

                    ESTER
          What is that?

                    IVAN
          It's a table. I was told it was made
          in America in the early nineteen
          hundreds, I think.

                    ESTER
          I see it's a table, a very big one at
          that. What do you plan on doing with
          it?

                    IVAN
          I'm gonna restore it. It'll be our
          dining room table and my writing
          table. A little piece of Americana or
          something like that.

                    ESTER
               (reading aloud)
          "Woodstock 69", "Jimmy lives",
          "Janis is hot". Honey look at all
          the graffiti carved into it. Do you
          really think this is salvageable?
          Where on earth did you get this
          monstrosity?

                    IVAN
          They closed the Crystal Palace on the
          canal and I bought it for a hundred
          euros at the Auction. This table has a
          lot of sentimental value to me, as
          well as history. Did you know the
          Stones partied at this table? Verdun
          Grey painted on this table. I have
          twelve years of writing at this table,
          as well. All those children's books?
          Done at this table.
                    (MORE)

                    IVAN (CONT'D)
You know the Honey movie that won
those awards in Russia and at Cannes?
Those stories, as well: at this very
table.

Ivan stares at Ester.

                    IVAN (CONT'D)
You were very proud of me when I
flew to Cannes to receive those
awards. And, it's all because of
this table.

                        ESTER
                    (lovingly)
Yes, I was very proud of you. And I
am still proud of you.
                    (under her breath)
I still think you paid a hundred
too much for this table.

                        IVAN
                    (laughing)
Excuse me honey? I can't hear you.

                        ESTER
                    (stuttering)
Nothing my love, I was saying that
I didn't think a hundred was that
much.

                        IVAN
You wait and see dear, I'm gonna take
this to my workshop and make it look
brand new. Of course, I'll have to
keep a few of the Woodstock/Hippy
references.

Ester points her finger at him.

                        ESTER
You do that buster, this table
stays in your workshop.

                        IVAN
Only kidding, my love. I'll make this
look like a brand new table, then I
can start writing my new story.

                        ESTER
New story?

                    IVAN
          Yeah, I'm writing a story about this
          talking Totem Pole in Alaska that can
          see and predict people's lives in the
          future. A tribal American Indian
          story, very epic. I'm gonna need to do
          a bit of research on this one though.
          Maybe we should think about taking the
          kids to Alaska. We could fit in a
          holiday the same time while I'm doing
          research. We've never been to the
          States, this would be a great
          opportunity for the kids. What do you
          think?

                    ESTER
          Wow, that would be awesome, the kids
          would love it.

                    IVAN
          Ok, let's talk more about in the next
          few months. We need to make sure we
          have enough money. Right now, I have a
          lot of work to do on this table. Go in
          the house and see what the kids are up
          to while I get these table pieces to
          my workshop. I can hardly wait to
          start this project.

                    ESTER
               (shouting as she walks
                away)
          And what a project it is! But, I am
          excited for you honey. Excited
          about Alaska, as well.

Ester opens the front door while shouting.

                    ESTER (CONT'D)
          Hey kids, start packing! Your
          father's taking us to Alaska.

Kids yell in the background.

                                        FADE OUT.

INT. WORKSHOP - DAY

Ivan works on the table. The door opens and in walks Ester.

                    ESTER
          Hi honey, I brought you some coffee
          and cake.

                         IVAN
                    (concentrating)
               Thank you, my dear.

Ivan puts on his reading glasses.

                         IVAN (CONT'D)
               Honey, take a look at this branding
               underneath the table. At first, I
               thought it was more graffiti...
                    (reading aloud)
               "This table belongs to Iris Cohen.
               This table has been in our family
               since 1937. Please contact Iris
               Cohen, Old Post Road, Scarsdale,
               New York, USA." Look, there are two
               Star of David on either side of the
               branding.

Ivan stares at Ester.

                         IVAN (CONT'D)
               This is pre-WWII, maybe this table
               was taken by the Nazis?

                         ESTER
                    (sarcastically)
               Yes, it was taken by the Nazis and
               given to the Crystal Palace Coffee
               Shop so all the druggies could
               smoke pot and carve their names in
               it.

                         IVAN
               I'm being serious, Ester. Look at this
               table. This table has real history. I
               was told it was made in America, but
               how did it end up in Holland? I'm just
               speculating, but maybe the owner -
               Iris - lived in Holland, then moved to
               New York, and never took the table
               with her. Ohh I forgot Steve said
               something about the owner being French
               and the table might have come out of
               Paris. Now I'm curious, where was this
               table made? Who is Iris Cohen? What is
               the importance of this table that they
               would put an ownership branding
               underneath?

Ester pours coffee.

                         ESTER
               You're thinking too hard.

Ivan caresses the table.

                    IVAN
          I have been working with wood for
          twenty-odd years, and I've never
          seen such a type of wood like this
          before. It's so dense and the deep
          rich colors are just amazing.

                    ESTER
               (interrupting)
          Maybe it's from Norway or Russia -
          not from America as you say.

                    IVAN
               (sarcastically)
          My dear, all the wood in Europe
          comes from Norway and Russia. This
          wood is special. I really feel it
          was harvested from the U.S.,
          probably New York. That might
          explain the Iris-Cohen-Scarsdale-
          New York-branding.

                    ESTER
          Would it make a lot of sense to ship a
          table from Scarsdale, New York, USA -
          wherever that may be - to Amsterdam,
          The Netherlands, Europe? It's only a
          table what's the big deal about a
          table? Other than that it's too large
          to fit in anyone's home.

                    IVAN
          Maybe this table has sentimental value
          - a family heirloom if you will.
          Perhaps I should contact this Iris
          Cohen and let her know we have her
          table. Now, I'm very curious about the
          correlation between this table, Iris
          Cohen, and the Crystal Palace.

                    ESTER
          You know, she might still want it.
          After all, you did sand out the
          Woodstock and Hendrix carvings. Maybe
          she carved them after she went to
          Woodstock. Iris, the Jewish tripping
          hippie. Wasn't that concert in New
          York? Maybe she doesn't want the table
          anymore because you sanded out her
          carvings, maybe-

                    IVAN
              (interrupting)
          Alright already! Thank you for
          taking up the one minute of my life
          I'll never get back. I'll search
          the internet tonight and look up
          Cohen on Old Post Road in
          Scarsdale. It shouldn't be too
          hard.

                    ESTER
          Now Ivan, you just got done telling me
          how much this table means to you, that
          you have twelve years of history with
          this table, and how the Stones partied
          at this table. Now you're looking to
          give it away? Just like that?

                    IVAN
          Ester, there's a reason I have this
          table in my possession right now.
          Maybe this is a sign. My destiny,
          maybe the table's destiny. My
          curiosity is running wild. I need to
          find out who Iris Cohen is and why
          she's missing her table. This could be
          a new book. The Table, or The Missing
          Table. Either way, I must find out who
          this Iris Cohen is and why this table
          might be so significant in the life of
          Iris Cohen. Now, please, let me be. I
          want to get this table ready, one way
          or another.

Ivan turns on the sander as Ester exits.

                                        FADE TO BLACK.

INT. LIBRARY - EVENING - LATER

Ivan in front of his computer, talking to himself.

                    IVAN
          This must be it. This must be the
          number. Everything matches up - the
          name, the address. Now I need the
          country code to dial the U.S. Ah, yes
          here it is, the number one. Ok, here
          goes nothing.

Ivan starts dialing.

                        IVAN (CONT'D)
                    (on the phone)
                Hello. Yes, I am looking for a Mrs.
                Iris Cohen?

INT. KITCHEN - NEW YORK - DAY - LATER

JACOB, a heavyset, middle aged man, and son of Iris Cohen,
answers the phone.

                        JACOB
                Hello? Yes this was - I mean, is - the
                house of Iris Cohen. How may I help
                you?

INT. IVAN'S LIBRARY - JACOB'S HOUSE - SPLIT SCREEN

Ivan in Holland chats on the phone with Jacob in New York. Ester
tries to listen in.

                        JACOB
                Hello.

                        IVAN
                    (nervously)
                Yes, hi. My name is Ivan van
                Koening. I was wondering if I could
                speak to Mrs. Iris Cohen please?

                        JACOB
                May I ask what this is regarding?

                        IVAN
                Well, uh, yes. I am calling from
                Amsterdam, The Netherlands, Europe. It
                seems that I have something that
                belongs to Mrs. Iris Cohen. May I
                speak to her please?

                        JACOB
                    (confused)
                What? What? What kind of something?

                        IVAN
                Well I was at an auction and purchased
                a very old, very large, and very heavy
                table. There is a branding mark burnt
                in the wood underneath the table with
                the name Iris Cohen. I would really
                like to speak with Mrs. Cohen, is she
                available by chance?

                    JACOB
              (excitedly)
          Table, table, did you say table?
          What kind of table? How big is this
          table? Where is this table?

                    IVAN
          Yes, uh. So is Mrs. Iris Cohen
          available?

                    JACOB
          No, I'm sorry she's not here right
          now, but you can speak to me. I'm her
          son, Jacob. So, you have the table?

                    IVAN
          Oh, hey Jacob my name is Ivan, very
          nice to speak with you.

                    JACOB
              (rudely)
          Yeah yeah, whatever Steven, what
          about this table?

                    IVAN
          No, no, my name is Ivan.

                    JACOB
              (angrily)
          Whatever, so what about the table
          whoever you are?

Ivan pulls the phone from his ear and shakes his head.

                    IVAN
          Yes, well Jacob. As I mentioned
          before, I was at an auction in The
          Netherlands. I purchased this very
          old, very large and very heavy
          table. There's a branding mark
          underneath with your mother's name
          and address. Iris Cohen, Old Post
          Road, Scarsdale, New York.

                    JACOB
          Yes that's where I live. I mean that's
          where we live. You found the table! I
          have been looking for this table for
          years. I spent endless vacations in
          Paris trying to seek out this table.
          Where did you say you found it? Where
          is the table right now?

                    IVAN
It's in my workshop in Amsterdam,
Holland.

                    JACOB
How did it get there? We were told by
the family, the last place this table
was seen was in Paris.

                    IVAN
I don't know. Like I said I purchased
this table at an auct-

                    JACOB
          (interrupting, yelling)
Listen here Steven, I don't know
who you think you are and I don't
care. You have my property. Where
is my table? I want my table! It's
my property. I'm calling the police
if you don't return my table to me
immediately.

                    IVAN
          (calmly)
Jacob, calm down, calm down. First
of all my name is Ivan, not Steven.
Secondly, this is the very reason
I'm calling. I saw that the table
belonged to your mother so I'm
calling to let her know it is in my
possession and if this table has
any sentimental value to her -

                    JACOB
Yes, it has a lot of sentimental value-

                    IVAN
Ok, I'll gladly return it to her
immediately. All I want, is to talk to
your mother and find out the story and
the origin of this table. It's very
important to me. I'm a writer. I wrote
a few books and award-winning stories
at this very table. I would like to
hear what your mother knows about this
table and would love to ask her a few
questions. This table could make a
great story in itself.

                    JACOB
My mother is not here. What do you
want for it?
          (MORE)

                         JACOB (CONT'D)
You're not going to extort me, I'll
not stand for that. I'll call the
police.

Ivan places his hand over the phone and whispers to Ester.

                    IVAN
Honey, he keeps saying he'll call
the police if we don't return the
table.

                    ESTER
               (whispering)
Call the police, over a table? What
do the police have to do with this?
It's only a table. Maybe this table
came from Woodstock and it really
is famous-

Ivan looks at Ester, then at the phone, then at Ester then
back at the phone.

                    IVAN
Jacob, Jacob, Jacob, stop. I'm not
trying to extort you or anything of
the kind. I'm trying to contact
your mother to find out the history
of this table and return it to her
if, in fact, that's what she wants.

                    JACOB
Well, what do you want so we can get
our property back?

                    IVAN
               (frustrated)
Look Jacob, I paid a hundred euros
for the table. This table means a
lot to me. If your mother really
wants the table, she can come to
Holland and give me back my hundred
euros. Before she picks up her
table, I have a bunch of questions
I need to ask her. By the way you
can also tell her I sanded the
table top for her and that's on the
house.

                    JACOB
               (very sweetly)
Ok, ok, Im sorry Steven-

                    IVAN
          (interrupting, angry.)
It's Ivan!

                    JACOB
I'm sorry, I'm sorry, I'm sorry. Now
calm down. If what you want is a
hundred euro we will gladly meet your
demands. Could you wrap this table up
and ship it to me? I'll give you my
address and pay for the shipping.

                    IVAN
No, I cannot wrap the table up and
ship it to you. You don't understand!
This thing is huge, it would need to
be shipped in a crate.

                    JACOB
I'll pay for the shipping and the
crate.

                    IVAN
I don't care if you pay for the
crating and shipping and you fly it
first class. I'm NOT shipping this
table anywhere. Like I said, it's
huge. It cost me more to get it
delivered to my workshop from across
town in Amsterdam then it did for the
table itself. And I'm not even asking
for the transport money back.

                    JACOB
How big is this table?

                    IVAN
Lets just say it can seat about
sixteen with room to spare. It's so
heavy it needs a middle support. Even
if I were to ship it to you I think it
would have to go by boat.

                    JACOB
Oyyveyy. That is a big table.
          (pause)
I have a great idea. What if you
cut up the table into smaller
pieces, packed it up, then shipped
it to New York? I would pay for the
shipping and packing. And as a
token of my goodwill, I would give
you and your family an all-expense-
paid vacation to New York.
                    (MORE)

                    JACOB (CONT'D)
          And give you your hundred euro
          back. Oh, I would also pay your
          moving charges you incurred to get
          it to your workshop. What do you
          say to that?

                    IVAN
          Wow, an all-expense-paid vacation in
          New York? That's very generous of you.
          That's like a dream come true. You
          mean for me and my family? There's
          four of us, you know.

Ester starts jumping up and down, then doing a few crazy dance
moves.

                    JACOB
          Yes, an all-expense-paid vacation for
          you and your family. No problem. Four
          of you, five of you, it
          doesn't matter.
               (weepy)
          The only thing that matters is
          getting this table back to my poor
          old dying mother.

                    IVAN
          Oh I'm sorry to hear. You didn't tell
          me your mother was dying. That being
          said, I'll have to put the table back
          together for her when it reaches New
          York. Which means I would need to ship
          my tools, as well. Unless you have
          tools I can use.

                    JACOB
          No, no need my friend. I know one of
          the greatest carpenters in the state
          of New York, maybe even the whole East
          Coast. Her name is Isabella Gallager.
          Her father was a carpenter, her
          grandfather was a carpenter, her great
          grandfather was a carpenter. When it
          comes to wood this girl knows wood.
               (pauses, then grins)
          The whole family can fix or build
          anything. All I ask is the table
          gets to me - I mean to my poor old
          dying mother - and I'll take it
          from here.

                    IVAN
A woman carpenter? I like that! I'll
get this table to you ASAP, and do you
one better. I'll make this table shine
for your mother. I'll get on it right
away and make it perfect. This way
Isabella only has to glue the pieces
back together and give it a light
sanding.

                    JACOB
First and foremost give me all your
information and I'll give you all my
information.

                    IVAN
Ohh yeah, right, my name is spelled I
V A N-

                                        FADE OUT.

INT. RENTAL VAN - MOVING - DAY

Ivan drives a rental van. Ester sits in the front seat, DAUGHTER
in the back seat asking questions. Jacob paces in front of the
house, disheveled and stressed.

                    ESTER
             (excitedly)
Slow down, it looks like we're
getting closer. Ok, that's the
house on the right. The big white
one.

                    IVAN
Wow, that's some house. Look at the
size of that thing. I've never seen a
house that size up close before. I can
hardly wait to see inside, see how the
other half of the world lives.

The horn beeps and Jacob runs towards the van. Ivan and Ester
exit the van.

                    ESTER
Stay in the car, kids.

                    IVAN
Hello, you must be Jacob. I'm Ivan and
this is my wife-

                    JACOB
              (interrupting)
         Yeah whatever, where's the table?

                    IVAN
              (surprised)
         Uh, in the back of the vehicle.

                    JACOB
              (annoyed)
         Where have you been Steven? I have
         been waiting for you all day. Do
         you know how valuable my time is?

Jacob opens the back door, grabs the table legs, and runs
back to the house.

                    JACOB (CONT'D)
              (screaming)
         Get the hell off my property. Get
         you and your horrible family out of
         here. Jump in that piece of shit
         rental van and get out of my
         driveway. Hurry up, the neighbors
         are looking. If you don't leave
         right now, I'll call the police.

Ivan, confused, looks at Ester. Then Jacob. Then Ester. Then
Jacob.

                    IVAN
         Jacob, Jacob. Can I speak with your
         mother please?

                    JACOB
         Did you hear what I said, bozo? Get
         out of here, or I'll call the police.

                    IVAN
              (screaming)
         I want to speak with Iris Cohen,
         please!

Jacob turns to his wife.

                    JACOB
         Call the police.

Ivan grabs Ester and jumps in the van, screaming.

                    IVAN
         I bet your mother's not even dying.

                    ESTER
          This is weird, this is surreal.

                    IVAN
          Let's get the fuck out of here.

Ester turns around to face the kids.

                    ESTER
          Everything's ok kids, just a little
          bump in the road.

                    IVAN
          What the hell just happened back
          there? WOW, that was like a bad movie.
          Honey? Please tell me I'm not in a
          dream. Please tell me that my jet
          lag's not hallucinogenic.

                    ESTER
               (whispering)
          I'm so confused. I thought he
          wanted the table, but he only took
          the legs and then he made us leave
          like we were a bunch of circus
          clowns with poisonous cotton candy.
          That was crazy strange.

                    DAUGHTER
          Papa, why didn't that man take the
          whole table?

                    IVAN
          I don't know, cupcake. Your mother and
          I are still trying to figure this one
          out.

                    ESTER
          Now what?

                    IVAN
          I don't know. He seemed so nice on the
          phone. I don't know what happened. I
          don't know what to make of this.

                    ESTER
          So what are we going to do?

Ivan looks in the rearview mirror at the kids, then at Ester.

                    IVAN
          We're going to return this rental van
          and explore New York. That's what
          we're gonna do.

                    ESTER
What about the table? What are we
gonna do with the table?

                    IVAN
You're right, I forgot about the darn
table. That table gave me a lot of
writing inspiration. I guess I'll get
a saw at the hardware store cut out
the corner that has the branding and
make my own little writing table back
home. I hope Mick and Keith sat at
that end of the table. The rental van
is under Jacob's name. Let's leave the
rest of the table in the back and get
out of the rental place as quickly as
possible. After all, it's his table
and his rental van. Let him take full
responsibility.

                    DAUGHTER
Papa?

                    ESTER
Not now, cupcake. Your father's trying
to think.

                    IVAN
And if he changes his mind about the
table he can go to the bloody rental
place himself to retrieve it. He'll
have to pay us a handsome chunk of
money for the corner of the table with
the branding. He'll also have to
apologize to us and let me meet with
Iris Cohen.

                    DAUGHTER
But Papa? Papa?

                    IVAN
     (aggravated)
Yes cupcake.

                    DAUGHTER
Why did that man only take the legs of
the table and not the whole table?

                    IVAN
I don't know, cupcake. People are very
strange sometimes.

                    DAUGHTER
          Papa, maybe that man only wanted the
          legs because they meant something to
          him. Maybe there is a note or message
          on the legs.

                    IVAN
          Maybe, cupcake.
               (then, to Ester)
          I'm still confused. You think the
          branding under the table would have
          had more significance than the
          legs. It had a name and an address.
          I wonder where Iris Cohen was
          during all this? I wonder if she
          was even told we were in New York
          with her table? Maybe she's dead
          and the legs are for her coffin.

                    DAUGHTER
          Papa?

Ivan rolls his eyes.

                    IVAN
          Yes cupcake.

                    DAUGHTER
          Papa, if that man thought the legs
          were so important, he forgot one.

Ivan adjusts the rearview mirror, looks at his daughter, then
looks at his wife.

                    IVAN
          Honey, she's right. Jacob only took
          four legs. He didn't take the fifth
          leg, I wonder why.

                    ESTER
          Ivan we have to turn around.

                    IVAN
               (seriously)
          We're not turning around. Not after
          the way he treated us.

                    ESTER
          Ivan, it's obvious that those legs
          meant something to these people. It
          could be a religious thing. Kinda like
          part of their Menorah or something.
          Honey you have to turn back.

                    IVAN
We're not going back, no way, no how.

                    ESTER
          (sweetly)
Honey, let's be better people than
them. It's obvious they need these
legs for their religious ceremony
or something. Like you said, maybe
the legs are for his mother's
coffin.

                    IVAN
Honey, I don't think they'd need five
legs for a coffin. He has four legs,
if it's for a coffin, I think he's
covered.

                    ESTER
Let's turn around. Please please
please.

                    IVAN
          (feeling a little guilty)
Ok, ok. But we are not turning
around. We will drop off the van
then head to the hotel. I'll call
Jacob from the room. If he wants
the fifth leg he can retrieve it
from the front desk in the lobby.
I'll tell him the rest of the
table's in the van, just in case he
changes his mind.

                    ESTER
Awww, that's my Pooh Bear. You know
something, he might be on medication
and he's not thinking clearly.

                    IVAN
Not thinking clearly? Clearly, he's
not thinking. Did you see the way his
wife and the zombie twins with the
same outfits cheered when Jacob
grabbed those legs? Then they started
waving their hands and shooing us away
when we were told to get out of there
before the police came. Maybe the
whole family is on medication.
But you're right maybe they need
the fifth leg for their religious
ceremonies. We'll let him know the
fifth leg is at the front desk and
then we're done.
                    (MORE)

                    IVAN (CONT'D)
We did what was asked of us and now
we are done. With a capital D.

                    ESTER
But, what if he changes his mind and
wants the whole table and you have the
missing piece he needs? Then what?

                    IVAN
Like I said, he can contact us and
we'll negotiate. But I'll be damned if
I give up this piece of the table
without a personal apology, a reward,
and a meeting with Mrs. Iris Cohen in
the flesh. Even if she's dead and I
have to go to the cemetery to see her.

Ester pouts.

                    ESTER
You don't really need that piece
more than them.

                    IVAN
Ok, I'll give him back the missing
piece, but only if I can speak with
his mother to get the whole story
about this table. I need closure on
this bizarre table story. I'm a
writer, I need a story to make sense.
If she's in the ground then I'll let
everyone Rest In Peace and we'll move
on.

                    ESTER
Aww, honey who's the best?

                    IVAN
You and the kids are, you and the
kids. You know something? This story
is so weird I should write a short
story or a book about these people and
their obsession with table legs.
        (gesturing with hands in
         the air)
The Mad Zombie and His Family of
Three. The only way they survive is
rubbing these certain table legs
with their foreheads.

                    ESTER
        (laughing)
Ohh honey, you're so funny. You
have a great imagination.

                         IVAN
          I have a great idea. After we drop off
          the table leg at the front desk, let's
          have the concierge book us dinner and
          a Broadway show.

Ivan looks in the rearview mirror.

                         IVAN (CONT'D)
          Who wants to go to a Broadway play
          tonight?

Everyone in the car starts screaming.

                                        FADE OUT.

INT. HOTEL LOBBY - LATER

Ivan, Ester, Daughter and SON walk through the lobby carrying
bags and pieces of the table. Ivan rings the bell and is greeted
by a very flamboyant, sarcastic RECEPTIONIST. Receptionist eyes
the family up and down.

                         RECEPTIONIST
          Yes, may I help you peoples?

                         IVAN
          Yes, we have a reservation under van
          Koening, Ivan van Koening.

                         RECEPTIONIST
          Ok, let me see. I am sorry, peoples,
          that reservation has been cancelled.

                         IVAN
            (confused)
          Cancelled? That can't be. We just
          got in, came all the way from
          Holland to bring a table to a
          gentleman in Westchester, New York.

                         RECEPTIONIST
          I see right here peoples, it was
          cancelled two hours ago by a Mr. Jacob
          Levine. The room was reserved with an
          American Express card. And yes it has
          been cancelled with a capital C.

Ivan looks back and forth from Receptionist to Ester.

                         IVAN
          This is some kind of joke, right?

                    RECEPTIONIST
          I'm sorry, sir, this is the Hilton,
          not Comedy Central. There are no jokes
          here. There are no hidden cameras,
          there are no bikini clad woman gonna
          jump out from behind that pillar and
          hand you a check for a million
          dollars. Your room has been cancelled,
          you get it? Got it? Good!

                    IVAN
              (shocked)
          Yeah I get it.

                    RECEPTIONIST
          If you would like to make a
          reservation, rooms start at four-
          eighty-five per night. That is FOUR
          HUNDRED and EIGHTY-FIVE US DOLLARS per
          night and no that is not a joke
          either. Would you like to make a
          reservation or not?

                    IVAN
          Four hundred and eighty five dollars
          per night? You're joking.

                    RECEPTIONIST
              (dramatically, waving his
               hands and fixing his
               hair)
          Oh my God, this is a joke, we're on
          TV! Where's the cameras? Where's
          the cameras? I need to look good
          for all my friends and fans in
          Chelsea. Where are the fucking
          cameras?

Ivan and the family walk away. The Receptionist continues to be
a drama queen in the background.

                    ESTER
          Wow, now what are we gonna do?

                    IVAN
          I knew we should have checked in
          before we went to Scarsdale to drop
          off the table.

                    ESTER
          Yes honey, but you know Jacob had
          strict orders to bring him the table
          first. After all, he was paying the
          bill.

                    IVAN
          Well I guess he was not paying the
          bill in the end. I hope our return
          tickets are still valid so at least we
          can get home.

                    ESTER
          Oh, don't be so negative, Pooh. Things
          happen for a reason. I've got a great
          idea. Since we're already in the
          States, why don't we rent a car or
          take a bus to Alaska? You said you
          wanted to work on the living totem
          story. We're already packed. What do
          you say, kids?

The kids and Ester jump up and down. Ivan shakes his head and
rolls his eyes.

                    IVAN
          Do you know how far Alaska is from
          New York? It has to be at least
          four thousand miles, give or take.
          We're not going to Alaska, we're in
          New York. We're just gonna make the
          best of the situation.

                    ESTER
               (confused)
          Four thousand miles? How far is
          that in kilometers?

                    IVAN
               (annoyed)
          It doesn't matter, we're not going
          to Alaska. We're in New York and
          we're gonna stay in New York.

                    ESTER
          I tried kids. Looks like there's no
          trip to Alaska. I guess we're not
          gonna pet bears anytime soon.

                    IVAN
          Let me get on my cell and look for a
          cheaper hotel. Honey, can you go to
          the receptionist and ask for the
          password for the internet please?

                    ESTER
          I'm certainly not going over there.
          He's gonna think we're playing another
          joke on him.

Ivan shakes his head and walks toward the receptionist.

                    IVAN
          I'll go.

Ivan walks back a moment later.

                    ESTER
          What did he say?

                    IVAN
          He kept saying -
               (mockingly)
          "Is this a joke? Is this a joke?
          You want the internet? You must be
          joking. Is this a joke?"
               (normally)
          It took a little persuading, but
          finally he handed me a piece of
          paper with the password.

                    ESTER
          I tell you. This New York place gets
          stranger by the minute.

                    IVAN
          That it does, that it does. Ok, I
          found a place in the East Village for
          around one hundred and fifty dollars.
          Much cheaper. Let's keep looking.

                    SON
          Let's stay in New Jersey next to Bruce
          Springsteen.

                    DAUGHTER
          Shut up and play your video game,
          brat. Bruce Springsteen don't live in
          New Jersey anymore he lives in Asbury
          Park where the first postcard was
          invented.

Ivan looks up from his phone and shakes his head.

                    IVAN
          Kids, we're not gonna stay in New
          Jersey or near Bruce Springsteen.
          We're gonna stay in New York and
          enjoy the sights. Here we go. I
          found a budget hotel in the East
          Village for one hundred and ten
          dollars per night. Let's get one
          room for a night or two until we
          can figure things out.

                        ESTER
          That's a great idea. Come on my little
          soldiers follow me.

Ester grabs her bag and the table leg and starts marching in
place. The kids follow suit.

                        DAUGHTER
          Mama, mama! Stop! Stop! You keep
          dropping and spilling metal pieces and
          everything all over.

                        SON
          Mama, you're dropping all your rings.

                                        FADE OUT.

INT. HOSPITAL ROOM - AFTERNOON

IRIS lays in bed watching tv. Jacob walks in holding table legs,
his wife, CAMILLO, and their TWIN KIDS follow behind.

                        JACOB
               (sternly, holding up table
                legs)
          Hi, mother dear, how are you?

                        CAMILLO
               (very cold and serious)
          Hi Mother.

                        TWIN KIDS
               (in harmony)
          Hi, Grammy.

Iris ignores Jacob and Camillo.

                        IRIS
               (New York accent)
          Hey kids how are ya? You two got
          really big, let's have a look at
          ya. Wow. Oh my my. If I remember
          correctly, today is both of your
          birthdays and next year you two
          will have your Bar Mitzvahs, or
          should I say B'Nai Mitzvahs. That's
          a very big step for a young Jewish
          person.

Iris turns to Jacob.

                    IRIS (CONT'D)
Why do you have to dress the twins
the exact same way? Hellooo! One's
a girl, one's a boy. They look like
fucking elves. So right after
Hanukah, they're gonna run around
with fucking Santa Clause?

                    TWIN BOY
        (interrupting)
It's alright Grammy, we like
dressing the same. We think it's
funny.

                    IRIS
        (snapping)
That's not funny, that's fucking
weird. Pretty soon, they'll put you
in a dress. Will you still think
that's fucking funny?

                    TWIN BOY
I don't know. Maybe.

                    IRIS
Thats alright, you kids will learn
soon enough. I said my piece. If I
knew you kids were coming over, I
would've gotten you a cake or
something.

                    TWIN GIRL
That's alright, Grammy.

                    IRIS
        (proudly)
But I will do one better I'm gonna
sing you a birthday song. I never
did like the traditional Birthday
song, so as a young girl while I
was in boarding school, I made up
my own birthday song. It goes like
this:
        (humming a little to get
         in tune)
Happy Birthday I am not the same.
My age don't matter, what's your
name?
You think that I am way too old.
I'm so damn young or so I'm told.
Happy Birthday, when I saw you
last.
You grew too quick and way too
fast.
                (MORE)

                    IRIS (CONT"D)
Your hair was short and now it's
long.
Your image changed, your body
strong.
Happy Birthday, kiss and smile
well.
The grey's set in or can't you
tell?
Another candle for my wish.
Smack that pastry on my dish.
Happy Birthday, wish you all the
best.
You're growing old like all the
rest.
You plant your friends inside the
earth.
Your grandkids now are giving
birth.
Well the birthday thing's for old
and young.
I wish you well on your next one.
I have to go I'm fading fast.
I hope this birthday won't be your
last.
Happy Birthday, Happy Birthday,
Happy Birthday.

                    TWIN KIDS
          (simultaneously)
That sucked, Grammy.

                    IRIS
Jacob give me that piece of wood, I'm
gonna beat some manners into these
genetic defects of yours.

                    JACOB
Enough with the kids, mother. Here's
the table legs. Remember the story you
told us kids for years? The legs, the
precious table legs. The legs that are
worth more than Marilyn Monroe and the
Lincoln Center Dancers' legs put
together? You know the legs that even
Loyds of London couldn't even afford
to insure?

                    IRIS
          (annoyed)
Yes Jacob, I know, I know, I can
see the legs. I saw them when you
first walked in. I may be an old
bat but I'm not a blind bat.
                    (MORE)

IRIS (CONT'D)
And yes I got your relentless phone
messages all week. But I thought
you came to pick me up and get me
out of this godforsaken place and
bring me to see a long lost table.
A piece of family history. Instead
you bring me only the table legs.

                JACOB
Why didn't you return my calls?

                IRIS
Enough, Jacob. So where's the rest of
the table and the lovely Dutch people
who returned our precious family
heirloom?

                JACOB
I got rid of them. Once they brought
the table, they became useless,
expendable freeloaders.

                IRIS
        (angrily)
They were kind enough to return a
very valuable piece of family
history and you threw them to the
street like a bag of old rags? How
could you?

                JACOB
        (defensively)
I gave them four round trip plane
tickets from the Netherlands! Well,
I actually used the Amex points you
had saved up, which you weren't
gonna use anyway. I also gave them
the hundred euros that they paid
for the table. That's almost a
hundred and fifty dollars which
came out of my own pocket and I'm
not even looking for that money
back.

                IRIS
My God Jacob. You're as cheap and
greedy as your fucking father.

                JACOB
Don't speak like that about Dad, he's
not here to defend himself.

                    IRIS
               (sarcastically)
          You're right. As my mother would
          say, we should always speak good of
          the dead. Your father's dead...
          good.

                    JACOB
               (Upset.)
          Mother, enough enough enough. So
          here are the table legs. I brought
          them like you demanded on my
          answering machine.

                    IRIS
          Yes, those are the four identical legs
          I remembered as a little girl. Out of
          the whole family, only I could tell
          which leg sat under which part of the
          table.

Iris picks up one leg and caresses it.

                    IRIS (CONT'D)
          So you got rid of the Dutch family,
          I got that. Now, where is the rest
          of the table? You can't eat off a
          few legs.

                    JACOB
               (confused, stuttering)
          Well, well, when you told us the
          relentless stories of you growing
          up in Paris, you always talked
          about this table and how these
          ornate legs were the most important
          part of the table. You always
          emphasized the legs, the legs, the
          legs, the legs. So here are THE
          LEGS.

                    IRIS
               (angrily)
          I will ask you one more time. Where
          is the rest of the table Jacob
          Levine?

                    JACOB
          Well, when the Dutch family finally
          arrived I grabbed the four legs and
          made them leave and I made them take
          that firewood scraps of table with
          them.
                    (MORE)

JACOB (CONT'D)
I didn't want that junk sitting on my
front lawn. What would the neighbors
think?

                    IRIS
          (furious.)
My front lawn, that is my lawn!
Just because you threw me in this
old folks' home with these
shriveled up, crinkly people
doesn't mean I no longer own my own
home. It was left to me by your
great grandfather, not to you. My
name is still on the deed. I am
leaving MY HOUSE to your sister. If
she wants to give you something out
of the goodness of her heart, it's
up to her.

Iris turns to the twins.

                    IRIS (CONT'D)
Hey kids, don't get comfortable in
that house you're living in. You
might have to move to an apartment
in Yonkers cause of your deadbeat
dad.

                    JACOB
          (embarrassed)
Ok mother calm down, calm down.
Let's not dwell on this, I have the
legs of the table that's all I
have.

                    IRIS
          (disappointed)
So you don't have the rest of the
table?

                    JACOB
No Mother, I'm sorry, I don't!

                    IRIS
You're sorry? I don't think you've
ever been sorry for a day in your
whole life. You make me sick. *I'm*
sorry. Sorry I brought you into this
fucking world.

Jacob looks at Camillo and the twins, then back to his
mother.

                    JACOB
Mother, please don't talk that way
about me in front of my family.

                    IRIS
Would you like them to leave the room?
Have a seat my bastard son and let me
tell you the real story about this
family table. That's right, Jacob.
Keep rolling your eyes inside your
head, you might actually see some
brains for once up there. Where was I?
Ohh, ohh.

It was just before World War Two
around the Great Depression. My
father was one of the richest men
in Paris. He moved from Belgium
when he was a little boy.
     (pointing to the twins)
About your age you little brats. He
worked in the gem and precious
metal industry thanks to my
Grandfather but that's a whole
other story.

My father worked twenty-hour days,
seven days a week, just so he could
perfect and master his craft in
jewelry design. He was one of the
best. He made the finest brooches,
necklaces and rings in all of
Paris. Hell, in all of Europe.
Everyone wanted his craftsmanship.
He was a true artist.

When the Great Depression hit, my
father was the only one left
standing in the jewelry industry.
Saving everything he ever earned
unbeknownst to him that he would be
in that position. His previous
employers went belly up, his
competitors went belly up, but he
stood there standing in an almost
depleted jewelry industry.

> That's when my father took over
> what was left of the industry to
> become the best jeweler in Paris,
> as well as all of Europe.

Jacob stands up.

> JACOB
> Get to the point, Mother.

> IRIS
> Shut up, sit your ass down, and pay
> attention.

She looks at the twins.

> IRIS (CONT'D)
> You ungrateful kids should be proud
> of your great-grandfather. He was
> the finest jeweler in the twentieth
> century.
> (staring at the ceiling)
> Ohh yes. There was this Italian man
> named Sal I'll never forget his
> name, he knew my father real well.
> I think my father had designed some
> jewelry for him throughout the
> years.He was this big shipping
> tycoon. He was the biggest shipping
> magnate in the world.
>
> I met this man personally when I
> was a little girl. He was a big
> man, not as big as my father but a
> very nice man. He always had kind
> words to say about me. I think he
> liked me.
>
> Anyway, with the Great Depression,
> Sal went bankrupt and lost
> everything. So, he contacted my
> father to sell him some jewelry,
> art, books, or something like that
> and this great big table, as well.
> This table was so huge and heavy it
> took maybe ten or twenty men to
> carry it into the house from what I
> remember.

Jacob, Camillo and the kids get fidgety.

> JACOB
> We know the story mother!

                    IRIS
This table sat in the dining room. We
did everything at this table. We ate,
we read stories, my mother would help
me with my studies, we would play
games. All my parents' guests would
sit around this table for endless
hours, talking, drinking and eating. I
sat around this table for endless
hours, days, even years doing all
sorts of things.

                    CAMILLO
It's a very lovely story.

                    IRIS
        (dreamily)
My father was so proud of that
table. I think he was also proud of
the fact that the table had been
made in America and shipped to one
of the wealthiest men in Italy.

Soon after the war started,
everything was confiscated from all
the families in Paris and around
France. My father didn't think he
and his family were in danger -
after all he was one of the richest
people in Europe. My father also
designed jewelry for a lot of high
ranking officials and gave lots of
gifts to the right people.

He was smart, very important and a
generous man.

Jacob stands, agitated.

                    JACOB
Ok Mother, we heard this story
before, get to the point please.

                    CAMILLO
Jacob, please.

                    IRIS
        (angrily)
Shut up and don't interrupt me, you
fat little toad.

Ohh yeah, so my father didn't think
our family was in any danger but to
be on the safe side, he melted down
half of his gold inventory and
poured it down the hollows of two
of these here legs.

Iris holds a leg in the air, and Jacob jumps to his feet.

                    JACOB
          So these four legs are filled with
          gold?

                    IRIS
          No! Not all four, only two, don't you
          ever listen? You see, he couldn't
          deplete all his gold inventory because
          it would have looked very suspicious.

                    JACOB
          So only two legs are worth anything?

                    IRIS
          Let me finish, you fat piece of crap.
          So my father, your grandfather, took
          two table legs and filled them three
          quarters with gold and he took the
          other two table legs and filled them
          all the way with lead.

          This way the table would have an
          even distribution of weight. He
          also put the two gold legs kitty
          corner from each other so each end
          of the table would have an
          undetectable amount of weight.

          My father was a smart man, he was
          always thinking.

Jacob picks up two legs.

                    JACOB
          So which two legs are filled with
          gold and which two are filled with
          lead ?

                    IRIS
               (angrily)
          Shut the hell up and let me finish.
          Put those legs down.

Iris looks at the twins.

                    IRIS (CONT'D)
Your father is always talking,
never thinking. I hope you two
don't grow up to be an asshole like
him.
          (then)
Ok, so my father was always
thinking. He was always thinking
about his designs, his family and
even the table. So my father in his
shop designed a branding iron like
the kind you brand horses or cows.

                    JACOB
Yes, that's what the Dutch guy Steven
said, there was a branding under the
table.

Iris glares at Jacob.

                    IRIS
As I was saying, my father branded
underneath the table just in case
we had to part with the table for
any reason. Those were very
troubling times. But my father was
always thinking ahead, a very smart
man.

So as a little girl I would always
go under the table and read that
branding.

Jacob mouths the words as Iris recites.

                    IRIS (CONT'D)
"This table is the property of Iris
Cohen, Three-Fifty-Five Old Post
Road, Scarsdale, New York. Please
return to the rightful owner for
this table is a family heirloom."

Those were the first words I ever
learned in English. I was so proud
of that table knowing that my name
was stamped underneath. I used to
look at that branding every day and
ask the same question to my father
over and over. Why is my name under
the table with grandfather's
address when I live in Paris?

> And my Father would repeat the same
> thing time and time again: "One day
> my princess you will be living at
> that address in Scarsdale, New
> York."

Iris stares at Jacob with a mean look.

                    JACOB
               (interrupting)
          Ok Mother that's-

                    IRIS
               (snapping)
          I'm not fucking finished, you
          hippo.

Iris looks at the twins, who are playing with their phones.

                    IRIS (CONT'D)
          Sorry children, that you have a
          father like that. So where was I?
          Ohh, so after my father branded the
          table with my name, he took the
          middle support or as we might call
          it the fifth leg.

Iris stares at Jacob with eyes filled with hatred.

                    IRIS (CONT'D)
          And he filled the fifth support leg
          with rings, brooches, necklaces,
          cut and uncut diamonds, rubies,
          emeralds, sapphires, and my
          mother's second wedding ring.

Iris continues to stare back at Jacob with an evil look.

                    IRIS (CONT'D)
          So I shall ask the question once
          again. Where is the rest of the
          table? Where is that fucking fifth
          leg? Where is my mother's wedding
          ring?

                    JACOB
               (white as a ghost,
                stuttering)
          Fifth leg? I didn't know this table
          had five legs. All tables have four
          legs. I have always seen tables
          with four legs.

He points to the different tables around the room.

JACOB (CONT'D)
Look this table has four legs. That
table has four legs. So does that
one. I never heard of a table with
five legs.

IRIS
This isn't just any table this is my
table. Don't make me ask again. Where
is the rest of the table and that
fifth support leg?

JACOB
I don't know.

IRIS
(shouting)
What do you mean, you don't know?

JACOB
(scared)
I sent it off with the Dutch
people. I said they could keep it.
I didn't want all those scraps of
wood on my front lawn.

IRIS
That's my front lawn, my front lawn.
Now call those Dutch people and tell
them you made a mistake and get my
table and my fifth support leg back.

JACOB
You see Mother, it's not that easy. I
don't know where they are.

IRIS
What do you mean you don't know where
they are? Call their hotel, call their
cell, email them, do something.

JACOB
I don't know which hotel they're
staying in and I deleted their emails
with all their info.

IRIS
You said you gave them flights from
Holland using my Amex points. I am
assuming you gave them a hotel as well
with my Amex points?

                    JACOB
                (embarrassed)
          No. I didn't want to use the Amex
          points because they're non-
          refundable and we're going to
          London next month. You see,
          actually, I put the reservation on
          your Amex card but after they
          delivered the table legs, I
          cancelled their hotel reservation
          and Amex refunded the full amount
          back to your card.

Jacob points at himself, very proud.

                    JACOB (CONT'D)
          You see, I was trying to save you
          money, and this is the thanks
          I'm getting?

                    IRIS
                (angrily)
          Well call their fucking cell
          numbers, email these fucking
          people. Do something.

                    JACOB
          Like I said, unfortunately I deleted
          their email address and cell numbers.
          I also put a block on everything so
          they wouldn't bother us.

                    IRIS
          What? You did what? Let me understand
          this. These nice people called you up
          out of the blue saying they wanted to
          return a table to our family, a table
          that's worth a few million dollars.
          You get them all the way here, take a
          few pieces of the table, and kick them
          out on the street? You are a horrible
          human being Jacob Levine.

Jacob holds his head down. Camillo and the twins stare with
their mouths open.

                    IRIS (CONT'D)
          Jacob you blundering idiot, give me
          your phone.

Jacob holds up his phone. Iris snatches the phone and dials an
old friend, Seth.

                    IRIS
              (very sweetly)
          Hello Seth, this is Michou.

                    SETH
              (surprised)
          Well hello Michou, lechaim lechaim
          lechaim. And to what do I owe this
          phone call? I thought you were
          retired.

                    IRIS
          Retired? Who's retired when it comes
          to jewelry? You know me, I was always
          a shaker and a mover on 47th.

                    SETH
          That you were, and you are well missed
          - even by the Belgian. You know he
          always had a thing for you, he didn't
          like anybody, but when it came to you,
          you commanded respect.

                    IRIS
          Yeah, that's cause my father was from
          the same neighborhood in Belgium.
          Seth, quick question this is very
          important. Did a Dutch family come to
          your store or around the street trying
          to offload a large amount of goods?
          Like cut and uncut stones, rings,
          brooches, necklaces to name a few?

                    SETH
          Wow, how did you know that? That only
          happened twenty minutes ago. Word
          travels fast. You're truly a shaker
          and mover.

                    IRIS
          Seth, this is very important. Where
          are these people now?

                    SETH
          I don't know. They came walking around
          the district with this piece of wood,
          which looked like an old table leg. It
          was filled with goods. Very odd. They
          walked into a few stores then they
          walked in the Belgian's store and
          started speaking, I guess in Dutch or
          Flemish? It wasn't French, that's for
          sure, and the Belgium whisked them
          away in a limo.

                    IRIS
Shit shit shit shit. Did you get a
look at any of the goods?

                    SETH
I sure did. I was probably the first
to get a peek. Once these people hit
the street Isaac called me up and I
ran right over. This load was way over
the top. I wish I could have been part
of it.

                    IRIS
     (voice quivering)
Seth? Was there a ring that looked
like a rose that had three
different colored diamonds, which
only a royal family could afford?

                    SETH
Exactly. Were these your clients? Were
those your goods?

                    IRIS
Let's just say, I knew the designer.

                    SETH
You know the designer? You know the
designer? Where is he right now, I
have a job for him right away.

                    IRIS
Yes I did know the designer. He
passed, he was my father.

                    SETH
Wow. I'm sorry to hear. Your father
was a true artist. I am so sorry to
say this Michou, but those pieces are
probably lost forever. Once that
shrewd Belgian gets his hands on
something, it's gone forever. Those
pieces are probably on a plane as we
speak, off to some rich, oil-drinking
country.

                    IRIS
     (disappointed)
I know, you're probably right. Even
if I had the Belgian's cell number
and called him, he wouldn't deal
with me. He might have liked me as
a Belgian, but he never got over
the Tiara redesign I took from him.

> SETH
> Yes and he does hold grudges.

> IRIS
> That he does, that he does. Seth do me
> a favor - if any of these pieces hit
> the street again, could you give me a
> call, please? Especially the rose
> ring.

> SETH
> Michou, anything for you.

> IRIS
> Seth, you're a doll. You're the only
> one I ever trusted on that street.
> Take care.

Iris hangs up the phone and throws it in the corner of the room.

> IRIS (CONT'D)
> Now the Belgian has the fifth leg
> and everything is lost forever. You
> see, the fifth leg was the second
> most important thing about that
> table besides the memories. Now I
> don't have the fifth leg or the
> table of memories. Now the only
> thing that's left is four table
> legs and the long lost memories.
> Like I promised you, Jacob, two
> legs go to you and two legs go to
> your sister.

Looks at the four legs, hesitates, grabs two legs and holds them
in the air.

> IRIS (CONT'D)
> Now here are your two legs. Take them
> and do whatever you want, but don't
> ever come around here again. I'm sick
> of looking at you.

> JACOB
> (concerned)
> Mother, how do you know which legs
> are filled with gold and which legs
> are filled with lead?

Iris stares at Jacob.

> IRIS

                         IRIS (CONT'D)
          I know, I know. I've been around these
          legs my whole childhood. Now take
          those legs and get out of here and let
          me be. I'm too young for all this
          excitement. I guess the next time I'll
          see you people is at my funeral. Take
          care twins, don't grow up to be like
          these two scumbags you're calling
          parents.

The twins give Iris a hug and a kiss, Jacob and Camillo head
straight for the door. Jacob holds the door open, angry.

                         JACOB
          Come on kids let's get a move on.

                         IRIS
               (yelling)
          I hope the door hits you in the ass
          on the way out you bastard. You two
          little monsters better get an
          education cause you're probably not
          gonna get shit from your father.
          And don't wreck my house you pagan
          squatters.

The twins exit, Jacob slams door, and Amanda walks in.

                         AMANDA
               (confused)
          Hello Mother, I just saw Jacob,
          Cammy, and the twins leaving. Jacob
          came to visit you? I thought you
          hadn't seen him in five years?

                         IRIS
               (sarcastically)
          Yeah, that was your good-for-
          nothing brother trying to bother
          me. I think he's trying to get on
          the good side of me so when I get
          to heaven I can put in a good word
          for him. He should be talking to
          his father so when he goes to hell
          his father doesn't turn up the heat
          on him.

                         AMANDA
               (changing the subject
                awkwardly)
          Now, Mother!! Would you like to
          take a stroll around the grounds
          today?
                         (MORE)

AMANDA (CONT'D)
It's a beautiful day outside. That
would make it the sixth time this
week I got you out of this room.
I'm hoping tomorrow will be the
seventh.

IRIS
I'm sorry, I don't think I feel up to
that today. I'm exhausted after your
brother's visit.

AMANDA
Mother, what did he say or do to you?

Amanda pulls out her cellphone.

AMANDA (CONT'D)
I'm gonna call him right now.

IRIS
No no nothing, put down the phone.
Your brother Jacob is just being Jacob
that's all. Don't worry yourself in a
tizzy.

AMANDA
Ok ok, so mother what do you say we go
outside?

IRIS
Not now Amanda I'm a little tired.
thanks for trying.

Amanda gazes lovingly at her mother.

AMANDA
Ok, that's fine, no problem. So
let's chat then. What are these two
pieces of wood doing in your room?

IRIS
(smiling)
Your brother Jacob brought them
over. They're for you.

AMANDA
They're for me? I don't understand.

IRIS
Did I ever tell you the story about
the table that used to be in our
family?

                    AMANDA
          Yes you did Mother, since my
          childhood, but tell me again. I know
          you love telling that story and I like
          hearing it, as well.

Iris looks up at the ceiling.

                    IRIS
          Well, it all started in Paris
          around the Great Depression and
          there was this shipping magnate
          named Sal.

                                        FADE TO BLACK.

Warming up backstage before my mime gig (I miss Polaroids!) at the Empire State Building for a new store opening. They say nobody likes a mime but, I got paid for that gig. So, someone out there at some point liked a mime.

Me in my Verdun Gray character at
Sequoia National Forest in California.

ART DECAY

BY

GLENN TRIPP

EXT. BACKYARD - AFTERNOON

SYLVAIN, a young boy, plays by a stream in his backyard. MAMA is
seen through the kitchen window washing dishes.

                    MAMA
               (yelling from window)
          Syl! What are you doing back
          there?!

                    SYLVAIN
          Nothing!

                    MAMA
          Why are you digging in the dirt?

                    SYLVAIN
          Just looking!!

                    MAMA
          Looking for what?

                    SYLVAIN
               (aggravated)
          Nothing much, just looking!

                    MAMA
          Well, stop looking. Come in the house
          and wash up for dinner.

                    SYLVAIN (V.O.)
          If only you would leave me alone. I'm
          old enough to take care of myself,
          stop treating me like a little kid.

                    MAMA
          What did you say Syl?

                    SYLVAIN
          I didn't say anything.

                    SYLVAIN (V.O.)
          What, are you hearing things? Why
          don't you stop bothering me for once?

                    MAMA (V.O.)
          Yes, I heard you, I would leave you
          alone if you were older and more
          responsible, my dear Sylvain.

Sylvain stares at his mother. He hears her speaking, but her lips don't move, realizing for the first time he has the same telepathic gift as her.

                    MAMA (V.O.)
          I'm your Mama doing what I'm
          supposed to do, just being your
          Mama, that's all. You remind me so
          much of your father.

Sylvain becomes introverted and spacey when he realizes that Mama can read his thoughts.

                    SYLVAIN
               (mumbling)
          Ok, I'm coming.

                                        FADE OUT.

INT. KITCHEN - LATER

Sylvain sits at the dinner table with Mama.

                    MAMA
          Syl, why did you have those cans of
          house paint by the stream?

                    SYLVAIN
          Just experimenting.

                    MAMA
          What kind of experimenting?

                    SYLVAIN
          Just bored, something to do.

                    MAMA
          You know if you keep pouring that
          paint in the stream, you're gonna kill
          the fish and the frogs. When they're
          all dead this place will be overrun
          with mosquitoes.

                    SYLVAIN
          I wasn't pouring it in the water. I
          was drizzling it, checking out the
          different patterns as they floated
          with the current. I don't think that
          little bit is hurting any ecosystem.

                    MAMA
          Well, whatever you're doing it can't
          be good for nature!

                    SYLVAIN
          I don't think doing laundry with all
          that bleach and detergent is good for
          nature, either.

                    MAMA
          Well, I have to get the laundry
          cleaned. Besides it doesn't go
          directly into the stream. It goes into
          the septic and ruins that bio-world.

                    SYLVAIN (V.O.)
          I can't listen to this anymore.

                    MAMA
          You have something to say?

                    SYLVAIN
          No Mama, may I be excused, please? I
          don't have much of an appetite right
          now.

                    MAMA
          Ok, I'll put it in the fridge you can
          warm it up later.

                                        FADE OUT.

EXT. CEMETERY - EVENING

Sylain sitting in the cemetery leaning against the headstone
with a pad and pencil, feverishly drawing in frustration. Dozens
of sheets of drawings scattered around him.

                                        FADE TO BLACK.

EXT. CLASSROOM - MORNING

Sylvain daydreams in MR. BOLAND's history class.

                    MR. BOLAND
          Ok, class, when was the French
          Revolutionary War? Sylvain?

                    SYLVAIN
          Huh? A what?

                    MR. BOLAND
          The year, please!

                         SYLVAIN
                    (confused)
               Why do snakes and worms have the
               same- Sorry, what? What was the
               question?

                         MR. BOLAND
                    (annoyed)
               We're not talking about snakes and
               worms, son. We're talking about
               history. History, my son! The
               subject is the French Revolutionary
               War. This is not a science class.
               This is a history class.

                         SYLVAIN
               I'm sorry, I thought- I mean- I was
               thinking about something else, sir.
               Sorry.

                         MR BOLAND
               Well, pay attention in my class, son,
               because I'm here to teach and you're
               here to learn. This is not just a
               history class, it's a history
               experience and you, you mindless
               sphere are going to retain this
               information. Do you understand that,
               little boy?

                         SYLVAIN
                    (embarrassed)
               I guess, I do, sir!

PRINCIPAL enters.

                         PRINCIPAL
                    (annoyed)
               Mr. Boland, may I have a word with you
               in the hall, please?

                         MR. BOLAND
               Okay, class, open your books to
               chapter eleven. I'll be right back.

Sylvain stares at Mr. Boland as he exits.

                         SYLVAIN (V.O.)
               Now see what it's like to have someone
               yell at you, you bald headed cue ball.

Mr. Boland turns around and stares at Sylvain, as if he heard
something.

                    SYLVAIN (V.O.)
          That's right, keep staring jack-ass,
          it's the only time you'll see a
          brilliant human being in your life.

As Mr. Boland exits the classroom, Sylvain gives him the middle
finger.

                    SYLVAIN (V.O.)
          Fuck you and your French Revolutionary
          War.

                                        FADE OUT.

EXT. HIGH SCHOOL - LATER

Sylvain bumps into a friend, PHIL.

                    SYLVAIN
          Hey Phil, what's up? Where you going?

                    PHIL
          To art class!

                    SYLVAIN
          Wow, I'd love that class. How come you
          get to go to art class?

                    PHIL
          Because I signed up for it! Didn't you
          sign up for an extra class this year?

                    SYLVAIN
           Didn't know I had a choice.

                    PHIL
          There'll be a lot of choices in life
          that'll pop up that you may never know
          about. Ask and you shall receive,
          Syl.

Sylvain freezes in mid-step.

                    SYLVAIN
          I'll keep that in mind.

                    PHIL
              (arrogantly)
          Got to go. Can't keep art waiting!

Phil walks away.

                    SYLVAIN
          You're so right. Can't keep art
          waiting.

                    SYLVAIN (V.O.)
          I'll show you how to mix colors. You
          spoiled brat.

Phil turns around like he heard something and stares at
Sylvain.

                    PHIL
          Sorry?

Sylvain walks away with his head down.

                                        FADE OUT.

EXT. MAMA'S HOUSE - AFTERNOON - TEN YEARS LATER

Sylvain lookS like a hippy artist. Mama showS some gray.

                    MAMA
          Sylvain, where you going?

                    SYLVAIN (V.O.)
          Out.

                    MAMA
          Out where?

Sylvain looks at his mother and leaves.

                    MAMA
              (shouting)
          I know where you're going!

Mama stares out the window.

                    MAMA (V.O.)
          You're going to that new art
          gallery that opened in the city. I
          don't think you're gonna like what
          you see there. I guess you'll have
          to find out the hard way, just like
          the rest of your life.

Sylvain creepily turns around towards Mama, stares at the
ground, turns back, and then walks away.

                                        FADE TO BLACK.

EXT. LIVING ROOM - MORNING

Mama paces the floor. Sylvain enters, looking disheveled.

                    MAMA
          Where have you been? I was crazy-sick
          worried about you!

Sylvain hurries for the stairs.

                    SYLVAIN
          I was out. You didn't see or feel
          where I was?

                    MAMA
          I'm not happy right now! When you live
          under my roof, you must obey my rules.
          You can't just say you were out
          and have me worried sick for three
          days.

Mama follows Sylvain upstairs.

                                        FADE TO:

INT. BEDROOM - MOMENTS LATER

Sylvain starts packing.

                    MAMA (V.O.)
          What are you doing?

                    SYLVAIN
          Mama, I'm going!

                    MAMA
               (confused)
          Where, where, where you going?

Sylvain drops a plan ticket on the bed.

                    SYLVAIN
          Holland, I'm gonna to start my
          future.

                    MAMA
               (nervously)
          Holland? Like in Holland, the
          Netherlands, Europe?

                    SYLVAIN
          Yes, Mama!

                    MAMA
God damn it, Syl! Why are you going to
Holland? What's in Holland? I left
Holland as a pregnant young woman
because I saw no future for you and
your brother. Now you're going to
Holland for what? Your future?

                    SYLVAIN
I'm gonna learn how the great artists
got inspired. Then I'm gonna be as
great as they were and you're gonna be
so proud of me.

                    MAMA
Are you crazy? How long you going for?
And, you're gonna stay where?

                    SYLVAIN
I'm gonna stay with Uncle Piet!

                    MAMA
You're gonna stay where? Do you really
think my baby brother's gonna deal
with you waking up at three in the
afternoon and going to bed at three in
the morning?

                    SYLVAIN
That's when I get my inspiration,
Mama. In the day I feel like a blob
but at night I'm ready show the world
my talents.

                    MAMA
Piet has a very high profile job. He
has to be up early every morning, he
works till really late! How you gonna
find him anyway? Holland's a very big
country you know? I don't even know
where he's staying and he's my
brother!

                    SYLVAIN
For the last eight months I've been
corresponding with Uncle Piet through
e-mails and Facebook. Not only did he
think it was a great idea, he was the
one who made all the arrangements.

                    MAMA
You've been planning this trip the
whole time without telling me?

                    SYLVAIN
          Yes, Mama. I always had a dream to
          visit Holland and now's my chance.
          Besides if I told you about my plans
          eight months ago you would have tried
          to stop me every day for eight months.

                    MAMA
          Honey!

Holds her hands out.

                    SYLVAIN
          I'm not your little honeybee anymore,
          Mama. I'm a grown man. I need my
          freedom, I need to show my free
          expression in my art and in my sole.
          The only reason I stayed for as long
          as I did was because of you. I don't
          even like Tuxedo, New York! This town
          gives me the creeps - and I love
          creepy things!

                    MAMA
               (emotionally)
          I love you.

                    SYLVAIN
          I love you too, Mama. Don't start
          crying.

                    MAMA
          What do you want me to do?

                    SYLVAIN
          I don't want you to do anything, Mama.
          Just want you to understand that as an
          artist I need your blessing for this
          journey, as well as my freedom.

                    MAMA
          What about all your paintings in the
          cellar?

                    SYLVAIN
          I'll take care of them.

                    MAMA
               (panicking)
          You can do what you want here.
          Don't go! You can hang your
          paintings all over the house. You
          can stay out for as long as you
          want. I need you here.

                    SYLVAIN
It's not about any of that, Mama, it's
- just, about, what I believe in. I
need to follow my dreams. You followed
your dreams when you made the journey
to America with a teenager and me in
your belly. Now it's my turn to follow
my dreams.

                    MAMA
But that was different. Those were
different times.

                    SYLVAIN
Yes and these are different times and
this will be a different journey. My
journey!

                    MAMA
I'll be all alone in this big old
house! Who's gonna take care of me
when I get old? Your brother Shepard
has been gone for years traveling the
planet. And now you? I feel so alone
already!

                    SYLVAIN
I'll be back, Mama. I'll be gone a few
months, perhaps a year, tops. I
promise.

                    MAMA
That's what you think. You're never
gonna come back I can feel the air.

Mama stares at Sylvain and starts crying.

                    MAMA (V.O.)
I'm gonna miss you. Your art is more
important than everything, even me.

                    SYLVAIN
     (yelling)
That's not true.

                    MAMA (V.O.)
As you say, but not as I think.

                    SYLVAIN
Mama? Speak to me, don't think to me!

                    MAMA
This house will always be yours, you
know!
            (MORE)

                         MAMA (CONT'D)
               I always wanted the best for my
               children. I'll send you money if you
               need it.

                              SYLVAIN
               I don't need money, Mama. I saved up a
               little more than two grand.

Mama stares at the floor and starts crying.

                         SYLVAIN (CONT'D)
                    (tenderly)
               Mama, ik hou van jou! That's Dutch
               for I love you.

Mama laughs and cries at the same time.

                              MAMA
               I know what it means. Ik hou van
               jou!

Mama and Sylvain stare into each other's eyes, both start
crying, as they hug.

                                        FADE TO BLACK.

EXT. CEMETERY - AFTERNOON

Sylvain sits on grass, dozens of paintings propped against
headstones.

                              SYLVAIN
                    (crying)
               Well, I'm leaving tomorrow. I don't
               know when I'll be back. You all
               keep a look after my Mama for me,
               please. Eventually you'll be on her
               walls to look after both of us all
               the time, I promise. I'll never
               reproduce any of you. I'll always
               look at every one of you as my very
               close friends. Friends that'll
               never turn on me. Thanks again, I
               love each and every one of you.
               Each one of you holds a special
               place and a special day in my
               heart. I will never forget.

Sylvain pulls out a marker and writes something on every
painting.

                                        FADE OUT.

EXT. SCHIPHOL AIRPORT - MORNING

Sylvain with large backpack and map talking to TOURISTS.

                    SYLVAIN
          Excuse me, I want to get to Herring
          Street in Den Haag. Can you tell me
          where to go, please?

                    TOURIST
          Sorry mate, not from around here,
          never heard of the place.

A tourist "over here's" Sylvain, looks at Sylvain's map, points
him in the right direction.

                                        FADE OUT.

EXT. STREET - AFTERNOON

Sylvain walks down the street.UNCLE PIET, a middle aged man with
GQ looks walks out of the building.

                    UNCLE PIET
               (surprised, excited)
          Yo, Syl, you finally made it! When
          I spoke to your Mama, she said you
          were gonna be early. I kept looking
          at the monitor and every hour you
          were delayed another hour. I was at
          the airport for four hours and
          finally I had to run, just couldn't
          wait any longer. How you been?

                    SYLVAIN
          Sorry Uncle Piet. We had a huge
          layover in Iceland, I figured I missed
          you at the airport so I decided to do
          a little tourist thing before we met
          up.

Both men hug.

                    UNCLE PIET
          No worries, youngster. You're safe and
          that's what matters. Let's grab a
          coffee, then we'll get my car so I can
          take you to your new place.

                    SYLVAIN
          I'm not staying with you, Uncle Piet?

                    UNCLE PIET
          I just said that so your mother
          wouldn't worry. I really have no room
          for two people. Besides, I have a
          really crazy job I need to concentrate
          on. Can't have any distractions. You
          understand, right?

                    SYLVAIN
               (confused)
          Yeah, sure, I understand. So where
          will I stay?

                    UNCLE PIET
          Everything's all arranged. You'll stay
          at Ivo's house. He's a good friend of
          the family.

                    SYLVAIN
          Ok, I'm following your lead, sir.

Sylvain and Uncle Piet walk down the street laughing.

                                        FADE TO BLACK.

EXT. STREET - LATER

Sylvain exits Uncle Piet's car.

                    UNCLE PIET
          Here we are, his name is Ivo, spelled
          I V O. Just ring the bell, he's
          expecting you. Tell him I had to get a
          flight to Switzerland, I'll catch up
          with you two in a few weeks.

Sylvain slams the door.

                    SYLVAIN
          Ok, thanks for everything, Uncle Piet.
          When you come back I'll take you out
          to dinner, my treat. See you in a few.

                    UNCLE PIET
          No problem youngster, I'm looking
          forward to catching up on how your
          mother and brother are doing. Keep the
          paint flowing, hope you paint the
          world red or whatever color it needs
          to be painted.

Uncle Piet stares at Sylvain crossing the street then drives away.

                                        FADE OUT.

EXT. STEPS - MOMENTS LATER

Sylvain stands on the steps and knocks on door. IVO, a tall thin guy with blond hair, answers.

                    IVO
          Hoe gaat het met jou?

                    SYLVAIN
          Sorry?

                    IVO
          Just fucking with you. I heard you and
          Piet talking in front -

Ivo looks around.

                    SYLVAIN
               (interrupting)
          Uncle Piet left. He had to catch a
          flight to Switzerland. I think he's
          running late. He said he'd meet up
          with us in a few weeks.

                    IVO
               (sarcastically)
          Piet is always running around the
          world. Thailand, New Zealand,
          Switzerland. What else is new? So,
          you're Auntie Kay's little boy?
          Come on in you little bastard.

                                        FADE OUT.

INT. LIVING ROOM - MOMENTS LATER

Sylvain and Ivo enter the living room.

                    IVO
          Put your bag over there, have a seat,
          make yourself at home. So you're
          Sylvain? I heard a lot about you.

                    SYLVAIN
               (nervously)
          Yeah I'm Sylvain. You know my
          Mama?

                    IVO
          I knew your mama when I was a little
          boy. She use to live next door and
          mind me. Everyone called her Auntie
          Kay. I haven't seen her in many years
          though. So, Sylvain's your real name?
          What kind of name is that?

                    SYLVAIN
          I don't know. My mother named me after
          a neighbor, I think.

                    IVO
          What the hell did she do that for?

                    SYLVAIN
          I don't know. He saved her life or
          something.

                    IVO
          That's a fucking weird name!

                    SYLVAIN
          What the hell is your name? Ivo? I V
          O, what the hell's an Ivo?

                    IVO
          My name is not IIIIIVO. It's really
          pronounced EEEEEVO.

Sylvain stares at Ivo curiously as if he's reading his mind.

                    SYLVAIN
          I was told you have a place to stay
          while I'm doing my art, which room's
          mine?

                    IVO
          I have so much room you're going to
          wish you never tasted hash. Your rooms
          up stairs.

Sylvain looks at him like he's weird.

                    SYLVAIN
          Very cool, thanks.

                    IVO
          Ik kan geen Nederlands meer praten met
          jou.

                    SYLVAIN
               (frustrated, tired)
          I don't know what that means! I
          don't speak Dutch.

Ivo laughs and hits Sylvain in the arm.

                    IVO
          I know. I'm just fucking with you.
          Your Mama never spoke Dutch in the
          house?

                    SYLVAIN
          Only when she cursed. She thought
          it was rude to speak another
          language that no one understood
          while living in America. She'd
          always say -
               (in a woman's voice with
                an English accent)
          Not quite right, let's be polite.
               (resumes with normal
                voice)
          Like I said, I don't know the
          language but I'm hoping to learn. I
          just know a few words.

                    IVO
          That's a start. Everyone speaks
          English anyway, you have nothing to
          worry about. It just helps meeting
          Dutch chicks.

                    SYLVAIN
          Well, I guess I should start
          practicing right away then!

                    IVO
          There's a good idea. It's not like
          you're in France where if you didn't
          speak the language, you'd starve to
          death. I've lived there, I know, I was
          really skinny back then!

                    SYLVAIN
               (disgusted)
          Aren't the French violent people?

                    IVO
          Well, they did make a lot of history:
          Hundred Year War, French Revolution,
          World War I, World War II. Weren't
          they the troublemakers of Vietnam? Not
          sure about that one?

                    SYLVAIN
            (irritated, looks faint)
        History? Ugh, I hate that one,
        especially French history! Look,
        man, I'd really like to lay down
        for a while if that's all right.
        Just a little jet lagged, I guess.
        We can catch up in the morning over
        breakfast.

                    IVO
        Like I said, got you covered,
        Klootzak.

                    SYLVAIN
        Sorry?

Ivo shakes his head and laughs.

                    IVO
        Shakes his head and laughs.
        Come up, youngster, I'll show you
        your kamer.

Ivo walks up stairs.

                    SYLVAIN (V.O.)
        This guy is a strange one.

Ivo turns towards Sylvain.

                    IVO
        Wat zeg je?

Sylvain looks at Ivo like he understood.

                    SYLVAIN
        Huh?

Ivo shakes his head as if he's hearing things.

                    IVO
         Nix.

Both men walk up the stairs.

                                        FADE OUT.

INT. LIVING ROOM - AFTERNOON

Sylvain is upstairs, working. Ivo enters the front door with an
old white bicycle.

                    IVO
           (happily, yells upstairs)
        Yo, Sylvain, come up.

Sylvain enters hallway.

                    SYLVAIN
        Yeah, Ivo, what's up?

                    IVO
        Look what I have for you. It's a gift
        from the neighbor.

                    SYLVAIN
        A gift, for me? From the neighbor? I
        don't even know the neighbor! What is
        it? That bicycle?

                    IVO
        That's right this bicycle, from our
        lovely neighbor. They heard you were
        from the States and didn't have a
        fiets so they gave you their son's old
        bike. It's from the 60s. A real
        charmer, heh?

                    SYLVAIN
        That was very nice of them, but they
        didn't have to do that.

                    IVO
        I know they didn't have to, but they
        did. Besides, this bicycle is from the
        government. The white bicycle law.

                    SYLVAIN
        The what?

                    IVO
        The white bicycle law. I'll tell you
        about it later. Come on, let's take a
        ride.

                    SYLVAIN
        I haven't rode a bicycle since I was a
        kid.

                    IVO
        Aaaaah man, you're in Holland now.
        Everyone rides a bicycle in Holland.

                    SYLVAIN
        Yeah, I guess they do. I almost got
        hit a few times.

                    IVO
          Kom op, youngster. Let's go to the
          coffee shop for a splash of tea, let's
          try out your new bike.

                    SYLVAIN
          That's nice of you, but I'm kinda in
          the middle of something.

                    IVO
          Come on, youngster, It can wait, you
          haven't even seen the town yet. You
          need to take a break from your work,
          it'll give you more inspiration. I'll
          tell you all about the history of your
          new/old bike.

                    SYLVAIN
          Alright, you got me. Let me wash the
          paint off my hands.

                                        FADE OUT.

EXT. COFFEE SHOP - LATER

Ivo and Sylvain pull up to a coffee shop and sit on the terrace.

                    IVO
          I love this terrace. You can see all
          the girls go by on their bicycles,
          have a hash cigarette, a cup of tea,
          and no one bothers you.

                    SYLVAIN
          Yeah, this is a nice spot, very cozy
          with the ivy hanging down and the old
          buildings.

                    IVO
          So what are your plans, Syl? This is
          really the first time we got the
          chance to chat.

                    SYLVAIN
          I don't know, I just want to be an
          artist. I want to be recognized for my
          talents and art. What I want is for
          people to look at my paintings and
          say, "that was done by Sylvain." You
          know, the same way when they look at a
          Van Gogh or a Mondrian.

                    IVO
I read you loud and clear, brother.
They're gonna know you're an artist by
all the paint on your clothes.

They break into contagious laughter.

                    IVO (CONT'D)
I'm just fucking with you! I wish
you success. If there's anything I
can do to help, let me know. I
think I have some old brushes and
paints in the shed, help yourself.

                    SYLVAIN
I appreciate it, Ivo-

                    IVO
        (interrupting)
Also, don't underestimate your
Uncle Piet either. He's a very well-
connected man. He's got a lot of
contacts all over the world. He
might be a man of mystery, but he's
definitely a person in the know.

                    SYLVAIN
He probably is, but I don't want to
bother him. He's done enough for me
already. Besides, I need to do this on
my own. I think I'm on the right
track, though. I just need time,
patience and a lot of paint.

                    IVO
It sounds like you're on the right
track. You can stay at my place for as
long as your art needs. Don't forget
me when you're rich and famous!

                    SYLVAIN
I won't. Thanks again for everything,
and thanks for getting me that
bicycle, as well.

                    IVO
 I didn't get the bike for you. The
neighbor offered it.

                    SYLVAIN
Ohh yeah, I have to go to the neighbor
and thank her. What's the story about
the white bicycle you started telling
me?

                    IVO
          Well, the neighbor was saving that
          bike since the 60s for her son's
          return, from the Vietnam War. She
          promised herself to keep the bike till
          he got back, he was missing in action.

                    SYLVAIN
          That's awful. You mean I'm riding a
          dead man's bike?

                    IVO
          Yep, that's a dead man's bike.

                    SYLVAIN
          That's creepy, man. I don't want it
          anymore. I'm gonna return it to the
          neighbor right away.

                    IVO
          Are you foolish, man?

                    SYLVAIN
          I don't care if it is a free bicycle.
          I'm not gonna ride around on a dead
          man's bike. I can see it now, every
          time the neighbor looks out her
          window, she'll see me riding her dead
          son's bicycle and start crying.

                    IVO
          Youngster, I was just fucking with
          you. That's not a dead man's bicycle.

Sylvain angry, punches Ivo in the arm.

                    SYLVAIN
          What the fuck did you do that for,
          man? I was all upset for this woman
          and her missing son, you just want to
          make up stories and play games.
          Everything's a joke in your eyes.

Ivo laughs hysterically.

                    IVO
          Man, you are gullible! I thought
          you knew, Holland wasn't in
          Vietnam. You'll believe anything.
          You're like a sucker in paint
          clothes.

                    SYLVAN
How the fuck am I supposed to know? I
don't know Dutch history. I thought
you were being straight with me.

                    IVO
That was funny, man. You should have
seen the look on your face when you
thought you were driving a dead man's
bike.

                    SYLVAIN
Yeah, real funny. I knew I should've
stayed home and kept working on my
project. Instead, I come out for a cup
of tea to listen to bullshit.

                    IVO
Aahh come on, man. It was a joke. The
real truth about that bicycle is that
it's from the sixties. There's not too
many of those bicycles left,
especially in that condition.

                    SYLVAIN
What's so special about a sixties
bike?

                    IVO
In the sixties, the government made a
law called the White Bicycle Law. They
bought a million or so bicycles and
scattered them around the major cities
of Holland for the public to use,
free. If you went to the pub, you
would leave the bike you were riding
in front unlocked. When you came out,
if that bike was gone, you'd grab
another one. If you passed by
someone's house and saw a bicycle on
the front lawn, you could just take it
and so on. The white bikes were share
bikes for everyone to use. The Dutch
honor system.

                    SYLVAIN
So what happened with all the white
bicycles? Why's that one so special?

                    IVO
They disappeared. People started
painting them, putting locks on them
to make them private.
                    (MORE)

                    IVO (CONT'D)
Also, people would get drunk and throw
them in the canals or when they were
damaged people wouldn't report it to
the government - they'd just dump it
and grab another bike. One year, the
city workers dredged the canals in
Amsterdam and they pulled out over
thirty-thousand bicycles, that's just
Amsterdam. Imagine all the other
cities with bicycles in the canals.
The government program couldn't keep
up with the upkeep.

                    SYLVAIN
Wow, that's a lot of metal.

                    IVO
It sure is. So you see, you have one
of the few existing bicycles from the
White Bicycle Law in mint condition.

                    SYLVAIN
So why did the neighbor give it to
me?

                    IVO
Her son grew up and moved to Berlin.
She had no use for it, she wanted to
make room in her shed. She heard you
were from the States and didn't have a
bicycle.

                    SYLVAIN
That was very nice of her. I should
get her flowers or chocolate.

                    IVO
You really don't have to get her
anything, but as you wish. The reason
I thought you might get a kick out of
your bike is you like art and that
bike is like a piece of art, from the
sixties!

                    SYLVAIN
Yeah. It's pretty cool. I'm gonna
paint it red with black dots.

                    IVO
You're not right, man. When the
neighbor sees you painted her son's
bike, she's gonna crap her knickers.

They both laugh hysterically.

                                        FADE OUT.

INT. LOFT – MIDDAY

Sylvain, painting. IVO yells upstairs.

                    IVO (O.S.)
              Oi, Sylvain! You have some post that
              came for you.

                    SYLVAIN
              Cool. I'll be right down.

Sylvan stops working, face lighting up.

                    SYLVAIN (CONT'D)
              Mama! Mama!

                                        FADE TO BLACK.

INT. LIVING ROOM – MOMENTS LATER

Sylvain runs downstairs. Ivo looks through the mail and squeezes
an envelope.

                    IVO
              Your mother must really like to
              write. There's a novel in here.

Sylvain grabs the envelope.

                    SYLVAIN
              Thanks.

                    SYLVAIN (V.O.)
              This is not just an ordinary envelope,
              hash brain.

                    IVO
              Well, open it!

                    SYLVAIN
              Yeah, I will... It's probably mushy,
              I'd rather read it in private.

Sylvain runs upstairs.

                                        FADE TO:

INT. LOFT - MOMENTS LATER

Sylvain opens the letter, hundred dollar bills fall out.

               MAMA (V.O.)
     My dear Syl, how's everything? I miss
     you so much! It's hard to count the
     days when you're coming home. I hung
     all your paintings on the living room
     walls to give me an everyday reminder
     of how special you are in my life. I
     love you so much.

Sylvain cries.

               IVO (O.S.)
     (yelling)
     Ya, is she doing well?

               SYLVAIN
     (startled)
     Yeah, she's doing fine. She sends
     her love.

Sylvain collects the money, puts it under the pillow.

               IVO (V.O.)
     Ja, lekker.

               MAMA (V.O.)
     I sent you some money to help fund
     your art career. I hope it serves you
     well. I was wondering if I have to
     spend the holiday by myself this year?
     I would love for you to come home. I
     just want to feel the warmth of your
     eyes and hold the talent that spills
     out of your hands while enjoying each
     other's thoughts together.

He puts the letter on his chest and closes his eyes.

               FADE TO BLACK.

INT. MAMA'S LIVING ROOM (DREAM SEQUENCE) - LATER

Sylvain holds Mama's hands as they dance around the living room
to classical music until the beauty of his mother's face and the
serenity of the room disappear.

               FADE TO:

EXT. FRENCH BATTLEFIELD (DREAM SEQUENCE) - LATER

A melee rages during the French Revolution, Sylvain runs with
paintings under his arm being chased by soldiers. Red paint
spills everywhere.

                                        FADE TO:

INT. LOFT - LATER

Sylvain wakes up sweating from the nightmare, pacing the floor,
talking to himself. He picks up the clock

                    SYLVAIN
          It's midnight? I must have slept
          for six hours but only dreamt a few
          seconds of Mama and the war. Or a
          few seconds that I can remember. I
          need to paint.

He paints like a mad scientist.

                    SYLVAIN (CONT'D)
          If I just take this apple and tie it
          to the canvas -

He punctures two holes in canvas with scissors.

                    SYLVAIN (CONT'D)
          I'll just tie this up here.

He paints with strong colors and long brush strokes.

                                        FADE TO BLACK.

INT. LOFT - NOON

Sylvain wakes up in paint clothes. He hurries to new apple
painting, writes in journal.

                    SYLVAIN (V.O.)
          So, the apple took on a different
          appearance today. It's been 12 hours
          since the apple was made into a piece
          of art and now this masterpiece has
          taken on a more decayed look. With the
          moisture being leached out of the
          apple by the warm air of the room, we
          should see another piece of art in a
          matter of days.

Sylvain closes his journal. A look of genius comes over his face.

                    SYLVAIN
          I need to get more food.

Sylvain grabs his jacket and runs downstairs.

                              FADE OUT.

INT. LIVING ROOM - MOMENTS LATER

Ivo reads the paper. Sylvain runs past him.

                    SYLVAIN
          Hi, Ivo.

                    IVO
          Hey, where are you going? What's your
          hurry?

                    SYLVAIN
          Gotta get some more food.

                    IVO
          We have food here!

                    SYLVAIN
          No, that food's for eating!

Sylvain runs out the door.

                    IVO
               (yelling)
          What do you normally do with food?
          Stick it in your- Never mind, I
          don't even want to know.
               (talking to himself)
          He locks himself in his room for
          several days then runs out of the
          house like it's on fire, yelling,
          "I have to get food you can't eat!"
          Crazy New Yorker!

                              FADE OUT.

INT. LOFT - MORNING

Sylvain paints. He hears a triggered mousetrap, moves the dresser, and finds the trap with a dead moust in it.

                         SYLVAIN
          Ohh you poor creature! You will
          work fucking brilliantly for my
          next piece! A short-lived time in
          this dimension but forever
          immortalized in my artistic
          creation.

Sylvain opens his journal and writes feverishly.

                         SYLVAIN (V.O.)
          Today, April whatever, I caught a
          mouse in a trap. The mouse was dead
          instantly from the trigger bar
          crushing its fragile little skull. A
          little blood is evident, but no real
          severe bleeding. I shall accent this
          subject with lots of red. I'll call
          this "Slow Decay."

Sylvain fastens the mousetrap to the canvas and starts painting
in red.

                         SYLVAIN
          There, that's kinda done. I'll put
          this aside and see what the next few
          months bring for this masterpiece.

Sylvain stares at the canvas.

                         SYLVAIN (CONT'D)
          I might come back in a week or so and
          add a little yellow and orange, make
          it look like a sunburst Stratocaster
          guitar. We'll see the feelings in a
          few weeks.

Sylvain turns back to his journal.

                         SYLVAIN (CONT'D)
          The fur was not very friendly towards
          the paint. It seemed like it was
          clumping up in places, I guess the oil
          in its fur is not consistent
          throughout the whole creature. The red
          did the subject real justice with the
          nature of its death. On this same day,
          I hung a melon on the wall to watch it
          slowly dry and decay. After one week,
          I will take the melon off the wall and
          incorporate this semi-dried fruit onto
          a new canvas.
                         (MORE)

SYLVAIN (CONT'D)
This will create a new form of art I
shall call, "Rot Decay." That's what I
shall call it! "Rot Decay.".

Sylvain throws the journal on the desk.

SYLVAIN (CONT'D)
I need more food.

Sylvain grabs his jacket and hurries out of the room.

FADE TO:

INT. LIVING ROOM - MOMENTS LATER

Ivo sits on the couch watching tv as Sylvain runs downstairs.

SYLVAIN
Hi, Ivo.

IVO
Where you off to now? It seems like
the only time I see you is when you're
running out of the house.

SYLVAIN
Got to get some more food.

IVO
This is like fucking deja vu.

SYLVAIN
Did I get any mail?

IVO
No, your mother didn't send you a
letter. You know, it seems like the
only time you and I talk is when
you're asking if the postman brought
you a letter or if your Mama called.

SYLVAIN
I'm sorry, Ivo. Im just so deep into
my work, I don't realize what I'm
doing half the time. The days go into
nights, the nights go into days. Top
it off, I haven't heard from Mama in
eight months. Her phone's not working,
she doesn't reply to my letters... I'm
really stressed and worried about her.
Again, I'm real sorry for acting the
way I am.

                    IVO
          It's okay Syl. I know you're trying to
          do the right thing. I'll let you know
          when your mother calls or sends you a
          letter. I'm sorry for getting upset
          with you.

                    SYLVAIN
          Cheers brother, it's all good.

                    IVO
          I'll call your Uncle Piet and see if
          he can contact your Mama for you.

Sylvain stands by the doorway, lost in thought.

                    SYLVAIN (V.O.)
          She hasn't written in eight months, no
          phone calls, no reply. So she probably
          thinks that'll get me home sooner.

Ivo leans forward and stares at Sylvain.

                    IVO
          Are you ok, Syl?

Sylvain snaps out of it.

                    SYLVAIN
          Yeah, sure. Yeah, yeah, yeah, just
          fine. That would be great, contact
          Uncle Piet. I really hate to bother
          him, but...

                    IVO
          No problem, Syl. Besides, Uncle Piet
          loves to do things like this.

Sylvain's eyes fill with appreciation.

                    SYLVAIN
          Thank you, Ivo. Well, I gotta go.

                    IVO
          I know, you're gonna get more food you
          don't eat.

                    SYLVAIN
               (laughing)
          You got it. Take care, thanks
          brother.

Sylvain grabs his bicycle in the foyer and slams the door behind him.

                              FADE TO BLACK.

INT. BUTCHER SHOP - LATER

Sylvain enters an old world butcher shop, greeted by a Bavarian dressed BUTCHER who speaks with a heavy accent.

                    BUTCHER
          May I help you?

                    SYLVAIN
          Yes, please, I'm looking for a cow's
          head or a lamb's head for an art
          project. I was wondering if you might
          have something lying around I can
          buy?

                    BUTCHER
          You are English?

                    SYLVAIN
          American.

                    BUTCHER
          Good men those Americans are. During
          World War II, my father worked with
          the Allied forces, always spoke good
          about those American soldiers.

                    SYLVAIN (V.O.)
          I just need a cow's head, not a
          history lesson. Next you'll be talking
          about the French and their war. Oh
          wait, World War II was a French war
          wasn't it?

                    BUTCHER
          I think we can spare a cow's head for
          a patriotic American, let's see what
          we have in back.

                    SYLVAIN
          Thank you, sir.

The butcher comes back moments later with a plastic bag.

                    BUTCHER
          Will this work for you?

Sylvain looks inside the bag.

                         SYLVAIN
              That's great. How much?

                         BUTCHER
              Nix. My pleasure to help an American.
              Besides, I just love those American
              movies. Did you see-

                         SYLVAIN
                    (interrupting)
              Thank you, thank you, thank you
              sir. I have to keep moving, can't
              keep art waiting!

                         BUTCHER
              No problem, young man. Say, what are
              you gonna do with that head anyway?
              You say it's for your artwork?

                         SYLVAIN
              I'm gonna wire it to a canvas, paint
              the head psychedelic colors, give it
              lipstick and fake eyelashes. Gotta
              run, gotta go shock the rest of the
              world. Thanks again.

Sylvain exits the shop. Butcher stares at Sylvain getting on his
bicycle.

                         BUTCHER
              Papa always did say some of those
              Americans were strange. I finally met
              one.

                                             FADE OUT.

INT. LIVING ROOM - EARLY EVENING

Ivo yells upstairs.

                         IVO
              Hey, Sylvain!

Sylvain comes to the top of the stairs.

                         SYLVAIN
              Yeah, Ivo, What's up? Did the mail
              come?

                         IVO
              No, Syl. There's no post today, it's
              Sunday!
                    (MORE)

                    IVO (CONT"D)
          Just wanted to let you know, there's
          an awful odor coming from those paints
          you're using, and it's starting to
          stink up the house.

                    SYLVAIN
          I don't smell anything.

                    IVO
          That's because you're in your room
          twenty-four-seven, you're probably
          used to it.

Ivo throws a can of spray to Sylvain.

                    IVO
          Use this, please. I have a few friends
          coming over later. Don't want to scare
          them off.

                    SYLVAIN
          You got it, Ivo. I'll use this all the
          time. I didn't realize. I won't let it
          happen again.

                    IVO
          It's all right, it's just the smell is
          starting to get to me. What's the
          paint made of? Dead animals?

                    SYLVAIN
          Yeah, something like that.

Sylvain sprays towards Ivo and closes the door.

                                        FADE OUT.

EXT. SIDEWALK- MIDDAY

Sylvain sits on a blanket with paintings, a sign on one side
that says Art Decay. On the other side, a sign reads "Handmade
paintings - fifty euro." A tip jar stands in the middle.
PEDESTRIAN walks by and drops a tip. Sylvain drinks wine out of
the bottle as he shouts at pedestrians.

                    SYLVAIN
          Hand made paintings. Art Decay! Be
          the first on your block. Start the
          new trend. Don't be like the rest
          of the Wallies you went to school
          with. Art Decay, Art Decay. Works
          well on bathroom walls as well.

A man stops and stares at the paintings.

                    PEDESTRIAN
              (in an English accent)
          What is Art Decay?

                    SYLVAIN
              (like a salesman)
          Art Decay is a form of art that I
          invented. I take living matter and
          incorporate the composition onto my
          canvas, then I paint over the
          subject. As the years go by, my art
          takes on a different form and
          appearance, then, you have a
          different piece of art altogether
          called, "Art Decay."

                    PEDESTRIAN
          Sounds like a very interesting and
          novel idea.

The pedestrian reaches into his pocket.

                    PEDESTRIAN (CONT'D)
          My opinion, I think your art needs
          work. Although... it is very
          beautiful. Unique in its own
          special way. One day it will
          probably be worth a great deal of
          money. For now, you being an up-and-
          coming artist, I think your art is
          overpriced. Good luck and have a
          good day.

The pedestrian drops a few coins in the jar and walks away.

                    SYLVAIN
              (mumbling)
          Overpriced? You probably would have
          said the same thing to Van Gogh or
          Mondrian, you stupid cow.

Sylvain looks at his sign and back at the man walking away. He
takes out a marker, crosses out fifty, and puts twenty-five. He
looks in his tip jar.

                                        FADE TO BLACK.

INT. LOFT - MORNING

Sylvain writes in his journal on a makeshift desk, filled with
Anatomy books. Sylvain studies his painting, writing feverishly.

SYLVAIN (V.O.)
It's been three weeks since I've
incorporated the cow flesh onto
this painted canvas. Maybe I should
have put lipstick and eyelashes on
it! Anyway, I'm noticing a new
decomposition stage in the subject.
As the flesh starts to deteriorate
the paint is starting to shrink and
separate in spots. Where I've
applied vast quantities of paints,
there seems to be some preservation
to the -

IVO (VO)
(interrupting)
Oi, Sylvain, there's a phone call
for you.

SYLVAIN
Sylvain working in his Journal, yells.

Okay, just a minute.

Eyes wide open, runs to the door.

Mama! Mama!

FADE OUT.

INT. LIVINGROOM- MOMENTS LATER

Sylvain runs downstairs picks up the phone, talks to Uncle Piet.
Ivo walks out front door.

SYLVAIN
Thanks, man. Hello, Mama?

Ivo opens the front door.

IVO
It's Piet!

UNCLE PIET (V.O.)
Hey, Syl. It's me, Uncle Piet.

SYLVAIN
(confused, disappointed)
Huh, what? Oh, hi, Uncle Piet. I
don't usually get phone calls, I
thought it was my Mama.

                    UNCLE PIET (V.O.)
Hey, Syl, I had someone in the States
contact your Mama to make sure she's
alright.

                    SYLVAIN
          (excited)
Really? How's she doing? I haven't
.spoken with her in over a year. She
slowed down with sending letters
and doesn't have a phone anymore.

                    UNCLE PIET (V.O.)
Yeah, I know. Ivo told me. Like I
said, I got someone to get in touch
with her. To make sure all is good.

                    SYLVAIN
And? Is she okay?

                    UNCLE PIET (V.O.)
          (uncomfortably)
She's doing fine, she said she's
not sending anymore letters. She
disconnected the phone. Said if you
can't come home and spend some time
with her then why be tortured with
letters and phone calls? She also
said you promised her that you
would be back within a year, and
it's going on two.

                    SYLVAIN
          (angrily)
It's not two, it's almost one-and-a-
half.

                    UNCLE PIET (V.O.)
          (sympathizing)
I'm just the messenger, Syl.

                    SYLVAN
That's insane. I'm not asking her for
money or anything. I just want to
speak to her, or for her to at least
write me back!

                    UNCLE PIET (V.O.)
I know Syl. After knowing your mother
my whole life, I can't figure her out,
either. I can't figure out any women
for that matter. I told her to come to
Holland, I'd put her up and pay for
the plane ticket.
                    ((MORE))

UNCLE PIET (V.O.) (CONT'D)
She wanted no part of my scheme. She
just wants to see you back in the
states. Back in Tuxedo, New York.

                    SYLVAIN
         (whinily)
I can't go back now. Things are
just starting to happen for me.
Besides I don't really have the
cash to travel.

                    UNCLE PIET (V.O.)
Syl, like I said in the past, if you
need money, let me know. I'm there for
ya.

                    SYLVAIN
I really appreciate it, Uncle Piet,
but if I go back now, my Mama will
find some sort of excuse to keep me
there. I'll never get back here again.
Everything I've done here will be in
vain. Besides, I have this new form of
art that people are starting to groove
on. I just can't let go now!

                    UNCLE PIET (V.O.)
What can I say Syl? Again, I'm only
the messenger.

                    SYLVAIN
I know, Uncle Piet. I didn't want you
to get involved in the first place.
She's a stubborn old woman that thinks
she can always get her way.

                    UNCLE PIET (V.O.)
You can say that again.

                    SYLVAIN
She can turn off her phone and stop
sending letters. I'll write her
whether she likes it or not. I'll even
double up on the letters I'm sending.

                    UNCLE PIET (V.O.)
There you go Syl, turn the tables.
Listen, if you want to go to Amsterdam
to clear your head and make some art,
I have a flat there I hardly ever use.
I stop in now and again with a lady
friend, so if I did come by you would
have to leave for the night. But, like
I said, I'm hardly ever there.
                    (MORE)

                    UNCLE PIET (V.O.) (CONT'D)
You pretty much could stay as long as
you like.

                    SYLVAIN
Wow, that would be great, Uncle Piet.
I could use a little time away from
this tiny, one horse town. I need the
big city for a little action and
inspiration. Let me finish up this one
project before I go though.

                    UNCLE PIET (V.O.)
No problem, youngster, as you will.
I'll leave you a set of keys with my
neighbor, Monique. Grab a pen, I'll
give you the address.

Sylvain looks for a pen, sliding his books to the floor.

                    SYLVAIN
I can never find a pen in this
place. I got a paint brush, shoot.

He paints the address on canvas.

                                        FADE OUT.

EXT. TRAIN STATION - AFTERNOON

Ivo walks off a train and runs into Sylvain with a backpack and
some stretched canvases. TRAIN CONDUCTOR speaks in the
background. Ivo sneaks up behind Sylvain.

                    IVO
Hey, Syl, where you going?

                    SYLVAIN
          (startled)
Hey Ivo, you scared the shit out of
me! I'm heading to Amsterdam for a
spell. Uncle Piet said I could stay
at his flat to get some painting
done.

                    IVO
Yeah, I've been there. That's a great
place to collect your thoughts and
bring a chick. It seems like your
Uncle Piet has a flat in every city,
almost! A very mysterious man, that
Uncle Piet. Well, enjoy yourself,
mate. I have to get back.
          (MORE)

IVO (CONT'D)
Im meeting Raven at Polly Magoo's
happy hour to see the band, the
Exploding Bedroom.

SYLVAIN
Now that's a cool band. Well, take
care, have a pint for me. Tell Raven I
said hello.

Ivo walks away.

IVO
Will do.

Sylvain goes into a trance while the express train goes by.
Sylvain stares at the train.

SYLVAIN (V.O.)
If I threw a bucket of red paint in
front of the train, it would give
it an eerie blood-splattered look.
All the spray would get all over
the people on the platform, and
finally they would be wearing
trendy clothes. I could start my
own fashion line. I would call it,
"The Pieces of Shit Who Were
Standing Too Close To Art." Yeah,
that's what I would call it.

A train pulls up on the other platform.

TRAIN CONDUCTOR (VO)
Next stop, Den Bosch.

Sylvain walks toward the train.

FADE TO BLACK.

EXT. APARTMENT BUILDING - LATER

Sylvain rings doorbell. MONIQUE, an older woman in a nightgown,
looks out the window.

MONIQUE
May I help you?

SYLVAIN
Hello, I am looking for Monique?

MONIQUE
I am she. You must be Piet's nephew
from New York.
(MORE)

MONIQUE (CONT'D)
He told me you were coming over. I
have keys for you. One moment, please.
I'll throw them down.

SYLVAIN
Thank you.
(mumbling to himself)
I thought with a name like Monique
she would be this hot, blonde-
haired, blue-eyed model chick with
a nice rack. Not an old hag.

MONIQUE
Use the long silver key, dear, and
come up to the third floor.

SYLVAIN
Alright.

Sylvain opens the door to a steep and narrow staircase.

SYLVAIN
Holy shit. I have to climb these
stairs for the next few days? This is
gonna be a fucking workout.

FADE TO BLACK.

INT. TOP OF STAIRS - MOMENTS LATER

Monique opens the door as Sylvain arrives, out of breath.

MONIQUE
Good exercise for you lad, eh?

SYLVAIN
I guess, but it's a bit tiring when
you have a rucksack on your back and
canvases under your arms. My name is
Sylvain, mijn plezier.

Sylvain shakes Monique's hand.

MONIQUE
The pleasure is mine. You speak Dutch?

SYLVAIN
No, sorry, only a few words.

Sylvain holds up the keys.

                         MONIQUE
          That's okay, we both speak English.
          Now, the short silver key opens the
          apartment door, but you have to wiggle
          it a bit.

Monique struggles with the key.

                         SYLVAIN
          I can do that. Don't want to bother
          you. I think I bothered you enough.

                         MONIQUE
          I got it, I got it.

Monique opens the door, leaving the keys in the lock.

                         MONIQUE
          That's your set of keys. If you see a
          hanger on the door, that means Pieter
          is staying for the night. Keep a
          lookout for a hanger. Pieter really
          likes his privacy.
                    (winking)
          Know what I mean?

Monique turns to exit.

                         SYLVAIN
          Loud and clear.

                         SYLVAIN (V.O.)
          But do you really know what Uncle Piet
          is doing?

Monique turns around.

                         MONIQUE
          Excuse me?

                         SYLVAIN
          Sorry? I didn't say anything!

                         MONIQUE
          Nothing, I thought I heard something.
          If you need anything I'm right next
          door. Oh, by the way, there's a
          grocery store around the corner.

                         SYLVAIN
          Got it.

> SYLVAIN (V.O.)
> Ok, already. I'm a big boy, leave me
> alone.

> MONIQUE
> Don't worry about making any noise, I
> sleep through anything.

> SYLVAIN
> That's good to know. Thanks for
> everything.

> MONIQUE
> Mijn plezier.

Monique goes to her apartment. Sylvain fumbles with the key,
closing the door.

                                        FADE OUT.

INT. AMSTERDAM FLAT - MOMENTS LATER

Sylvain throws backpack and art supplies in the corner. He looks
around, amazed.

> SYLVAIN
> Wow, look at this place. This is so
> awesome. I've only seen places like
> this in books. This is very art
> inspiring. I think I'll set up shop
> right here so I can look out the
> window at the cool rooftops and
> cozy streets. This is truly an
> artist's dream.

Sylvain lies down on the couch. His eyes fade.

                                        FADE OUT.

EXT. WAR ZONE - MOMENTS LATER

Sylvain dreams he's in the middle of a battlefield, carrying two
paintings, running for his life. Bombs explode around him, smoke
everywhere.

                                        FADE TO BLACK.

INT. AMSTERDAM FLAT - MOMENTS LATER

Sylvain wakes up, sweating. Sylvain looks at the clock. He's
only lost a few minutes, shakes his head, paces the floor.

43.

                              SYLVAIN (V.O.)
          Wow, that was a crazy dream. I hate
          the French, they're so destructive.
          Let me go and take a stroll around
          Amsterdam. That should keep my mind
          off the stupid French. Let me see what
          I can find for my new Amsterdam
          masterpieces.

                                          FADE OUT.

EXT. STREET - LATER

Sylvain walks up the street and strolls into a coffee shop.

                                          FADE OUT.

EXT. STREET - LATER

Montage of Sylvain walking around the streets of Amsterdam,
looking in windows, taking in the sights.

                                          FADE OUT.

EXT. STREET - LATER

Sylvain approaches the Van Gogh Bridge. Lots of TOURISTS walk
around.

                              SYLVAIN (V.O.)
          So I guess that, old Vincent boy stood
          about here when he created every
          stroke with precision.

Sylvain sits down on the curb, closes his eyes taking in the
sun. Tourists stand over him.

                              TOURIST
                    (with an English accent)
          Excuse me, sir. Would you take our
          picture in front of the Van Gogh
          Bridge, please?

                              SYLVAIN
          Yeah, sure. I'd be more than happy
          to.

The tourist hands Sylvain a camera.

                              TOURIST
          Thank you very much, sir.

Sylvain hands back the camera.

                    SYLVAIN
          Enjoy. Have you guys seen the Van
          Gogh Museum yet?

                    TOURIST
          No, not yet. Where's it located?

Sylvain grabs their map.

                    SYLVAIN
          Let's see. It's over here. You can
          take the three or the five tram. I'm
          gonna check it out tomorrow when I
          have more time. Little late in the day
          for me. I wanna catch the whole
          experience.

                    TOURIST
          Us as well, thanks for the tip. And
          thanks again for the photo.

                    SYLVAIN
          No problem, enjoy the day.

Tourists walk away, Sylvain walks onto the Van Gogh Bridge,
staring down the canal.

                           FADE OUT.

EXT. CANAL BEHIND RESTAURANT - MORNING

Sylvain walks up the canal, stopping to look over the rail.

                  SYLVAIN (VO)
          I should drop a few drops of blood and
          a few drops of paint at the exact same
          time. When they hit the water, I
          should take multiple pictures in its
          various stages. The first contact with
          the water, separating with the flow of
          the current, spreading out across the
          surface of the water. Then a boat
          would probably go by and kill my
          vision.

Sylvain continues walking along the canal, sees some garbage
cans at the back of a restaurant. The OWNER of the restaurant
comes out with trash while Sylvain is putting rotten food in a
bag.

                         OWNER
          Hey, you. Get out of here. Go, eat out
          of someone else's garbage.

                         SYLVAIN
          This isn't for me, this is for my art.

                         OWNER
          You're crazy, kid. Get out of here.

                         SYLVAIN
              (a little nastily)
          Ya, ya, ya. Pipe down old man.

Sylvain flips him the bird and walks away.

                                        FADE TO BLACK.

EXT. STREET - LATER

Sylvain walks down a side street, stumbling upon a small red
light district. He slows down to look in the windows and catches
the eye of a PROSTITUTE. She stands in the doorway

                         PROSTITUTE
              (rudely, with an accent)
          Are you looking or buying, my
          friend? If you have no money be on
          your way.

Sylvain walks up to her.

                         SYLVAIN
          You know what I'm thinking?

                         PROSTITUTE
              (snottily)
          How could I possibly know or give a
          fuck about what you're thinking?

                         SYLVAIN
          Then I guess nothing really matters,
          does it?

Sylvain takes rotten food from his pocket and smears it all over
her window making finger painting designs.

                         PROSTITUTE
              (screaming)
          What the hell are you doing? What
          are you, crazy? I'm gonna call the
          police!

Sylvain points at the window.

                    SYLVAIN
          That's art. Now, that's Art Decay.
               (like a salesman)
          Now, if you let that decay for about
          two weeks, it will take on a new
          appearance, a new form. This my
          friend, will take on a new meaning of
          how rude you are, you fucking bitch!

Sylvain turns around, walks away.

                    PROSTITUTE
          You fucking psycho weirdo! They should
          lock you up in the zieken huis!

People stop and stare. Sylvain walks down the street, picks up a
paper bag. He whips his hands and throws the bag. The prostitute
continues yelling in the background.

                                        FADE OUT.

INT. UNCLE PIET'S APARTMENT BUILDING - EVENING

Sylvain walks up stairs, gets to the top, and sees a coathanger
hanging on the door. Sylvain lightly knocks on the door.

                    SYLVAIN
          Uncle Piet, hello -

He slowly opens the door.

                    SYLVAIN (CONT'D)
          Hello, Uncle Piet?

Sylvain hears the shower running, grabs a sleeping bag, and
leaves.

                                        FADE TO BLACK.

EXT. AMSTERDAM STREET - MORNING

Sylvain sleeps on the cobblestone between two cars. A young
woman named GRETCHEN tries to get into her car.

                    GRETCHEN
          Pardon, sir? Sir, Pardon.

                    SYLVAIN
               (waking up)
          Oh, yes, I'm sorry.

Sylvain gets up quickly with sleeping bag in hand.

                    SYLVAIN (CONT'D)
               (confused, trying to speak
                Dutch)
          Sorry. Hoi, ik hou van jou.

                    GRETCHEN
          Excuse me!

                    SYLVAIN
          Meneer, how goes it? Pardon.

                    GRETCHEN
               (with an English accent)
          You are English?

                    SYLVAIN
          Well I speak English. I'm from New
          York.

                    GRETCHEN
               (smiling, very excited)
          American? Very nice. How do you
          know how to speak Dutch?

                    SYLVAIN
          What made you think I speak Dutch?

                    GRETCHEN
          Because when you woke up you said you
          love me in Dutch.

                    SYLVAIN
               (mesmerized)
          And maybe I would like to say it in
          English, as well.

                    GRETCHEN
               (shyly)
          You're crazy.

                    SYLVAIN
               (staring creepily)
          Yeah I have been told that lately.

                    GRETCHEN
               (bubbly)
          You live on the streets?

                    SYLVAIN
          No, no. I live permanently in Tilburg,
          but I'm staying in Amsterdam for a few
          days or maybe weeks, not sure. I was
          just resting by your car.

                    GRETCHEN
          Strange place to rest.

                    SYLVAIN
          Yeah, that's what I thought at first.
          Then I thought, it's a great place for
          now.

                    GRETCHEN
          Why did you move to Holland from the
          US?

                    SYLVAIN
          I wanted to live and breathe like my
          artist heroes. You know, Rembrandt,
          Van Gogh -

                    GRETCHEN
               (interrupting)
          So you moved from New York to the
          south of Holland... Tilburg? You
          rest on the streets in Amsterdam?
          I'm confused.

                    SYLVAIN
          Something like that, when I'm in
          Amsterdam I stay at a my uncle's flat,
          but when he's cheati- I mean... has a
          lady friend over... I have to leave
          for the night. You're so beautiful. My
          name is Sylvain, what's your name?

                    GRETCHEN
          Gretchen! So you're a painter?

Sylvain looks down at his paint clothes.

                    SYLVAIN
          No. Uh, yes. I mean, I don't paint
          houses or buildings. I paint on
          canvas.
               (like a salesman)
          You see, I incorporate living matter
          into my art. It's a new thing.

                    GRETCHEN
          Living matter? What do you mean?

                    SYLVAIN
              (excited)
         I take food, attach it to my
         canvas, and paint it. In time, the
         food decays, revealing a different
         image, so, as the painting gets
         older it starts distorting and
         makes a new art form called "Art
         Decay".

He stands proudly with arms folded.

                    GRETCHEN
              (disgusted)
         Sounds a little on the smelly side,
         with all that rotting food.

                    SYLVAIN
         It's a little complicated to explain
         right now. Maybe I'll show you one day
         or invite you to my opening.

                    GRETCHEN
         I'd like that!

                    SYLVAIN
         What do you do?

                    GRETCHEN
         I, I, I'd rather not say.

                    SYLVAIN
         Why?

                    GRETCHEN
         Just because.

As Gretchen pauses, both of them stare at each other.

                    SYLVAIN
         Cause you work in the Red Light
         District?

                    GRETCHEN
              (surprised, stuttering)
         How did you know that? I mean- no.
         Yes, whatever. How did you know
         that?

                    SYLVAIN
              (astutely)
         Because, when you have a job that
         you're not so proud of, you usually
         lie.
                    (MORE)

                    SYLVAIN (CONT'D)
But, in your case, you opted for
the answer of, "I'd rather not
say." Therefore, it led me to
believe you worked in an occupation
that was a little clandestine. My
choice was fifty-fifty. With your
beautiful looks, I didn't think you
worked in a hash house, so my
second choice was the Red Light
District.

                    GRETCHEN
          (awestruck)
That's amazing.

                    SYLVAIN
          (cockily)
No big deal!

                    GRETCHEN
That doesn't turn you off?

                    SYLVAIN
Well, let's say it doesn't turn me on,
but to each his own. Live and let
live, I always say.

                    GRETCHEN
You're funny and smart too. I like
you.

                    SYLVAIN
Do you happen to know a black girl
that works in the Red Light-

Gretchen gives him a puzzled look.

                    SYLVAIN (CONT'D)
Never mind. Would you like to go for a
cup of tea?

                    GRETCHEN
That'd be nice. First let me move my
car for the sweeper machine.

                    SYLVAIN (V.O.)
Nice legs and buttocks. Now that's
art.

Gretchen turns around, thinking she heard something.

                    GRETCHEN
          Sorry?

                         SYLVAIN
                    (startled)
          Nee, pardon. Nothing- I didn't say
          anything!

                         GRETCHEN
          Well, jump in. We have to drive a few
          blocks.

                                        FADE OUT.

INT. GRETCHEN'S APARTMENT - MORNING

Gretchen and Sylvain sit in bed.

                         SYLVAIN
          What made you start working for the
          district?

                         GRETCHEN
          Just bored, I guess!

                         SYLVAIN
          Bored? People don't go there cause
          they're bored. People go to the
          district to pay for school, support a
          child, or drugs. You went there
          because you were bored?

                         GRETCHEN
          Well, maybe not bored just... lost.
          When I was a child, my family
          disappeared on a business trip in the
          Middle East. My Auntie took care of me
          until I was a teenager, then she
          passed away. I felt so all alone in
          the world. The only thing I really
          wanted in life was a family and to be
          loved.

                         SYLVAIN
          And you thought the district was that
          path?

                         GRETCHEN
          No... I wouldn't say a path... but a
          stepping stone! It seemed like they
          were the only real friends and family
          I had until I met you.

                         SYLVAIN
          You haven't even known me for twenty-
          four hours.

                    GRETCHEN
          I usually get the chance to know
          someone for only an hour. You really
          taught me a lot in a day: how to love,
          and be loved, and how to respect what
          little you have. I really like that
          philosophy.

                    SYLVAIN
          Yeah, it's a tough road whichever path
          you take, I guess.

                    GRETCHEN
               (talking fast)
          So how about you? What's your deal?
          Do you have a big family back home?
          Why are you living in Holland? Tell
          me more about your art and
          everything?

                    SYLVAIN
          I told you about Mama. Don't know what
          else to tell you. I lived in a small
          town in the states called
               (hillbilly accent)
          Tuxedo, New York.
               (normal voice)
          The place had no warmth. Big old
          cemetery in the center of town with
          big old rotting oak trees, a couple
          old shops in ill-repair, a train
          station. I hated that town. It was
          kinda creepy. Unfriendly people. It's
          just my opinion though. My Mama on the
          other hand loves the town. She thinks
          it's great, very cozy. She also has a
          lot of friends.

                    GRETCHEN
          If your mama thinks it's cozy, then it
          sounds nice and cozy to me, girls know
          best.

                    SYLVAIN
          Believe me, if I brought you there,
          you'd come back to Holland in a
          flash.

                    GRETCHEN
          I'd probably want to stay forever.
          It'd be my first real home.

                    SYLVAIN
The only cool thing about that area
was being close to Harriman State
Park. And of course, New York City.

                    GRETCHEN
Harriman Park? What kind of park is
that? An amusement park?

                    SYLVAIN
A nature park, with a lot of lakes.
Cool hiking trails, hidden caves, it
was the highlight of my growing up.
Didn't experience New York City till I
was much older.

                    GRETCHEN
That must have been a great place to
show your art, no? New York City, The
Big Apple, the city that never sleeps.

                    SYLVAIN
It seemed like there was no art scene
there at the time. Like you, I just
got bored with the whole thing, had to
get out.

                    GRETCHEN
Did you have any art openings in New
York?

                    SYLVAIN
Yeah, just one. I really didn't get a
very warm welcome in the art world.
Did get a couple articles in some
trendy art magazines, that was nice.
Mama was quite proud of me. The New
York art world is a very cold and
snobby industry.

                    GRETCHEN
Sounds it. And what about your family?
You told me about your Mama. What
about the rest of your family?

                    SYLVAIN
              (seriously)
I wasn't born yet when my Pop
passed. I think it was an airplane
accident. The prop cut him, or
something like that. So I'm told.

                    GRETCHEN
Oh, I'm sorry to hear.

                    SYLVAIN
No need, it was long ago. I have no
memory. My Mama ended up raising me
along with my stepbrother, Shepard.
She never remarried. She was totally
devastated for years. I guess she
really loved my Pop!

                    GRETCHEN
Any other family members?

                    SYLVAIN
Well, my mother's side of the family
is all scattered around Holland. I
don't know any of them except for her
youngest brother, Piet. My father's
side either passed or we never kept in
touch. They're American Indians living
on reservations.

                    GRETCHEN
So it was just you, your brother and
your mother?

                    SYLVAIN
Yeah, pretty much.

                    GRETCHEN
Is your brother older or younger?

                    SYLVAIN
He's much older then me, almost twenty
years.

                    GRETCHEN
Wow, that's a big gap! Were you close?

                    SYLVAIN
We never really got to know each
other, when I was young he was
traveling the globe getting plants for
his work.

                    GRETCHEN
Plants? What kind of work does he do?

                    SYLVAIN
He was a botanist and curator for The
New York Botanical Gardens. He's
retired now, living in the Catskill
Mountains with a bee farm.

                    GRETCHEN
          That sounds interesting. And your
          mother?

                    SYLVAIN
                (lovingly)
          Yeah, like I told you earlier,
          she's the most amazing person on
          the planet. She has long blond
          hair, silky smooth skin, and a
          beautiful smile. Growing up we
          would do everything together. She
          was my best friend. We even think
          alike.

                    GRETCHEN
          Think alike? What do you mean?

                    SYLVAIN
          Well, it's a long story, kinda
          complicated. I'll tell you another
          time.

                    GRETCHEN
          No worries, another time. I'm
          forgetful, what brought you to
          Holland?

                    SYLVAIN
          I wanted to see where my roots were
          from - my family and my artist family.
          You know, Van Gogh, Mondrian, de
          Kooning, Rembrandt... these are my
          heroes. But most of all, I wanted to
          live and breathe like the great
          artists of Holland. That's the real
          reason I'm here.

                    GRETCHEN
          Oh, yeah, that's right, you said that
          before.
                (grabs her hair)
          Blonde. You're very funny, and
          special. Do you have a kiss for me?
                (Gretchen kisses Sylvain)
          I'm going to the shower.

Gretchen gets out of bed as Sylvain checks out her butt.

                    SYLVAIN (V.O.)
          That's art.

Gretchen turns around and catches Sylvain checking her out.

                                        FADE OUT.

INT. IVO'S LIVING ROOM - EVENING

Sylvain walks into the house. Ivo reads the paper.

                    IVO
          How was Amsterdam, youngster?

Sylvain hangs up his jacket.

                    SYLVAIN
          I had a blast. I met this hot
          chick. I think her and I hit it
          off.

Sylvain runs excitedly around the couch and shakes Ivo.

                    SYLVAIN (CONT'D)
          I think I'm in love!

                    IVO
          Four days in Amsterdam and the
          American's in love. What, is the girl
          a tourist from the States?

                    SYLVAIN
          No, she's a Dutch chick.

Sylvain holds his head in the air, as if dreaming.

                    SYLVAIN
          Her name is Gretchen. Isn't that a
          fucking cool name? Gretchen, you know
          like the Gretch Guitar with a chin, or
          something like that.

Ivo stares at Sylvain as if he's crazy.

                    IVO
          And where does this bird live?

                    SYLVAIN
          In the Rembrandt's Plein overlooking
          this beautiful Canal.

                    IVO
          She must have money to afford the
          Rembrandt's Plein.

                         SYLVAIN (V.O.)
              Maybe she is rich. She has a car.

                         IVO
              She has a car?

Sylvain looks at Ivo like he read his mind.

                         SYLVAIN
              Yes, by the way. She does.

                         IVO
              Then she must be rich. What does she
              do for a living?

                         SYLVAIN
                    (embarrassed)
              I am not sure. I think she works
              for the government or something.

Ivo reads the paper.

                         IVO
              Well, I'm glad you had a good time.
              Hey, lover boy, there's some food on
              the stove. It's still hot and it's for
              eating only.

                         SYLVAIN
              I can't eat now. I'm in love, I need
              to paint.

Ivo shakes his head as Sylvain runs up stairs.

                         IVO
                    (mumbling)
              Probably gonna be painting fucking
              hearts all night?

                                             FADE OUT.

INT. GRETCHEN'S APARTMENT - MORNING

Sylvain enters the apartment, Gretchen in other room.

                         SYLVAIN
              Oi, Gretch.

                         GRETCHEN (V.O.)
              I'm in the bathtub.

                                             FADE TO:

INT. BATHROOM - MOMENTS LATER

                    SYLVAIN
          Hi, baby. Sorry I'm late, I missed the
          transfer in Den Bosch. Had to wait the
          hour.

                    GRETCHEN
          I thought that's what happened. I
          figured I would take a soak for a
          while. Why don't you just move up to
          Amsterdam and stay with me? All this
          running back and forth must be killing
          you.

                    SYLVAIN
          Uncle Piet said the same thing. I
          can't just move to Amsterdam right
          now, baby. All my artwork and supplies
          are in Tilburg. Besides, you work most
          nights and I get my artistic energy at
          night. We would never see each other
          anyway.

                    GRETCHEN
          I don't work nights any more.

                    SYLVAIN
          You took on the day shift?

                    GRETCHEN
          No, I quit my job. I paid them off and
          I'm free and clear from the district.
          I'm finally alive again! I have more
          good news. I applied for a government
          position and I was accepted. I start
          Monday part-time with full benefits
          for me and you, they said we can apply
          for your work visa right away then we
          can work on your permanent residency.

                    SYLVAIN
          Wow, that's great. Start of a new
          life.

                    GRETCHEN
          And with benefits, they said that the
          medical aid would help you with your
          sleeping thoughts.

                    SYLVAIN
          Nightmares, baby. Nightmares.

                    GRETCHEN
          You don't speak Dutch that well and I
          don't speak American that well.

Sylvain rolls his eyes.

                    SYLVAIN
          That's ok, baby, I love you just the
          way you are. I have some good news as
          well. Yesterday I was selling some art
          on the street and a lady walked up to
          me without saying a word she bought
          all my paintings at full price. She
          threw 100 Euro in my tip bowl as well,
          the only thing she said was, enjoy
          your newfound fame and fortune, my
          son.

                    GRETCHEN
          See, I told you, you were gonna be
          famous. Now give me a celebration
          kiss.

Sylvain kisses Gretchen and falls in the tub.

                                        FADE OUT.

EXT. AMSTERDAM - DAM SQUARE - DAY - SIX MONTHS LATER

Montage of Gretchen and Sylvain walking hand-in-hand in Dam
Square. They look at the Museum posters and kiss.

                                        FADE OUT.

EXT. AMSTERDAM - REMBRANDT'S PLEIN - DAY

Gretchen and Sylvain walk hand-in-hand out of an expensive
designer store with shopping bags. She hugs him, and he kisses
her on the head.

                                        FADE OUT.

EXT. AMSTERDAM - VAN GOGH BRIDGE - DAY

Gretchen and Sylvain walk hand-in-hand down the street, over the
bridge and into an exclusive restaurant. He holds the door and
hits her buttocks on the way in. She jumps and giggles.

                                        FADE OUT.

EXT. AMSTERDAM - LEIDSEPLEIN - DAY

Sylvain rides a bicycle with Gretchen on the back, both laughing
as they ride down the bike path. Gretchen hugs and squeezes
Sylvain.

                                        FADE OUT.

EXT. AMSTERDAM - DAY

Gretchen and Sylvain walk hand-in-hand sharing a bottle of wine.
They stop at the canal watching the boats go by. Sylvain takes a
sip of wine and shares the sip with Gretchen in a kiss. It
spills all over, and they both laugh.

                                        FADE OUT.

EXT. AMSTERDAM - LEIDSEPLEIN - DAY

Gretchen and Sylvain walking hand-in-hand through the Square.
They stop to watch a street act. A tourist asks for Sylvain's
picture, and Gretchen takes the photo.

                                        FADE OUT.

EXT. AMSTERDAM - CENTRUM - DAY

Gretchen and Sylvain walk hand-in-hand into a gallery. They're
seen through the window talking with the owner, they walk out
laughing and kissing.

                                        FADE OUT.

INT. GRETCHEN'S APARTMENT - DAY

Sylvain writes a letter.

                    SYLVAIN (V.O.)
               Dear Mama, I miss you so much. I
               really love it here. I want you to
               come to visit me soon. I have plenty
               of room, and so does Uncle Piet. I
               cannot leave the Netherlands right now
               in fear they will not let me back in
               the country. They say I need a work
               visa to do my art. Uncle Piet and
               Gretchen are working on that.
                    (MORE)

SYLVAIN (V.O.)   (CONT'D)

I know I wrote you a lot about
Gretchen, I think I really want to get
serious with her. You and her are the
only women in my life that I ever
loved. It breaks my heart to not share
this joy with you right now. I'm not
sure when I'm gonna ask her the
question. I want the wedding to be in
Tuxedo, we can have the reception in
the backyard.

Sylvain wipes tears from his eyes.

                    SYLVAIN (V.O.)
Mama, you're gonna really love
Gretchen. She's the kindest,
sweetest girl you'd ever wanna
meet. I told her all about you.
She's in such a hurry to meet you.
Mama, please, please call or write
me. I miss you so much.

Gretchen enters with groceries and sees Sylvain crying.

                    GRETCHEN
What's the matter, love?

Sylvain holds his head down, covering the letter.

                    SYLVAIN
Nothing.

                    GRETCHEN
Are you writing your Mama again?

                    SYLVAIN
     (long pause)
Yes, I miss her so much. I just
want to talk to her.

                    GRETCHEN
Syl, that's the third letter this
week. You know how upset you get when
you write your Mama.

Gretchen grabs the pen and paper from Sylvain.

                    SYLVAIN
What? What are you doing-

Gretchen slams the pen and paper down.

                         GRETCHEN
                    (interrupting)
               Let's drop everything right now!
               Let's get on a plane and go to the
               States so you can hug your Mama.
               You need to hug your Mama.

                         SYLVAIN
               I can't leave the country right now,
               I'll jeopardize my work visa and my
               residency.

                         GRETCHEN
               Who cares about that bloody visa stuff
               anyway?
                    (pause)
               Syl your destiny is your art. Your
               love is to me, but your destiny and
               your love is to be with your Mama
               forever. Myself and your art would
               like to share that destiny and love
               with you and your Mama.

Gretchen cries with hands out for a hug.

                         SYLVAIN
                    (sobbing)
               One day, baby, one day.

                                        FADE OUT.

INT. GRETCHEN'S APARTMENT - DAY

Sylvain paints as Gretchen walks in the room.

                         GRETCHEN
               Hey honey, I'm gonna take your art in.
               It's starting to rain.

                         SYLVAIN
               No, no, no. I'm leaving it out so the
               elements get to it, I want to log the
               effect in my journal.

                         GRETCHEN
               Aren't you afraid the paints gonna run
               and ruin the look and the surprise?

                         SYLVAIN
               That's what I'm hoping for. I call
               this one, "Quick Decay."

Sylvain rolls a joint.

                    GRETCHEN
          Let's get out of the house, I'm going
          stir crazy. Syl, let's check out that
          new gallery that opened up. What's it
          called, Star 58, I think? Maybe they'd
          be interested in curating your next
          show.

                    SYLVAIN
          Funny you mentioned that, I bumped
          into the owner of the gallery at the
          Crystal Palace Coffee Shop. I think
          his name is Jost. Anyway, we got
          talking, he said he's interested in
          showing my work at his gallery in a
          few months. He was very excited to
          meet me. He was practically begging.

                    GRETCHEN
          You never told me that Syl!

                    SYLVAIN
               (nervously)
          Yeah, well, I smoked a little and
          must have forgot.

                    GRETCHEN
          That's great news, Syl!

                    SYLVAIN
          Also while I was there I bumped into
          that writer Ivan van Koening. He said
          he wants to write my life's story. I
          meet a lot of really cool people
          hanging at that enormous table in the
          Crystal Palace.

                    GRETCHEN
          Wow, it sounds like you and hash meet
          a lot of stoned people.

                    SYLVAIN
          Did you know that the Crystal Palace
          was one of the first Coffee Shops in
          Amsterdam? I spoke to the owner,
          Steve. He's a really cool guy, says
          he's good friends with Izzy from Guns
          'n Roses.

                    GRETCHEN
          That place always gets celebrities.

Sylvain drops the joint and changes the subject.

                         SYLVAIN
          Come on, grab your jacket. Let's check
          out that new gallery. I've never been
          inside.

                         GRETCHEN
                 (excitedly)
          You know, Syl, if we can get him to
          show your work, you'll be the top
          cat in all of Amsterdam.

                         SYLVAIN
          That's top dog, sweetheart. Top dog.

                         GRETCHEN
          Oh, yeah, "the cat's meow", "top dog".
          Well, you know what I mean. That place
          has always filled up with celebrities -
          Ronny Wood, Bowie, those guys from
          Golden Earring! The list goes on and
          on. Everyday someone new pops in that
          gallery.

                         SYLVAIN
          I know. Ok, let's go. I'm excited.

                                   FADE TO BLACK.

INT. ART PARTY - EVENING

Party guest CREEPY MAN introduces himself to Sylvain.

                         CREEPY MAN
                 (British accent)
          Hello, Sylvain. Your name comes
          from the guitar player from the New
          York Dolls.
                 (pausing)
          I've seen them in London when-

                         SYLVAIN
                 (interrupts, snottily)
          That can't be, sir, because I was
          born in the late sixties and the
          Dolls didn't come out until the
          early seventies, so therefore, my
          parents must have gotten my name
          from somewhere else.

                         CREEPY MAN
          I know your real name, Verdun. You are
          part American Indian. You use your
          middle name as a disguise.
                         (MORE)

                    CREEPY MAN (CONT'D)
I'm not sure what you're hiding from,
but the truth will soon come clear. If
you want to be truly remembered for
your art, use your given birth name.

                    SYLVAN
          (shocked)
You don't know what you're talking
about old man.

                    CREEPY MAN
          (eerily)
Sylvain, Sylvain, your work is
dangerous. It's not normal what
you're doing.

                    SYLVAN
You know nothing about my Art Decay.

Gretchen interrupts.

                    GRETCHEN
Pardon. Hey, Syl, there's a gentleman
over there that would love to meet
you. He's from the magazine, Art
World.

                    SYLVAIN
Really?

Sylvain turns to Creepy Man.

                    SYLVAIN (CONT'D)
          (with an English accent)
If you will excuse me, kind sir, I
believe I am being summoned. By the
way, nice dress. It matches your
lipstick.

                    CREEPY MAN
Duty calls.
          (sinisterly)
Sylvain!

                    SYLVAN (V.O.)
          (fearfully)
You're a creepy old man.

                    CREEPY MAN
I'll be watching out for you, Sylvain
Sylvain... or shall I say Verdun? You
have red paint on your hands... like
your brother's wife.

Gretchen pulls Sylvain away, scared.

                    GRETCHEN
          What the hell was that all about?
          That guy was weird!

Sylvain turns to glance at Creepy Man.

                    SYLVAIN
          I don't know, something about me
          taking the guitar player from the
          Doll's name or something like that.
          What's with all the guys wearing
          dresses and lipstick?

Gretchen shakes Sylvain's arm.

                    GRETCHEN
          I'm not sure about that, either.
          New fashion statement, I guess.
          There are some really strange
          people here tonight. They say the
          weirder the people, the more
          success you have.

                    SYLVAIN
          That means I must be rich and famous.
          These people are the bottom of the
          pickle barrel in the weird department.

                    GRETCHEN
               (whispering)
          Okay, this is it. The eccentric guy
          walking towards us is Dr.
          Vanderhoff. Keep cool and don't
          forget to bow.

                    SYLVAN
          Bow? For what?

                    GRETCHEN
          Hello Doctor. I would like to
          introduce you to Sylvain. Sylvain,
          this is Dr. Vanderhoff. He started the
          magazine Art World back in the
          sixties.

The Doctor and Sylvain shake hands and bow.

                    DOCTOR
          It's a pleasure to meet someone with
          such a wild and crazy imagination.

                    SYLVAIN
          Likewise, Doctor.

                    DOCTOR
          My publication would like to do an
          exclusive interview with you, we are
          prepared to give you a handsome
          advance. We would like to purchase
          some of your paintings and display
          them in our lobby.

                    SYLVAIN
          I'm sorry, I don't do advertisement
          art, Sir.

                    DOCTOR
          No, no, no, no. We would like your
          originals that have been decaying
          nicely for several years. We are
          interested in your art that is in
          second, third, and fourth generation
          decomposition stages.
               (sinisterly)
          We like it. Very controversial.

                    SYLVAIN (V.O.)
          You're trying to exploit me and all
          other artists for your magazine's
          gain.

                    DOCTOR
          You are thinking. That is a good sign.

          Gretchen nervously pulls Sylvain away from the Doctor.

                    GRETCHEN
          Yes he has a lot on his mind right
          now. We'll contact your office this
          week to set up a schedule. It was nice
          chatting with you, Doctor. I have your
          card.

                    SYLVAIN
               (sarcastically)
          Yeah, it was really nice talking to
          you three.

                    GRETCHEN
               (whispering angrily)
          What is wrong with you? You start
          trouble with these people, they
          will crush you.

                    SYLVAIN
          These people are pretentious assholes.
          They think they're so artsy and
          sophisticated. It makes me sick.

                    GRETCHEN
          Who cares what these people think?
          They're gonna push your work into
          overseas markets and territories.
          These people are very rich, very
          powerful, and very well-connected.

                    SYLVAIN
          Yeah, I guess. I saw the same bullshit
          in New York, it was just with a
          different accent. It made me sick to
          my stomach. That's another reason I
          split the New York art scene.

                    GRETCHEN
          I understand. Oh look, I see my friend
          Shari. Let's go over and chat with
          her, she works for Associated Press. I
          told you about her! We definitely have
          to talk with her before we go. We'll
          have one more drink then we'll get out
          of here, so we don't get sick of these
          people in front of them.

                                        FADE OUT.

INT. GRETCHEN'S APARTMENT - MORNING

Gretchen and Sylvain sit on the bed reading magazines and
newspapers. Gretchen is in a lace top and Sylvain with a scarf
around his neck.

                    GRETCHEN
          I can't believe we got an advance copy
          of every magazine before it hit the
          newsstands. Look, your dopey mug is on
          every front cover. Newsweek, Time, The
          Art Reporter, Art and You. This one's
          in Japanese.

She holds up the magazine to her face, making fun.

                    GRETCHEN (CONT'D)
          There're papers from halfway around
          the world interested in what you're
          doing. I bet it's all because of
          your chat with my friend Shari at
          Associated Press.
                    (MORE)

GRETCHEN (CONT'D)
You were very professional chatting
with her. A real celebrity artist.
I owe that girl big time.

                    SYLVAIN
What's really great is, I didn't have
to do an exclusive with that dickhead
Doctor from Art World, either.

                    GRETCHEN
Yeah, he was an asshole. But Shari is
fucking brilliant.

                    SYLVAIN
That girl is awesome. How do you know
her again?

                    GRETCHEN
          (embarrassed)
I told you about her. Her and I
used to share a storefront in the
district. She had the day shift and
I had the night shift. She got
pregnant by this New York guy. He
swept her away and married her.

                    SYLVAIN
You and her kept in touch all this
time?

                    GRETCHEN
Yeah, a little. She sends me pics of
the kids through Facebook and we
FaceTime now and again. It's tough
with a six-hour time difference.

Gretchen grabs Sylvain's arm.

                    GRETCHEN
That's why when I met you, I
thought you were my New York knight
in shining armor, ready to sweep me
away.

                    SYLVAIN
          (sarcastically)
That's me, a knight, all-night
sweeping. All kidding aside...
pretty soon, I'll take you to New
York so you can catch up with Shari
and meet Mama.

                    GRETCHEN
I'd really like that.

She throws the magazines around while bouncing on the bed.

                    GRETCHEN (CONT'D)
          You're gonna be famous! You're
          already famous! I still can't
          believe the fanfare you're getting.
          This is just too much. Everyone
          wants to know what the surprise is
          behind your paint.

                    SYLVAIN
          Isn't an artist supposed to be famous
          after he dies?

                    GRETCHEN
          That's not always true. You said so
          yourself, look at Peter Max, Marc
          Kastobbi, Keith Herring, Andy- oh, no,
          he's dead. Anyway, none of them ever
          received the Paris Arts Council Award
          before. Matter of fact, you're the
          first American in history. In the next
          few weeks, your art will be touring
          around the world in every famous
          museum.

                    SYLVAIN
          Yeah, how am I suppose to travel
          around without my Dutch visa? I'm not
          gonna leave this country in fear they
          won't let me back in. I'll lose all my
          artistic expression if I can't come
          back.

                    GRETCHEN
          Well, I wanted to surprise you. I did
          a little private investigating. I
          phoned your Uncle Piet and told him
          about your award ceremony. He made the
          right phone calls and you'll be
          getting your temporary visa in two
          days. The catch is, you can't leave
          the country for more then ninety days
          at any given time until you get your
          permanent. If you do you'll have to
          start the process all over again.

                    SYLVAIN
               (shocked)
          Are you serious? You are serious!

Gretchen kisses Sylvain.

GRETCHEN
I love you, baby.

SYLVAIN
(excitedly)
In two days, let's get the hell out
of here. Let's go to Morocco for a
few days. I need to paint there, I
had a dream. Then we'll go straight
to New York to see Mama so we can
dance around the living room.

GRETCHEN
Yes, that sounds like a great idea.
Right after the Paris Art Convention,
though. We stay a few days at the
Paris Hilton, compliments of the
Council. Then we check out some of the
sites, Morrison's grave, Eiffel Tower,
Mont Mart. Then you get your
achievement award, we leave straight
from there to Morocco, if you want.
Then off to New York to visit Mama.

SYLVAIN
(whining)
I don't want to take a pit stop in
Paris, I want to go straight to
Morocco for a few days, then
directly to New York to see Mama
for a month or so.
(angrily)
I don't like Paris, I don't like
the French. Those people give me
nightmares.

GRETCHEN
(motherly)
You have to go to Paris. They're
expecting you, love. You'll get
more worldwide press than you know
what to do with. The news will get
back home to Mama in the States
before you do. She'll be so proud
of you, Sylvain. You can ring her
doorbell and surprise her with the
biggest bouquet of flowers money
can buy.

SYLVAN
I can't stay a few days in France.

                    GRETCHEN
          Okay we stay a few hours in Paris, get
          the award. Then go straight to
          Morocco, stay a few days and then fly
          straight to New York.

                    SYLVAIN (VO)
          I knew you'd see it my way.

                    GRETCHEN
          Syl, what are you thinking about?

Sylvain snaps out of it.

                    SYLVAIN
          Sounds great, this calls for a
          celebration. This afternoon, I'll
          get a couple bottles of wine and
          some mushrooms so we can trip and
          have a few laughs whilst enjoying
          our new found freedom and fortune.

                    GRETCHEN
          I don't know, I haven't tripped in a
          long time. I can't even smoke that
          hash you get, it has too much power.

                    SYLVAIN
          I won't get the strong ones, I
          promise.

                    GRETCHEN
          Do we have to get mushrooms? Can't we
          get a little powder, or just a few
          bottles of wine?

                    SYLVAIN
          I really want to celebrate, I want to
          expand my mind to help with the
          creative process of my art. Besides, I
          really don't want to trip alone.

                    GRETCHEN
          Okay, but don't go to the smart bar in
          the district. Go to the one by the
          Melkweg.

                    SYLVAIN
          It's all the same shit.

                    GRETCHEN
          Syl, they play with those soft drugs
          over in the district. They get the
          kids hooked so they buy more.

                    SYLVAIN
          Okay, okay, I'll go by the Melkweg. It
          just means I have to wait for a tram.

                    GRETCHEN
          It's only 15 minutes. You could take a
          bike!

                    SYLVAIN
          It's raining outside!

                    GRETCHEN
          It's Holland, it rains almost everyday
          here.

                    SYLVAIN
          Ok, ok. The tram it is. I'll leave a
          bit later.

                                        FADE OUT.

INT. GRETCHEN'S APARTMENT - MORNING

After three days of tripping on mushrooms, Sylvain wakes up in
his paint clothes to ringing church bells. He grabs an open
bottle of wine, takes a sip, and then spits it out.

                    SYLVAIN
               (mumbling)
          Wow, my head is spinning. What the
          hell happened?

He looks around the room at dozens of new paintings, paint
splattered everywhere.

                    SYLVAIN
          That's art. And that's art, as well.
          Wow I must have been really busy while
          I was out of my mind. I don't remember
          any of this work.

He looks closely at the paintings.

                    SYLVAIN
          What kind of vegetable is this? This
          is meat.

Sylvain's eyes roll down the row of painted canvases. The last
canvas looking like a woman's hand holding a pocketbook.

                    SYLVAIN (CONT'D)
          Oh, no. What the hell did I do? What
          did I do?

Sylvain hugs the painting. Paint smearing all over his face and clothes.

                         SYLVAIN
                    (tormented)
          Gretchen. What did I do? I didn't
          mean to do this. I'm so sorry. I
          love you. I would never do anything
          to hurt you.

Horrified, he throws the painting on the floor, flips all paints and paintings over, then runs out of the apartment, slamming the door.

                                        FADE OUT.

EXT. AMSTERDAM STREETS - MIDDAY

Sylvain roams the streets for two days, eating out of garbage cans. A female RESTAURANT OWNER comes out. Gretchen's voice can be heard in the background.

                    RESTAURANT OWNER
          Hey, you! Get out of there! Go eat out
          of someone else's garbage.

Sylvain, hunched over with a wild look, food hanging from his mouth, stares at the restaurant owner.

                    SYLVAIN (V.O.)
          I'm so hungry lady. Get inside before
          I eat you.

The scared woman goes in and slams the door.

                    GRETCHEN (O.S.)
                    (ghostly)
          Sylvain. Come with me.

Sylvain looks up at the sky.

                    SYLVAIN
          Gretch, Gretch, where are you?

                    GRETCHEN (O.S.)
          Sylvain, come with me. You'll like it
          here! I miss you.

                    SYLVAIN
          Gretch, I miss you too baby. Gretch, I
          didn't mean to do that to you I was
          high on drugs. I love you.

> GRETCHEN (O.S.)
> Syl, I want to let you know that I
> always understood your thoughts. It's
> not a bad gift that your Mama gave
> you. Come with me. We'll visit your
> Mama together.

Sylvain grabs some bread out of the garbage, walks down the
street, eating and talking to himself. People stop and stare.

> FADE TO BLACK.

INT. PORNO SHOP - LATE MORNING

Sylvain goes into a porn shop for bondage equipment. INGRID, the
red-headed, full figured, store owner greets him at the door.

> INGRID
> (surprised, sarcastically)
> Sylvain, what are you doing here?
> You all right? You look like shit.

> SYLVAIN
> (depressed, mumbling)
> Ingrid, I need some stuff. I'll pay
> you later?

> INGRID
> Naturally, Syl. Anything you need,
> luv. You and Gretchen's credit is good
> in my book. By the way, where is
> Gretchen?

Sylvain ignores Ingrid and walks over to the bondage apparel. He
grabs whips, chains, leather straps and walks out like a zombie.

> INGRID
> (excited, startled)
> Syl! Wait, I want to write down
> what you're taking. Syl, Syl! I
> need to write down what you're
> taking.

Ingrid follows Sylvain to the door, yelling.

> INGRID
> Sylvain, you need to come back, I need
> to write down the items you're taking!
> Sylvain, don't you ignore me! Get back
> here this instant!

Confused, she throws her hands in the air slams the door.

                    INGRID (CONT'D)
               (angrily)
          God damn, artist asshole!

                                        FADE OUT.

EXT. AMSTERDAM STREETS - LATER

Sylvain walks past coffee shop. GUY, an English rocker, stands
in the doorway.

                    GUY
          Hey. Sylvain. What are you up to,
          mate?
               (then)
          Sylvain, are you alright? You don't
          look good.

Sylvain, white as a ghost, is covered in paint.

                    SYLVAIN (VO)
          Alright? You don't know what alright
          is. You'll never know how to be
          alright.

                    GUY
               (puzzled)
          Hey, where you going with all that
          bondage gear? Coming back from an
          all nighter? Hey, where's Gretchen,
          man? I never see you walk the
          street without her. What, did you
          dump her cause you're a star now?

                    SYLVAIN
               (grunting)
          Yeah forever.

                    GUY
          Sorry to hear, man. Talk on the street
          says you missed a few TV and award
          shows. Sylvain? You're not acting like
          yourself. I think you need some sleep.
          Take care, Syl. If you need anything,
          let me know.
               (whispers, shaking his
                head)
          Fucking artists.

Sylvain stares at the sky while walking.

> SYLVAIN
> Gretch I never said to him we broke
> up.

Sylvain walks down the bike path, bicycles trying to get around
him. A photographer tries to take a picture, and Sylvain swats
him away with bondage gear.

> FADE TO BLACK.

EXT. AMSTERDAM STREET - EVENING

Sylvain, looking filthy, dragging the bondage gear while roaming
the streets. Goes behind some garbage cans to piss, then he lays
down with the bondage gear as a pillow.

> FADE TO BLACK.

INT. GRETCHEN'S APARTMENT HALLWAY - MORNING

Sylvain opens the front door to the apartment building, peeks
inside, and slams the door behind him. With his back against the
door holding bondage gear he sits down, looks up at the stairs
he has to climb and starts sobbing.

> FADE TO BLACK.

INT. GRETCHEN'S APARTMENT - LATER

Sylvain peeks inside the apartment and sees the trashed room
with paints and paintings everywhere. Still hallucinating, he
hears Gretchen and Mama speak with an angelic voice in the
background.

> SYLVAIN (V.O.)
> Ok, I have to clean this place up and
> get this room in order. Where do I
> start?

He sits on the bed, closes his eyes, and lays down.

> FADE TO:

INT. GRETCHEN'S APARTMENT - DREAM - MOMENTS LATER

Sylvain's dreaming. In the dream, he talks with Gretchen and
Mama.

> GRETCHEN (V.O.)
> You're English?

>   SYLVAIN (V.O.)
>   Well, I speak Eng- no, I'm from New
>   York.

>   GRETCHEN (V.O.)
>   American? Very nice, How do you know
>   how to speak Dutch?

>   SYLVAIN (V.O.)
>   Well, my Mama's from Holland. You're
>   so pretty.

Mama enters the dream sequence.

>   MAMA (V.O.)
>   Sylvain, who are you talking to?

>   SYLVAIN (V.O.)
>   (proudly)
>   Mama, I want you to meet my love. I
>   met her in Holland. Gretchen, this
>   is Mama, Mama, this is Gretchen.

>   GRETCHEN (V.O.)
>   Mama, you must be proud to have a son
>   as brilliant as Syl.

>   MAMA (VO)
>   Oh, I am, I am.

>   FADE OUT.

EXT. REVOLUTIONARY WAR - DREAM - MOMENTS LATER

Switching dreams, Sylvain dreams he's painting while in the
middle of the French Revolutionary War. Horses running by, smoke
everywhere, bombs explode. A toothless FRENCHMAN in the
background beheads a person and puts the head on a stick.

>   SYLVAIN
>   (scared)
>   What are you doing? I can't put
>   that in my painting!

Frenchman holds up the stick with the bloody head.

>   FRENCHMAN
>   That's art!

                         SYLVAIN
          Leave me alone, that's not art, that's
          death!

                                        FADE TO BLACK.

INT. GRETCHEN'S APARTMENT - MOMENTS LATER

Sylvain wakes up in a cold sweat to a trashed apartment. He runs
to the bathroom, turns on the shower, and starts vomiting.

                                        FADE TO BLACK.

INT. GRETCHEN'S APARTMENT - NIGHT

The apartment, semi-cleaned. All paintings neatly displayed.
Sylvain fastening, straps, chains, and bondage gear on a heavy
duty, life size canvas.

                         SYLVAIN (V.O.)
          Gretchen I never meant to do you no
          harm. Believe me when I tell you, I
          would never do you, no wrong. Before
          they take me away, I want to do one
          last piece for you, baby. Maybe I will
          call this one, "In Memory Of" or "My
          Dearly Beloved."

                                        FADE OUT.

EXT. STREET OUTSIDE GRETCHEN'S APARTMENT - MORNING

Guy walks up to Gretchen's building and rings doorbell. Two
gunshots heard in the background. Guy looks up, starts pounding
on the door.

                         GUY
                 (upset, screaming)
          Sylvain, open up! Sylvain! Gretchen
          open up, Gretchen, Gretchen.
          Someone call an ambulance, help
          help, call an ambulance. Gretchen,
          Sylvain!

                                        FADE TO BLACK.

EXT. STREET OUTSIDE GRETCHEN'S APARTMENT - LATER

POLICE CAPTAIN talks with Guy. More backup police arrive with
flashing lights and sirens. A large CROWD gathers.

                    CAPTAIN
          Hello, I'm Captain Baker. What is your
          name?

                    GUY
          Guy Hooper, everyone calls me Hoops or
          Guy - depends on who you ask.

                    CAPTAIN
          Cute. So, when did you see your
          friends last? Tell me times, dates,
          the way they were dressed-

AMERICAN EMBASSY INSPECTORS arrive and Captain stares Guy down.

                    GUY
          I saw Sylvain a few days ago. He was
          walking around like a zombie. When he
          wasn't with his girlfriend, Gretchen,
          I knew something was wrong. Those two
          are inseparable. I spoke to some
          friends on the streets and they said
          they saw him at the biker bar talking
          with some gang members. You know, you
          don't talk to the those guys unless
          you want drugs, guns, money or
          something crazy done-

A COP, hysterical, runs downstairs to the Captain.

                    COP
               (in Dutch)
          Captain, dit is gek!

Captain holds up his hand.

                    CAPTAIN
          Calm down, calm down, please, speak
          English. There're inspectors from
          the American embassy present. We'd
          like for everyone to understand the
          conversation. Were you the first
          officer on the scene?

                    COP
               (out of breath)
          That's correct, Captain.

                    CAPTAIN
               (calmly)
          Ok, so tell us what you observed on
          entering the building?

                    COP
Well, the neighbor came down and
opened the front door for my partner
and I-

             AMERICAN EMBASSY INSPECTOR #1
          (interrupting)
Where's your partner now?

Captain gives inspector a cold stare.

                    COP
Well, the local inspectors are
questioning him upstairs, they sent me
down to speak with you, Captain.

                    CAPTAIN
Very good, please continue.

                    COP
It's an awful weird sight up there
Captain. There's paint and blood
everywhere. The Inspectors can't tell
which is paint and which is blood. We
have one body, maybe two, or three
hacked to pieces and tied up to
sections of artist canvas. We have
another body strapped to this huge
artist canvas with bondage whips,
straps and buckles. That subject on
the large canvas has a gun in one hand
and a syringe in the other. There are
two buckets of paint hanging over the
body. From my prospective, it looks
like he shot the buckets of paint, as
they dripped on his body he injected
himself with drugs. Or the other way
around. The inspectors are still
trying to figure this one out. It
looks like some sort of masochism or a
cult that went wrong, or that it was
made to look like a suicide. Or, maybe
even a suicide. Maybe some sick,
perverted serial killer. It's really
hard to tell, the inspectors are
combing every inch of the place trying
to put the puzzle pieces together.

                    CAPTAIN
Good job, officer. The inspectors and
myself will take on the investigation
from here.
                 (MORE)

                         CAPTAIN (CONT'D)
          I want everything you told us or
          anything that you can remember written
          in your report and on my desk first
          thing in the morning. You're dismissed
          for now, stay -

                         AMERICAN EMBASSY INSPECTOR #2
                    (interrupting)
          With all due respect, Captain, we
          need to be exclusively on this
          case. It's a very high profile
          case.

                         CAPTAIN
          High profile? Sounds to me like some
          drug addicts and weirdos got a little
          out of control.

                         AMERICAN EMBASSY INSPECTOR #1
          We'll be the judge of this crime
          scene, Captain. It also involves a
          CSS agent's family member. We were
          told to take care of this very
          sensitive and high profile
          situation.

American Embassy Inspectors walk past the Captain and into the
building flipping badges at the police line.

                         CROWD
          That's where that crazy artist,
          Sylvain, lives. You know the one with
          the decaying art? I knew his
          girlfriend Gretchen. Those two were
          always up to no good.

                                                      FADE OUT.

INT. LAW OFFICE - MORNING - TWO YEARS LATER

Mama dressed in funeral clothes, sits across from LAWYER.

                         LAWYER
          Mrs. Vanderveen, we're sorry we have
          to meet under these circumstances. On
          behalf of myself and our firm, we send
          our condolences.

                         MAMA
          I appreciate that and I thank you for
          that lovely bouquet of flowers you
          sent me.

LAWYER

Our pleasure, it's the least we can
do. As you know, after two long years
of investigations and legal battles
with the Dutch Government, our firm
and certain high profile Dutch
political figures finally convinced
the Netherlands to release your son's
controversial art work.

MAMA
(sobbing)
Did they release all the pieces?

LAWYER
(sympathetically)
No. As you know, some of the pieces
were confiscated to be considered
part of the Netherlands homicide
investigation. Those pieces will
not be released into our custody
until they can figure out the
origin of the decaying matter
adhered to the art work. As the
executor of Sylvain's last will and
testament, his wishes were for our
firm to sell all the remaining
paintings and take the proceeds and
forward them to you, less our
standard fee of course. His wishes
were for you to travel the world or
just enjoy life with no more
financial burden. We have taken the
liberty to contact Sotheby's
Auction House, and they have agreed
to hold a private auction as a
courtesy to our firm.

MAMA
(crying, trembling)
Why does it have to be a private
auction? My son would have wanted
his art for the entire world to
see.

LAWYER
(apologetic)
I understand that, Mrs. Vanderveen,
but by having a private auction, it
makes the art much harder to obtain
so therefore, the pieces of art
increase in value.
(MORE)

                              LAWYER (CONT'D)
                    As stated in your son's will, we
                    will try to get the most money for
                    each individual piece that the
                    private auction will bring. And by
                    all means, Mrs. Vanderveen you are
                    welcome to attend the auction as
                    our guest. And by law, you may
                    purchase any piece that you so
                    desire with a small fee going to
                    the auction house. Our firm will
                    forgo our fees from your personal
                    purchases.

                              MAMA (V.O.)
                    You guys are not gonna screw me out of
                    my son's prized possessions. Not if I
                    can help it.

                              LAWYER
                         (stuttering)
                    I'm sorry Ma'am. Did you say
                    something?

                              MAMA
                    Excuse me?

                              LAWYER
                    Oh, nothing. I also wanted to let you
                    know that if you have any personal
                    paintings from your son's collection
                    you'd like to sell on auction day,
                    your welcome to submit them into the
                    collection at no charge.

                                                  FADE OUT.

INT. SOTHEBYS AUCTION HOUSE - MORNING

The AUCTIONEER stands behind a podium pointing to a large
painting under a sheet.

                              AUCTIONEER
                    Okay, ladies and gentleman. Our final
                    piece we have in the collection by
                    Sylvain, again one of the greatest
                    award-winning artists of the twenty-
                    first century, who took his New York
                    roots and brought them to Europe to
                    create his own form of art known as
                    Art Decay, with this being the only
                    piece called self portrait.

Auctioneer takes off the sheet, everyone in the room gasps.

                         AUCTIONEER
               Okay, ladies and gentleman, let's all
               settle down. It's just a replica of
               the artist himself. It was
               authenticated and it is formerly
               living matter but not of human
               substance.

The crowd raves on. The auctioneer angrily hits his gavel on the
podium. The crowd slowly settles down.

                         AUCTIONEER (CONT'D)
               Settle down, folks! This is our last
               piece on the block for the day. Lets
               start the auction! Okay, we saw the
               smaller pieces going for nearly a
               million up towards one point eight so
               lets start this priceless piece at one
               point five. Okay, one million five. Do
               I hear one million six? Okay one
               million six. Do I hear seven? Seven it
               is. Eight, do I hear eight? Eight.

Auctioneer points around the room.

                         AUCTIONEER
               Okay, two million, two five, do I
               hear two six? Seven, eight, three
               million. Three point two, three
               point three? Four, five, six,
               seven, eight? Do I hear three point
               nine million dollars, going once,
               going twice? Sold to number two-
               forty-nine. Ladies and gentleman,
               this has been the largest piece, as
               well as highest price paid for, any
               twenty-first century artist to-
               date. We've all just witnessed
               history in the making. Thank you
               very much for attending Sotheby's
               Auction House. Have a good day.

                                             FADE OUT.

EXT. SOTHEBY'S FRONT STEPS - LATER

REPORTERS look up steps at everyone leaving Sotheby's. Reporters
yell questions at Mama.

                         REPORTER NED
               Ma'am what is your name and why did
               you choose such an unusual piece?

                    MAMA (V.O.)
               (nodding)
          You might say that this one touched
          my heart.

Reporter Ned seems to be the only one to hear.

                    REPORTER NED
          Why this particular one ma'am? There
          must have been a plethora of artists
          on that auction block that might have
          touched your heart, but you chose this
          one particular artist and this one
          particular piece.

All reporters quiet down and stare at Ned and Mama. Mama stares
at Reporter Ned.

                    MAMA (V.O.)
          Why don't you come over my house
          some time and ask my son?

All the reporters stare at Mama nodding her head while only
Reporter Ned talks to her.

                    REPORTER NED
          Did you say something?
               (pause)
          I think I might stop by your house
          sometime if that's ok? You think that
          might be ok ma'am?

Mama stares at Ned, nods, then walks down the steps.

                                        FADE TO BLACK.

INT. MAMA'S LIVING ROOM - NOON

A large self-portrait painting hangs on the wall. Mama sits in a
chair staring at the painting.

                    MAMA (V.O.)
          I know you said you would be back in a
          few years, but did I really have to
          wait so long? Your Uncle Piet promised
          he'd get you and your art back in one
          piece. I have to say, he really loved
          you and me to put his career on the
          line. He's truly a man of his word. A
          what? A picture? Where?

Mama gets up and reaches behind the art and takes out a picture
of Gretchen.

                    MAMA (V.O.)
          So, this is the one that reminded
          you of me?

Mama starts to tear up.

                    MAMA (V.O.)
          Oh, she is so beautiful. Of course
          I'll hang her next to you. If you
          love her, then I love her.

She opens a nightstand for a push pin and hangs the picture.

                    MAMA (V.O.)
          Now you two look like one. I knew
          there was something missing. I read
          about Gretchen's picture in your
          journal, but didn't know what you
          were talking about. Oh, by the way,
          that reporter that I told you about
          wants to know if he could have a
          word with you and me?

Mama stares into the distance for a while.

                    MAMA (V.O.)
          I'll let him know he has to travel.

Reporter Ned stands outside, cleaning window glass and looking
in living room.

                                        FADE OUT.

EXT. BAY OF ISLANDS - NEW ZEALAND - NOON

Sylvain and Gretchen sit on the beach in beach chairs, staring
at the water. Sylvain has a shaved head and a goatee and
Gretchen has red hair.

                    SYLVAIN
               (excited)
          So where's the helicopter?

                    GRETCHEN
               (frustrated)
          I told you a few hours ago. It'll
          be here in a few hours!

Gretchen pours another drink.

                    SYLVAIN
          That's what I'm talking about, a few
          hours have passed already.

                    GRETCHEN
Syl- don't start!

                    SYLVAIN
Okay, I'm sorry, I'm sorry.

                    GRETCHEN
It's ok, I'm just crazy nervous.

                    SYLVAIN
Baby?

                    GRETCHEN
Yes Syl?

                    SYLVAIN
Why did you leave me wandering the
streets by myself half out of my mind?
I could have gotten hurt.

                    GRETCHEN
             (aggressive and buzzed)
Syl, I didn't leave you wandering
the streets half out of your mind.
After you dug up that corpse out of
the cemetery for your art, you told
me right then and there that you
were more than half out of your
mind. Wandering the streets was the
least of your problems.

Gretchen lights up a joint.

                    GRETCHEN
When you dug up the second corpse to
supposedly cover up your mistake,
that's when I realized you were
completely out of your mind. I was
flying hard, as well. I just couldn't
believe what you were doing at the
time! My mind was thinking one thing
but my eyes were seeing another. I
told you not to go to the district for
your mushrooms but you didn't listen,
again. You were so fucked up, I
couldn't even drag you to Paris to
pick up your art award. I was so
embarrassed when I had to get up on
stage and accept it for you with my
slurring speech.

                    SYLVAIN
I'm sorry love. How did you know I
went to the district?

                    GRETCHEN
               (angry, yelling)
          Because, mushroom brain, when you
          brought home the package it said
          Fuego on it. I used to work in the
          district remember? I know that
          scumbag Italian. He tries to get
          these kids hooked on anything to
          make more money, that greedy
          bastard!
               (then, more calmly)
          I'm sorry love, I'm so nervous
          right now, I don't know what I'm
          saying.

                    SYLVAIN
          Ah, love, ik hou van jou. No problem.
          I'm just happy I'm here with you right
          now.

A helicopter comes from the distance.

                    GRETCHEN
          Oh, shit, there's the helicopter. I
          think I just wet myself.

                    SYLVAIN
          Gretch, don't worry you have nothing
          to be afraid of.

                    GRETCHEN
          I have nothing to be afraid of? That's
          easy for you to say. I'm going in the
          water so it looks like I was swimming.

Gretchen runs toward the water. Sylvain waves his hands in the
air. The helicopter lands on the beach. Sylvain and Gretchen
start running towards the helicopter. Doors open and Mama walks
out dressed in a trench coat, hat, sun glasses, and a huge
purse.

                    SYLVAIN
          Remember don't tell Mama I'm using
          Verdun Grey as my new artist name. I
          want to confuse the art world, not
          her.

                    GRETCHEN
          I'm not like you, mushroom brain. I
          remember when people tell me things.

                    SYLVAIN
               (shouting)
          Mama, Mama!

Sylvain grabs Mama and gives her a big hug. They both start crying.

> MAMA
> (passionately)
> I missed you so much Syl. It's been four long years.

> SYLVAIN
> I think more than that, Mama. You had to wait another year for the Dutch government to release my artwork for auction. Five long years at least. I missed you too. Mama, I want to introduce you to my fiancé.

> MAMA
> Sylvain you don't have to say another word, I know that beautiful face anywhere. She doesn't need an introduction.

Mama gives Gretchen a hug and kiss.

> MAMA
> Ik hou van jou Gretchen, mijn plezier.

> GRETCHEN
> Ik hou van jou Mama, you are my love.

Helicopter Pilot walks toward Mama with her bags. Mama turns and points.

> MAMA
> Put down those money bags, buster.

> SYLVAIN
> Thats everything from inside self portrait?

> MAMA
> No, that's not even half of it. Your Uncle also stuffed it with gold, diamonds and assorted foreign currencies as well.

> SYLVAIN
> (excited)
> Where's Uncle Piet? I thought he was flying with you.

                    MAMA
          Calm down, he'll be here in a couple
          days, he had to tie up some loose
          ends. I want to introduce you to my
          boyfriend, Frank. I was looking for a
          good ride and Frank is a great ride -
          on the helicopter that is!

Everyone laughs.

                                        FADE OUT.

Circa 1988 at The Tunnel in NYC, hanging with Tiny Tim and my Dutch friend Lorraine.

RUBBER BABY

Press photo for Rubber Baby, my pop-punk project.
From left: Orlando, Ralpho, Me and Andy

Backpacking through the Peruvian Andes while eating coca leaves for altitude sickness, I strolled into a village call Huaraz. With time on my hands and seeing a non-spitting Llama, I decided to stop for a quick pic before getting rip-roaring drunk at the local cantina. Below: Another llama experience, somewhere in the South of France.

HONEY CURE

BY

GLENN TRIPP

FADE IN.

EXT. GARDEN - MORNING

SHEPARD, a white haired, spry old man with a goofy personality
and a crazy look, is dressed in a beekeeper veil accented with
American Indian beads, boxer shorts, work boots, and bee smoker.
Tending to his bee hives on his hundred acre valley of
wildflowers, house perched on the mountainside. Shepard opens
the hive and talks to the bees.

                    SHEPARD
          Why are all the hives filled with
          ladybugs? That's not typical, there
          are so many of you!
               (looking, then)
          I guess it's a good sign! I like to
          see that you ladies keep the hives
          clean and healthy, but why so many?
          What's this, ladies night out? In
          my opinion you guys - or shall I
          say ladies? - are the terror of the
          new varroa mite! Keep up the good
          work. Keep eating those nasty
          mites.

Shepard holds a ladybug in the air.

                    SHEPARD
          You're a pretty young ladybug.
          You're not eating all my honey and
          Royal are you? You're not making my
          bees sick are you? You can eat all
          the varroa mites you want, you are
          welcome in my hives anytime.

Shepard shakes the ladybug in the air.

                    SHEPARD (CONT'D)
          As the old saying goes: release a
          ladybug, make a wish. The farmer's
          best friend puts food on a dish.
          Come back anytime.

Shepard looks back in the hive.

                    SHEPARD (CONT'D)
          Now, why are all you bees so angry?
          You act as if you are Africanized.
          There is no need to be upset, those
          are just ladybugs, they are our
          friends.
                    (MORE)

                    SHEPARD (CONT'D)
          Now don't get angry with me, I just
          came to get a little honey, check
          up on everyone.. don't worry, I'm
          not gonna touch the Royal.

Shepard writes in his journal: "Wow, the hives seem really sick
and irritated. There are quite a few that passed in their
sleep."

As Shepard writes, bees fly up his shorts and he starts
squirming.

                    SHEPARD (CONT'D)
          Hey! Hey! What are you guys doing
          up there? Get out of there. What,
          are you guys crazy? I knew you were
          sick, but not that kind of sick.
          Get out of there.

Shepard lets out a big scream.

                    SHEPARD (CONT'D)
          Ouch. Now look what you two have
          done! You both just stung me in the-
          ouch that really hurts! I've been
          stung before, but never there! Or
          even there. That's sick!

Shepard looks down his pants.

                    SHEPARD (CONT'D)
          That really hurts, I'm very
          sensitive there.
               (pause)
          Look what you've done now, it's
          starting to swell.
               (then, pleased)
          It's starting to swell. This is
          new, this is very interesting, this
          is exciting.

Shepard poses like a body builder.

                    SHEPARD (CONT'D)
          Look at me now, I look young again.
          I feel like an eighteen-year-old
          man on his first date. Where are
          the ladies now? Bring on the
          ladies! Maybe I'm onto something
          new! Where are the reporters? Now
          this is news. Better than Viagra,
          bring on the Reporters.

                                        FADE OUT.

INT. LIVING ROOM - EVENING

Shepard sits in an armchair, TV NEWSCASTER in background.
Shepard reads the newspaper aloud.

                    SHEPARD
          "What has been slowly killing the
          honey bees? That's the question
          that has the world of bee keepers
          up in arms. Previously infesting
          the hives was a nearly harmless,
          varroa mite. But, this new varroa
          mite species has mutated and is
          killing off the European Honey Bees
          at an alarming rate.
          The mite has traveled as far as
          Papua New Guinea which has the
          Australian beekeepers fearing for
          their succulent future. Scientists
          speculate that this mite is from
          the Asian sector of the honeybee
          world, which is spreading like a
          plague from apiary to apiary."

Shepard throws the paper on table.

                    SHEPARD
          Rubbish, another news article
          written by someone that says a
          whole lot of nothing he knows
          nothing about.

Shepard looks up at the tv.

                    TV NEWSCASTER
          What's Happening and What's New:
          The mutant varroa mites are running
          rampant through Mann Lake in Papua
          New Guinea, wiping out up to half
          the country's honey industry-

Shepard turns off the tv, screaming at the ceiling.

                    SHEPARD
          I just fucking read that. Hey,
          those ladybugs from earlier..
          they're not the mutant varroa
          species are they? Disguised as
          ladybugs? No, no it can't be! Why
          are all my bees sick? I thought the
          ladybugs were taking care of the
          hive cleaning, not damaging their
          delicate internal systems. I have a
          big day tomorrow!
                    (MORE)

SHEPARD (CONT'D)
I need to check all the queens and
work my way down to the drones.

BEN MAGIC, an old, burnt out hippie, knocks on the door and
walks in.

                    BEN MAGIC
          Hello, any creatures stirring? I
          know you have mice.

                    SHEPARD
          Bennie, what brings you to this neck
          of the woods? Come in, would you like
          some tea?

                    BEN MAGIC
          What's up, you old salamander? How are
          the bees buzzing? I need something
          stronger then tea! Can you mix some
          Royal Magic in the hot pot?

                    SHEPARD
          You know me, sure can. Glad you
          stopped by, I was getting depressed
          about the new varroa mite, infesting
          the hives around the world.

                    BEN MAGIC
          Yeah, like, wow man. I read about
          that. it's tripping out all the old
          bee dudes.

                    SHEPARD
          Mint tea?

                    BEN MAGIC
          Yeah perfect, throw in an extra
          tablespoon of Royal for me, please.
          The girls like me sweet.

                    SHEPARD
          Extra sweet it is. What girls?

                    BEN MAGIC
          Never mind, dude, just extra sweet. I
          came by to let you know that the Kelly
          boys captured one of your swarms.
          They're real happy making the Royal
          Magic just not interested in sharing.

                    SHEPARD
          That's alright Bennie. Everyone's
          entitled to a little extra pleasure,
          especially those Kelly boys.
                    (MORE)

SHEPARD (CONT"D)
Those red necks need all the pleasure
they can get, gives them something to
talk about.

                BEN MAGIC
Yeah, but, those red nose dudes are
not sharing, that's not very hippie of
them.

                SHEPARD
Don't get your panties in a bunch. Let
me know if you need some Royal Magic
to take home.

                BEN MAGIC
        (distracted)
Panties? I don't wear panties,
dude. Why would you even say that?
Do people really think that way?
That's wrong on so many levels. I'm
a hippie, hippies don't run that
way, I think - . Ok, yeah, thanks
for offering, I could use some
Royal Magic. Wait, I have a list.

                SHEPARD
A list? I don't have enough jars for a
list.

                BEN MAGIC
I didn't think you would, so I made
everyone on the list wash out their
peanut butter jars. You know how
hippies love their peanut butter.

                SHEPARD
Yeah, because it's cheap and hippies
are poor.

                BEN MAGIC
Hey, bee dude, that's discrimination.
First our rainbow flag was stolen from
us, now we are cheap cause we eat
peanut butter? I'm sorry, what were we
talking about? I lost my train of
consciousness.

                SHEPARD
You were saying you have a list and
some peanut butter jars.

                BEN MAGIC
Ohh yeah, I have the jars in my truck,
let me get them. Here's the list.
        (MORE)

                    BEN MAGIC (CONT'D)
          One dude tried to give me a bed pan -
          he said, don't worry it's clean, but I
          told him that's not gonna fly with
          Shep the old Bee dude. You need to
          respect the Royal Magic honey.

Shepard looks at the list.

                    SHEPARD
          There's about thirty people on this
          list.

                    BEN MAGIC
          When you're good, you're good. The
          demand is hot. Right now, Shep, you
          and the Magic bee poop are hot.

                    SHEPARD
          Honey is not made from the bee's anus.

                    BEN MAGIC
          That's what I tried to explain to
          Larry. Bed pan dude.

                    SHEPARD
          Ok, Veronica and Monica each want a
          jar? You know what they're going to do
          with it, let them share a jar and-

                    BEN MAGIC
          Ok, ok, whatever you can spare dude. I
          said I had a list, I didn't say I had
          to fulfill it like Santa. Whatever you
          can spare. If it's only for me, that's
          cool dude, I'll act like the Kelly
          boys with my jar. Without the red nose
          of course.

                    SHEPARD
          Maybe you can act like the Kelly boys
          with Veronica and Monica. You know
          those girls wouldn't disappoint you
          with their show.

                    BEN MAGIC
          Wow, you're always thinking dude. Make
          it four jars, I'll tell the rest you
          had limited supply. Monica is always
          willing to let me watch, but Veronica
          on the other hand...
               (thinking)
          I'm gonna have to work on this, let
          me get the jars out of the truck.
                    (MORE)

BEN MAGIC (CONT'D)

I'll tell the bed pan dude that he
is banned for six months out of
disrespect for the Royal.

FADE OUT.

INT. CAR - MOVING - MORNING

MAX, a young man, drives with SUE, his Asian girlfriend. Max
hangs up the phone.

                    MAX
          There's no answer, he must be
          outside tending to the bees and
          flowers. He has a landline, but he
          won't pick up unless he's next to
          it. We'll chat to him when we get
          there.

                    SUE
          He only has a landline? Who has a land
          line these days! I don't trust anyone
          who doesn't drink and doesn't have a
          cell phone.

                    MAX
          Shepard is very happy there are no
          cell towers were he lives. The bees
          would have to instinctively fly under
          the radar of the cell signal so as not
          to disturb their body rhythms and
          honey-making performances.

                    SUE
          That's interesting, where did you hear
          that? Or did you make it up to be
          popular?

                    MAX
          No, it's true. Shepard told me, he's a
          very smart man - very knowledgeable
          about bees and flowers.

                    SUE
          How do you know he's going to be there
          at all? You know two hours is a long
          way to drive to turn around empty
          handed.

                    MAX
          He will be there, he's always there.

                    SUE
          If you say so. I'm just saying, two
          hours is very far and that's just one
          way.

Max takes a deep breath, relaxes.

                    MAX
          Like I said, there are no cell
          towers in the mountains. Check what
          you need to check, call who you
          need to call, we're getting close.

                    SUE
          I'm good, I'm relaxed. I don't need my
          cell. Unless your friend Shepard is
          not there, then I will need to call an
          ambulance when I kill you.

                    MAX
          Well, if you kill me, then you
          wouldn't call an ambulance, you would
          call an undertaker. Besides, who would
          drive you home?

                    SUE
          Let's hope Shepard is there, so we
          don't have to call anyone on our
          inoperative cell phones.

                    MAX
          Don't worry, Shepard is always there.
          He works, lives, and breathes those
          insects and flowers. He loves his
          honey! Speaking of honey, the doctor
          always calls the middle of July, when
          the honey is most abundant. The Summer
          of Avery - have you ever heard of that
          term before?

                    SUE
          The Summer of Avery? No, what is that?

                    MAX
          I'm not sure, I looked it up and it
          said "ruler of the elves." In French
          it means wise. The doctor would speak
          about it in a different context
          though.
               (mockingly)
          All the flowers bloomed because of
          the summer of Avery. All the
          flowers bloom because of the summer
          of Avery.
                    (MORE)

                         MAX (CONT'D)
                (seriously)
          He says that's the apex of our
          traditional summer, or the start of
          Indian summer, with perfect rain
          and perfect sun all the time. I
          think it only happens every twenty
          years, or every other year, I'm not
          sure. The doctor recites this all
          the time, like its his mantra.
                (making fun, hands going
                 wild)
          I rub myself in honey. Look at me!
          I'm a flower, the Summer of Avery,
          the Summer of Avery.
                (laughing)
          Then, I bet he touches his little
          elf.

                         SUE
                (laughing hysterically)
          Watch the road!

A car swerves and beeps.

                         MAX
          Wow, that was close.

                         SUE
          You're telling me!

                         MAX
          So, hopefully this is the year.

                         SUE
          Summer of Avery, is that from Latin? I
          thought Indian Summer is in September?

                         MAX
          Not sure about Latin. I thought Indian
          Summer started in fall as well. I
          think it's an autumn term in summer
          for Indians or something like that.
          Hey, by the way, do you like honey
          when you take away an E and throw in
          an R?

                         SUE
          What the fuck does that mean? Honey
          with an R? There is no R in honey!

                         MAX
          But what if you put the letter R, in
          the word honey and take away the E!

                    SUE
          I'm sorry, I'm not with you, I don't
          get it.

                    MAX
          Never mind, I was just trying to
          making a bad joke.

                    SUE
          I'm not finding you funny right now!

                                        FADE OUT.

EXT. DIRT ROAD - MOVING - LATER

Max and Sue drive on Shepard's property.

                    MAX
          So this is it. Indian Valley. The
          locals call it Woodland Valley, and
          Shepard calls it Valley of the
          Flowers, you can see why. This place
          is magical, so Shepard says.

                    SUE
          It looks very enchanting, almost like
          a story book. I like the stream on the
          side. Is that your friend Shepard? He
          looks crazy scary.

Shepard runs up to the car, excited, talking fast.

                    SHEPARD
          Max you'll never believe what happened
          to me yesterday! I got stung, I got
          stung in the you know what, you know?
          You know?

                    MAX
          Know what?

Max and Sue look confused. Shepard stares back and forth at Max
and Sue.

                    SHEPARD
          Never mind, Jeep Cherokee? I like
          this car, it's an Indian car. I'm a
          Cherokee, as well, you know. Well
          part Cherokee and part Lenape.
          Did you know the Lenape Indians
          were from New Jersey? And of course
          Delaware, Western PA, and New York.
                    (MORE)

SHEPARD (CONT'D)
But primarily New Jersey, where you
live, Max. Did you know they were
called the Lenni Lenape Indians in
Jersey?

Max looks at Sue and rolls his eyes.

                    MAX
Yes Shepard, I think I heard something
to that effect before.

                    SHEPARD
I'm so glad to see people. Who's the
beautiful young squaw?

                    MAX
This is my girlfriend, Sue.

                    SHEPARD
Very proud to meet your acquaintance.
Are you Indian? You look like an Inuit
Indian from Alaska!

                    SUE
         (sarcastically)
No, I am full fledged Korean-
Indian. Pleasure to meet you as
well, sir.

                    SHEPARD
Please don't call me sir. My name is
Shepard. Unless you want to call me
Sir Shepard. Then I would have to get
on the phone with England to make sure
it was ok to use that prefix. If I
wanted, I could use the prefix Doctor.
God knows I paid the University enough
to earn it- never mind. How can I help
you fertile and virile people?

Shepard starts walking away.

                    SHEPARD (CONT'D)
Would you like some tea? I can't
relax too long, I'm having
complications. I need to handle all
the queens in ways I never handled
them before.

                    MAX
Yeah, sure, tea sounds nice.
Complications? What kind of
complications?

                    SUE
          (whispering)
Handle all the queens? This
conversation is going weird, way
too quick.

                    SHEPARD
I can't explain right now, it's a
little complicated.

                    MAX
Ohh, ok.

                    SUE
This guy is weird, but I kind of like
him. He's like a kooky long lost
uncle.

                    MAX
Yeah very weird, I think he needs to
grow on you.
          (shouting towards Shepard)
When did you get that tepee by the
stream?

                    SHEPARD
I had that thing for years. I like to
move it around the property. That's
where I have my temascal, or, as you
call it, sweat lodge. Do you see the
totem pole next to the teepee?

                    MAX
Yeah, that's really cool, did you
carve that?

                    SHEPARD
No, no, no, thats a sacred totem that
was carved over three hundred years
ago by the local Indians. They call
that the Dancing Totem. Every full
moon that totem moves. When I say it
moves, it moves.

                    MAX
What do you mean by, it moves? It
sways?

                    SHEPARD
No, I mean, it really moves. Like it
gets up and dances two feet here,
twelve feet there, nine feet over
there.
                    (MORE)

SHEPARD (CONT'D)
There's no rhyme or reason to when,
where, how, or why it moves, it just
moves.

                    MAX
Not sure if I understand properly.
That huge totem pole gets up and moves
all by itself. No help from anyone,
just moves, all by itself?

                    SHEPARD
Yes sir, that's what I said. It moves
during every full moon. The best part
is, when it's the Year of the Avery,
it seems to move in leaps and bounds.
Dancing around the valley and sitting
anywhere it very well pleases. One
month, on the full moon it was by the
stream. The next full moon, thirty
yards up the stream. The following
full moon, next to the fire pit. Now
it sits by the teepee, very strange I
tell you.

                    SUE
Do you smoke funny cigarettes now and
again Sir Shepard?

                    SHEPARD
No, I don't need that stuff, I'm kooky
already can't you tell?

                    MAX
I can tell.

                    SUE
I can tell, as well.

                    SHEPARD
Ok, sometimes I smoke funny
cigarettes. But seriously, I would
stay awake endless nights, just to
watch the dancing totem, but I was
never graced with that magical
experience. I would blink and the
totem would be in a different
location, next full moon I would stay
awake and again, somehow I would miss
the totems relocation to another area
on the property. Very real, very
strange. It's almost like I was in a
trance or hypnotized, not to see the
miracle or not to remember seeing the
miracle.

                    SUE
Yep, funny cigarettes!

                    SHEPARD
No, this is real! It's been happening
for over fifty years that I have known
this land. You know, that totem, has
to be at least a thousand pounds,
that's almost half a ton, and yet it
transplants itself to a different
location around the valley every full
moon. Also, during the full moon, the
Indian spirits do the bee dance around
the totem to keep the bees fertile.

                    SUE
Indian spirits?

                    SHEPARD
Yes, I've seen these spirits with my
own two eyes but they don't scare me
anymore. My hair is already white.
        (laughing crazily)
This place amazes me every single
day of my life, blows me away. I
tell you, especially the totem. I
was told by my antique dealing
cousin that up in Alaska they have
a walking totem. Every full moon,
the Indians pack up camp and follow
their totem to different hunting
grounds. Did you know that every
Indian in the world has a totem
made in the bees honor?

                    MAX
I didn't know that, you've been saying
for years, this place is magical and
mystical, I never realized, I'm
starting to believe.

                    SHEPARD
You should believe my son, this place
is very spiritual and very magical.
Did you know the American Indians
never lived in this valley? They only
came here to hunt and fish, they
thought this place to be too sacred. I
am the only American Indian to ever
settle in this land. I am the
gatekeeper and beekeeper of this
valley. I watch the totem, the flowers
and the grave sites. Do you see that
small graveyard next to the totem?
                  (MORE)

                    SHEPARD (CONT'D)
          Can you believe those gravestones are
          over three hundred years old?

                    MAX
          Wow, three hundred years? That's older
          than our country.

                    SHEPARD
          Well, the American Indians have been
          in this country for hundreds of years
          before the pale face stole their land.

                    SUE
          Yes, we learned that in history.

                    SHEPARD
          I watch those gravestones for the
          Indian spirits and they watch over me.
          The gravestones and totem were carved
          by the Mohawk tribe. Those gravestones
          represent the chiefs of the highest
          order, which took care of the honey
          bees of North America. These tribes
          are the only tribes that had two
          chiefs stand council at the same time.
          Two chiefs! That's unheard of, they
          all agreed that the life of the honey
          bee and the existence of their people
          depended on a two-chief ruling. The
          tribal chiefs were named after honey
          bees with names like Chief Bee, Honey
          Mountain, Yellow Wings, The Pollinator-

                    MAX
               (interrupting)
          The Pollinator? The Pollinator?
          That's cool.
               (in a deep voice)
          I am The Pollinator. Step back
          girls or you will be pollinated by
          the stroke of my-

Max looks at Sue.

                    MAX (CONT'D)
          Uh, never mind. The Pollinator
          sounds like a movie character.

                    SUE
          I'll give you a pollinator.

                    SHEPARD
          I'm just playing, just seeing if
          you're paying attention.
               (MORE)

                    SHEPARD (CONT'D)
There was never an Indian or a chief
for that matter named The Pollinator.
But the other names are real, check
the epitaphs, read for yourself.

Shepard stares at Sue.

                    SHEPARD (CONT'D)
Actually, I should be called Sir
Pollinator. I grow the flowers, the
bees thank me by giving me honey,
the flowers thank me by giving me
more flowers. The greatest reward
is the Royal Jelly, which my bees
are trained to produce: a rare,
high grade Royal Jelly I call Royal
Magic. It's a beautiful cycle of
life in the valley.

                    SUE
Wow, that's for sure.

                    MAX
Yes, you are truly The Pollinator of
the Catskills.

                    SHEPARD
Did you know that in some countries,
the bees are so scarce, the people
have to hand pollinate the fruit
flowers so they can yield a bountiful
crop? Imagine, if I had to do that, to
this whole valley? It would take me a
life-time, which the bees can manage
to get the job done in a few days.

                    SUE
That's incredible if you think about
it.

                    SHEPARD
Very incredible if you think about it!
Without the bees we wouldn't have any
cucumbers, tomatoes, oranges,
pumpkins, sunflowers, the list goes on
and on. We wouldn't have any fruits or
vegetables, period. Did you know the
farmers with the big orchards rent
thousands of beehives every season for
pollination? The hives get delivered
by the tractor trailer load-

                    MAX
               (interrupting)
          Yeah, without the bees, you
          wouldn't have almonds, therefore
          you wouldn't have almond milk.

Max motions like he's milking a cow.

                    MAX (CONT'D)
          I want to meet the little people
          who are actually milking these
          almonds!

                    SUE
          Stop making jokes, this is serious.

                    SHEPARD
          Are you done having fun? I have to get
          back to the complications in my hives.
          Do you want some Royal Magic? Is that
          what you came for?

                    SUE
          Magic, of course!

                    MAX
          Yes, please.

                    SHEPARD
          Ok, but I'm limited on supply right
          now. I promised my friend that runs
          the Delridge Nursing Home a few jars.
          He seems to be going through the Magic
          like it's oxygen. Max, can you deliver
          six jars on your way back to Jersey?
          You'd save me a road trip and a half
          day chatting with the residents.

                    MAX
          Yeah, sure.

Max and Sue buy a few bottles and grab the package. Shepard puts
on his bee veil.

                                        FADE TO BLACK.

INT. DELRIDGE NURSING HOME - DAY

DOC, old hippy, Resident Doctor at Delridge Nursing Home, sits
with MRS. JO, an old lady, schizophrenic, and delusional washed-
up actress. NURSE, flighty, sarcastic, rude, stern, watches over
them.

                    DOC
Mrs. Jo, you have to leave Mr.
Stricklin alone, I can't have our
residents harassing other residents.

                    MRS. JO
I am not harassing Mr. Stiff One. I go
in his room and he is happy to see me.
You know how I know he is happy to see
me? Because he has a pup tent under
the sheets, he always has a pup tent
under the sheets. I help him out every
day by rubbing it out until it's a
lean-to. For an old man it's not a bad
pup tent either, but it is definitely
not a teepee.

                    DOC
Enough Mrs. Jo, I heard enough. Nurse,
reduce Mr. Stricklin's RM-35 by forty
percent, he's having a reaction.

                    MRS. JO
Why do you call it RM-35? Just call it
Royal Magic like everyone else. You
always have to make it sound
scientific or something you bone head.
Besides, that's no reaction Mr. Stiff
One is having, that's excitement baby.
That's excitement to see me. Don't
listen to him nurse, Mr. Stiff One is
doing just fine. I'm monitoring him
every morning and by doing so, my
wrinkles are going away. He's even
strengthening the grip on my right
hand so much, I'm ready to pitch for
the girls' softball team. Look at
these lips, they're much fuller these
days, don't you think so?

                    NURSE
Ohh, wow, you're right. Now that you
mention it, they do look a lot fuller
and your skin does look a lot
healthier, as well. You don't look
like a shriveled raisin anymore.

                    MRS. JO
I'll be honest with you, nurse, my
little button down there even pops up
a little more then usual.. or should I
say ever?

She points to her crotch.

                         NURSE
          Your little button? I thought that was
          an extra raisin you grew.

                         MRS. JO
          Nurse, upgrade Mr. Stiff One by ten
          percent that will make his pup tent a
          teepee. And give me a twenty percent
          upcharge on the side for my little
          button, I haven't felt like this in
          many years.

                         NURSE
          Ok Mrs. Jo, will do, I'll get right on
          it.

                         DOC
               (frustrated)
          Don't listen to her nurse, I'm the
          doctor here, not her. She's just
          the resident, she's not part of our
          conversation or our work force.

                         NURSE
          Oh yeah, right. Sorry about that. Only
          arsenic?

Mrs. Jo stares down the nurse.

                         MRS. JO
          If Noah was loading the Ark, He
          would only have to take you, you
          two faced son of a bitch.

                         DOC
          Enough, Mrs. Jo.

                         MRS. JO
          They should call the Royal Magic stuff
          Viagram.

                         DOC
          That's Viagra, and no, it's not like
          Viagra. It has similar side effects,
          but it is only simple bee honey.

                         NURSE
          I'm confused. Downgrade Mr Stricklin
          by ten percent or upgrade him by
          thirty percent? Do I give Mrs. Jo an
          upgrade? A downgrade? Or the arsenic?

                    DOC
No, no, ok, ok. I've heard enough.
Nurse, retract the dosage for Mr.
Stricklin. Nothing for Mrs. Jo, and I
mean nothing. Mrs. Jo, go to your room
right now, and I don't mean Mr.
Stricklin's room either. You know Mrs.
Jo, the night nurse, wrote you up
twice this week for running around the
halls in sexy lingerie. If you get any
more writeups I will have to restrict
you to your room for a month.

                    MRS. JO
You should have been there, I was
looking hot, like a Victoria Secret
model on acid.
        (proudly)
As usual, I gave Mr. Stiff One an
instant pup tent.

                    DOC
Enough Mrs. Jo, I've heard enough. I'm
getting a visual and it's probably
going to give me nightmares. You know
something? We can lock unruly
residents inside their room for an
undetermined amount of time. Did you
know that? It's in the rule book. Do
you want that? Is that what you want?

                    MRS. JO
        (interrupting)
Nurse, give the doctor a valium to
calm him down. You know doc, you
better calm down right now and be
nice to me or I'm gonna prescribe
something stronger. Do you want to
spend the rest of the day sitting
in the corner dribbling on
yourself?

                    NURSE
Yeah doctor, you better behave.

                    MRS. JO
Nurse, is he on Adderall? Maybe I
should prescribe him Adderall, as
well. That would calm the son of a
bitch down.

Doc throws the clipboard.

                    DOC
          Nurse, don't side with her. This
          place is insane.

Doc marches away.

                    MRS. JO
          Don't listen to him Nurse, I think
          he's losing it. Are Quaaludes still on
          the market? I used to like them. Three
          of those and he will be dribbling all
          weekend.

                    DOC
          I heard that Mrs Jo. Nurse, a jeep
          pulled up in the back. Take care of
          it, please.
                    (to himself)
          I'm out of here.

                                        FADE TO BLACK.

INT. COUNTRY BAR - LATER

BAR MAID cleans glasses. Doc enters and sits on stool at bar.

                    BAR MAID
          Hey Doc, what are you doing here this
          early? Having a rough day?

                    DOC
          Yeah, really rough. Vodka and tonic
          with a twist, make it a double.

                    BAR MAID
          That's a switch. Right away, Doctor
          Sadness.

                    DOC
                    (to himself)
          Why doesn't anybody listen to me?

                    BAR MAID
          I listen to you doc. Vodka and tonic
          with a twist, make it a double.

                    DOC
          I act professional. Very professional.

                    BAR MAID
          I bet you do. You seem very
          professional to me.

                    DOC
I should be in a regional medical
center, in Hawaii or New York running
the ICU or something exciting. Instead
I moved to the Catskills to work at
this crazy place next door.
          (making fun)
Delridge Assisted Resident Living.
With residents of the bizarre.

Turning serious, Doc stares at the Bar Maid.

                    DOC (CONT'D)
I have a ninety-year-old man with a
twenty-four hour hard on, an eighty-
year-old broken down actress that
thinks she's a doctor and runs
around in sexy underwear, and a
nurse that does whatever the hell
she pleases while taking orders
from the residents. The funny thing
is I don't even know the nurse's
name, she's been working for me for
over two years. She probably
doesn't even know her own name.

                    BAR MAID
That does sound bizarre.

                    DOC
That's just the tip of the iceberg. I
have people coming to my facility on
their death bed for assisted living. A
few weeks later, they are up and about
miraculously healed, getting out of
their beds and walking away from the
facility without signing out or even
saying goodbye, never to be heard from
again. I don't know if people are
coming or going in this place, it's
insane.

                    BAR MAID
Sounds insane, but sounds like you're
giving them the treatment they need!

                    DOC
          (ignoring her)
Little children living in the lobby
for days at a time while their
family members occupy a bed. The
next minute I turn around, the
place is empty like the plague hit.
                 (MORE)

DOC (CONT"D)
No patients, no children, the place
is quiet. I'm looking around and
all the rooms are empty. The only
ones in the facility are the
nurses, twenty-four-hour-hard-on,
the broken down actress, and
myself. I ask the staff, "Where is
everyone?" They're clueless! Two
weeks go by and I see another huge
raise in my pay check. Then all of
a sudden the place is full again.
It's like a fucking Steven King
movie.

BAR MAID
I wouldn't complain about the
paycheck. I wouldn't even bring up the
raise in fear they would think it's a
mistake and take it back.

DOC
I'm not complaining, but the place is
bizarre. When I speak to my superiors
regarding the four raises in six
months, they just keep parrot talking
the same phrase. "Keep doing what your
doing". I don't even know what the
fuck I'm doing to keep doing it. We
have millions and millions of dollars
pouring into the facility every year
and we don't even know where it comes
from. We're just a small nursing home,
if you will, in the Middle of the
Catskills, but we get grants larger
than some of the big medical centers
in major cities.

BAR MAID
Sounds like you're a great doctor.

DOC
I just can't explain it. I take off
for a two week vacation thinking the
place is going to go to the crapper.
Bam, the whole place is redone and
painted. New beds and furniture. New
lighting fixtures. A new facility
nearly. They even built me a science
lab in the back because I told them I
was a science professor during my
doctorate. And when I ask everybody
how and when did this remodeling
happened nobody has a clue.
(MORE)

                    DOC (CONT'D)
Like it's this big secret, this big
lie, this magic presto magic show.

                    BAR MAID
Doesn't sound like a bad gig to me at
all.

                    DOC
Again, I'm not complaining, but this
place is just so fucking odd. Ohh, you
want to hear the best part? I have a
friend in the Catskills that has a
large apiary and he gives me jars of
his Royal Jelly honey mix from his bee
hive. But it's no ordinary honey or
Royal jelly he calls it Royal Magic-

                    BAR MAID
          (interrupting)
I love honey.

                    DOC
So, I give this honey mix to the
residents in their tea and coffee
instead of sugar, thought it would be
a healthier alternative. They swear
it's a medicine. I guess it makes them
feel good enough to get up and leave
in the middle of the night without a
trace. So, it makes them feel good and
healthy but it has a side effect. Do
you want to know what the side effect
is?

                    BAR MAID
Yeah, what?

                    DOC
Ready? It makes them horny! That's the
side effect! It makes them horny. Now
there are all these healthy people
roaming around with these raging hard-
ons or God knows what. With my luck it
will probably lead to a population
explosion and I'll be responsible. It
feels like I'm living in a Peter Max
painting.

                    BAR MAID
Who? Never mind. I guess that explains
Mr. Twenty-Four Hour Hard-On and
Doctor Actress. I want some of that.
It makes everyone feel better as well?
                    (MORE)

                    BAR MAID (CONT"D)
Sounds to me like a win-win, sign me
up.

                    DOC
Yeah, a real win-win, the residents
say this Royal Magic makes them feel
better. So I decided to give it a
fancy medical name, I call it RM-35. I
prescribe it as medicine to the
residents, I guess it has that placebo
effect.

                    BAR MAID
The RM is for Royal Magic, I figured
that out all by myself. What's the
thirty five for?

                    DOC
Ohh, the thirty five? That's the
thirty five pollen compounds found in
the honey, when put under a
microscope. I wonder if the FDA would
consider this an Orphan Drug. Never
mind, I'm just thinking out loud. Let
me just say, it seems that, my
surroundings and my life is really
strange and a little surreal at this
point in time.

                    BAR MAID
Doc, you are a very smart man, can I
buy you a drink?

                                FADE TO BLACK.

EXT. GARDEN - MORNING

Shepard, Max, and Sue sit at a table.

                    MAX
We dropped off the jars to Delridge
the other day, the place was empty.
The few people that were there seemed
a little strange. There was an old
lady that kept winking at me, and when
we were leaving, she was standing in
the window taking off her clothes.

                    SUE
Very strange indeed.

                    SHEPARD
Yeah, that's Mrs. Johanson, or Mrs. Jo
as she likes to be called. She likes
doing the striptease thing.
So, I guess you don't buy for your
own consumption. You're a dealer? I
just sold you a few bottles of
Magic on Monday. You can't consume
that much Magic all in one sitting,
or you'll get sick. So you must be
a dealer, or a hoarder. Which one
is it?

                    MAX
Well, we're not actually dealers or
hoarders. We take care of our friends
and family. Everyone we give your
product to is no longer sick. It even
got rid of cancer in one of our
friends. Or so he says.

                    SHEPARD
Well I don't care what you do in your
spare time, just don't let people know
where I'm located. I don't want my
place to become a tourist trap. I'm
not putting on Mickey Mouse ears for
any kids that's for sure. Besides,
these are sacred Indian grounds. I
don't want them tainted.
     (beat)
But, if you're helping people I'll
give you a special rate. As long as
you don't tell anybody about my
valley.

                    MAX
You have our word.

                    SUE
That's for sure.

                    SHEPARD
Good.I just harvested a large supply
of Magic this morning. I also
harvested some cannabis. Do you think
your friends would be interested?
Now *that* is a plant that has
medicinal properties.

                    MAX
No, it makes us paranoid, but thanks
anyway.

                    SHEPARD
Ok, suit yourself. It seems like no
one is interested in cannabis these
days except for me and the bees. I
like to think it keeps the bees calm,
as well as me. Do you know my cannabis
flowers are red? This is the rarest
cannabis in the world, only grown in
this valley. And of course the
Bolivian Andes.

                    SUE
Is that what makes the Magic so
magical?

                    SHEPARD
I don't know, it might! It might not.
No one knows. I sent A Magic sample to
a lab and it came back with negative
cannabis results. My friend Doc and I
put the Magic under three different
microscope strengths and we couldn't
find any trace of cannabis or floral
compounds from the valley.

                    SUE
That's weird, now I'm really
intrigued.

                    SHEPARD
We put a sample in our do-it-
yourself DNA kits and nothing came
back cannabis or valley floral
positive. And yet, the bees are
pollinating the cannabis and
flowers like crazy, making large
quantities of magic honey. I truly
think it's the rare flower pollen
combination that makes the Magic
magical.

                    SUE
Why don't you keep doing tests till
you come up with a positive match?

                    SHEPARD
I can't spend twenty years trying to
figure out the right percentage of
pollen from each specific flower that
makes up its DNA. Most of the exotic
flowers I planted in the valley are so
rare they don't even exist anymore and
have a multi-dimensional pollen count.
Do you want to know something?
                    (MORE)

                    SHEPARD (CONT'D)
I planted two rare flowers from Africa
twenty years ago and they are just
starting to bloom. They both have a
nine to twelve lateral pollen count.
This is definitely the Summer of
Avery.

Max turns to Sue.

                    SHEPARD (CONT'D)
Some of the flowers I planted have
such a high pollen and sugar
content that the bees can produce
double the honey in half the time -
like those flowers I smuggled into
this country from Borneo. No other
bees on the planet are as highly
advanced and developed in medicinal
honey production as my bees.

                    SUE
I didn't realize that some flowers can
produce a higher output of pollen than
others. I guess I never really thought
about it.

                    SHEPARD
Oh yes! Not just pollen, but sugar, as
well. We tested every flower's DNA in
the valley, nothing came back
medicinal Magic positive. So, I've
given up on the search for answers and
devoted all my time to production.

                    MAX
Well, looks to me like you're doing a
fine job.

                    SUE
Max, tell him about the ladybugs.

                    MAX
Ohh yeah, the last time we were here,
there were ladybugs all over the hood
of our car. When I say all over, I
mean all over. Is that normal, to see
so many ladybugs in one group like
that? We thought that was very
strange, it creeped us out.

                    SUE
Yeah, I didn't even want to get in the
car, Max had to get the ice scraper to
clear them off.

                    SHEPARD
Anywhere else that might be strange,
Max, but not here in the valley. They
eat other insects and between the
flowers and the bees, there is a lot
of extra unwanted insects.

                    MAX
Ohh, ok, just checking. Speaking of
strange... you've probably told me
before, but where does the name
Shepard come from? It's not very
common, it's actually kinda strange.

                    SHEPARD
As you know, my parents were American-
Indian.

                    SUE
So why the name Shepard? That doesn't
sound very American-Indian!

                    SHEPARD
Well, when an American-Indian child is
born, the father leaves the teepee and
the first thing he sees, that's what
he would name his child. My father
must have seen a shepherd grazing his
animals. Some names are even stranger
to the pale faced people, like Soaring
Eagle , Dancing with Wolves, Honey
Mountain, Blue Sky, and so forth. I am
glad the first thing my father saw
wasn't Two Dogs Fucking. Can you
imagine that? How do you explain that
one in life?

Shepherd gestures to himself, then Max.

                    SHEPARD (CONT'D)
          (as if he's Max)
"Hello, I am Max and this is my
friend Two Dogs Fucking." Or... "k
class, does anyone have the answer?
Yes, I call on you Two Dogs
Fucking."

Everyone starts laughing.

                    SUE
Seriously, were you the only child?

SHEPARD
No, I have a half-brother named
Verdun.

SUE
That's a strange name, as well, and
not very American-Indian either. Where
does that come from?

SHEPARD
I'm not sure where the name comes
from. My stepmother probably read it
in a book. She loved to read. Actually
I think it's French. It means a fort
on a hill. I think they thought he was
going to be a warrior or something.

MAX
Did he, in fact, end up being a
warrior in the military?

SHEPARD
No, no, no, he's an artist and a
really good one at that, I think!

MAX
I really like that name Verdun. That's
a really cool name. Verdun the
Pollinator.

SUE
I really like that name, as well.
Without the Pollinator bit of course.

SHEPARD
Yeah, the name Verdun has a ring to
it, I guess. So, Verdun moved to
Europe, south Holland, when he was a
young man and never kept in touch. I
miss him dearly. I had an uncle that
watched out for him, but he passed.
Then I had a cousin watching out for
him, but he left Holland for Alaska to
research the walking totem. I also had
a childhood friend look him up, but my
brother pretended he didn't know him.
He changed his life and his last name,
as well, he calls himself Verdun Grey.
Now, I don't think that's very
American-Indian at all. I heard he
even changed his stories about his
life growing up. I heard it through
the grapevine that he has this new art
form called Art Decay.

                        SUE
          I think I heard of Verdun Grey with
          Art Decay.

                        SHEPARD
          Really? Wow, that's a first. I've
          never seen the Art Decay. I heard he
          even wrote a book called *The Ghost of
          Granite* but I can't find a copy
          anywhere. He had a special gift as a
          child, he could read minds and
          feelings. He got that gift from my
          step-mother. When you put those two in
          the same roomm your hair stood up on
          the back of your neck. That lad Verdun
          is a little strange, very smart, but
          he has some twisted issues. I guess we
          are all a little strange in our own
          little way. Maybe the apple doesn't
          fall far from the tree.

Max and Sue quickly look at each other. Shepard walks away,
still talking.

                                        FADE OUT

INT. LIVING ROOM - EVENING

Shepard, sits down, turns on the tv, volume very loud.

                        NEWSCASTER
          The new super mite is a strain of
          varroa mites which had never before
          been able to breed on the European
          honeybee, and thus had never been a
          threat to honey production.

Shepard stares in disbelief.

                        NEWSCASTER
          The mutation of the varroa mite is
          believed to have originated from a
          single female mite in South East
          Asia. Scientists say, based on
          experiences in the past, the mites
          will also be carrying exotic viral
          diseases. The scientists also
          believe -

Shepard turns off the tv.

                    SHEPARD
          Another news commentator that says
          everything he knows nothing about.

Shepard slumps down in seat as the phone rings.

                    SHEPARD (CONT'D)
          Hello? Hey Grace, how's everything?
          Ohh yeah, the art party tomorrow?
          Yeah, I'll try to make it, I'm a
          little busy. Ok, ok, let's chat
          tomorrow, I have someone knocking at
          the door.

Doc walks in.

                    DOC
          I thought you'd have been in your
          garden, there's still a little more
          sunlight left in the day.

                    SHEPARD
          No, I'm done for the day, wanted to
          keep moving on this new project. Lots
          of research needs to be done.

                    DOC
          What are you working on? Maybe I can
          help.

                    SHEPARD
          No, not right now. I'll lay it on you
          when I have more than just the
          foundation. You want something to
          drink? Beer, wine, tea? The tea is
          fresh from the garden, and the wine is
          homemade - I crushed the grapes with
          my own two feet.

                    DOC
          With those cloven hoofs? Thanks
          anyway, Shep, but I'll pass on the
          wine. I'd love to stay, but my girl's
          making me dinner as we speak. I
          stopped by cause a resident brought
          two pet chickens in the facility. Can
          I drop them here, if that's cool?

                    SHEPARD
          No problem, I always have room for
          another creature in the valley.
                    (MORE)

SHEPARD (CONT'D)
Especially chickens, they can feast on
some of the nasty bugs plaguing the
hives. Does the resident want the
chicks back?

                DOC
No, I explained they were leaving on a
one way trip to paradise.

                SHEPARD
What would you have done if I said no?

                DOC
I would have pulled up to the Kelly
boys' house, beeped the horn, and
tossed them out the window. Then, I
would have sat there for twenty
minutes watching those two
knuckleheads chase them around in
their underwear while my dinner was
getting cold.

                SHEPARD
That sounds like a lot more fun than
coming here.

                DOC
Yeah, I thought so as well. Let me get
the chicks out, I have to keep moving.

                SHEPARD
Sounds great. There's some bird seed
by the front door - throw that down
first to distract them so they don't
run away.

                                DISSOLVE TO:

EXT. GARDEN - MORNING

Shepard cuts flowers as Max and Sue enter the garden.

                MAX
Hey Shep, what are you doing? You need
a hand?

                SHEPARD
Hey kids you're back! Sure thing, I
can always use a hand. You should
bring a tent next time, stay a while.

MAX

We had some free time with school and work so we thought we'd take a ride, see what you're up to.

SHEPARD

You missed a good shindig in town yesterday! I went to an outdoor gathering on the village green, sponsored by the Art Cafe. With the scent of Royal still on my clothes from the cutout I did earlier, bees were saying hello to me all day. I was sitting in the shade having a beer when this little bee landed on my shirt. I let her crawl onto my hand where she sat and groomed herself for about 15 minutes from head to toe while I studied her. Her wings were tattered and one antenna partially gone. An old worn out bee for sure. I imagine it was a bee left from the cutout sitting in my truck. While at the shindig, I got a chance to educate the young kids on bees and how they're not out to sting, if not bothered. Anyhow, it was a fun and exciting experience educating kids and getting to watch a bee groom itself. I got more out of that, than I did the function itself. I pointed out that when you see a bee in town, it's probably my bee making really good honey.

SUE

Sounds like you had fun. Why is your honey so different in texture and color then normal honey in the stores?

SHEPARD

First of all, my bees are foraging on exotic flowers that I planted from around the globe, plus this is a very magical valley. As everyone knows, normal bees make hexagon shaped cells for their brood and honey. Having the hex design is as old as the bee itself, but that poor design allows the important Magical darker honey to be left behind in the corners.

                    MAX
I did not know that.

                    SHEPARD
Did you know that normal bees cannot
make honey in a cylindrical shaped
honey comb? It's a fact. But I trained
my bees to produce their brood and
their honey in cylindrical shaped
honeycombs, which makes all the Royal
Magic equally distributed throughout
the honey cell. My bees are the first
on the planet to have this happen. I
scientifically and singlehandedly
reshaped Mother Nature without any
genetic alterations.

                    SUE
Wow, that is something to be very
proud of. You've made history.

                    SHEPARD
Did you know it takes twelve honey
bees to make a teaspoon of honey in
their six week lifespan? That means it
takes 12 bees a lifetime of their hard
work and devotion to sweeten your cup
of tea this morning. Did you know a
bee can visit up to 1,500 flowers in a
single day? That's roughly 63,000
flowers in their lifespan. If you
times that by twelve, that's roughly
756,000 flowers to make a teaspoon's
worth of golden nectar. So you see,
that's why I have so much pride,
admiration, and devotion for my bees,
as well as my flowers.

                    MAX
Wow, that's crazy hard work for one
teaspoon of honey.

                    SHEPARD
Yes, that is very hard work for bees
making normal honey. But, my bees are
working just as hard making Royal
Magic honey, and there's the
difference.

                    MAX
Yes, I can see the difference. I
didn't know those facts about the hard
working bees, very interesting.

                    SHEPARD
You think that's interesting? Did you
know that there are up to 50,000 bees
in a colony during the Summer of
Avery, and most bees are female? To
make honey, bees drop nectar into a
honeycomb and evaporate it by fanning
their wings. Everybody thinks bees
poop in the honey comb to make honey,
and that's just not true because I
don't eat poop. Honey is the only food
that includes all the substances
needed to sustain life, including
water.

                    SUE
I thought honey was bee poop.

                    SHEPARD
I can keep going all day. Bees are
covered in tiny hairs which helps to
spread pollen from flower to flower
for the flowers' growth process. Bees
are 100 times more sensitive to the
smell of flowers than humans. Each bee
will fly over 600 miles in their six
week lifespan. About a third of the
world's food supply depends on
pollinating insects like the honey
bee. When a bee finds a great patch of
flowers, she tells the other bees in
the hive with a wiggle dance. Imagine
if we did a wiggle dance for -
     (starts dancing)
a pizzeria down the road.
     (and another dance)
Burger King and McDonald's, three
blocks away.

                    SUE
That's very interesting.

                    MAX
That's very funny.

                    SHEPARD
          (in an English accent)
If you will excuse me, please.

Sue and Max stare at Shepard walking toward the house.

                    SUE
He is odd and interesting at the same
time. Again, where did you say you met
him?

                    MAX

He was my sixth grade science and
horticulture teacher.

                    SUE
And you decided, ohh, ok, let me hang
out with this crack job that was my
sixth grade teacher?

                    MAX
Something like that. Sooo, a couple
quick little creepy facts. When
Shepard was a child about eleven or so
he saw Indian ghosts dancing around
him in the forest by his campfire. He
was so scared that he lost speech for
over a year and his jet black hair
turned pure white, just as you see it
today.

                    SUE
Wow, that is creepy. That might
explain the three hundred year-old
cemetery as well as the dancing Totem
pole that he worships. This place is
very creepy but very calming at the
same time. I don't know what it is, I
can't put my finger on it.

                    MAX
Also another fact: Shepard and Doc,
who you met last week at the nursing
home, grew up together and went to
Yale. Both studied biology and
medicine and were top of their class.
In the sixties they invented something
to do with medicinal cannabis and were
nominated for a Nobel Peace Prize but
the board members took their names out
of the running because cannabis was
too controversial at the time.
          (pauses for effect)
Shepard ended up working at the
botanical gardens as curator and
his friend Doc moved to Hawaii to
run a hospital. Twenty years later,
they bumped into each other grocery
shopping and realized they were
neighbors in the Catskills.
                    (MORE)

                    MAX (CONT'D)
            Well, if you can call fifteen miles
            away neighbors.

                        SUE
            This is a small world. And in the
            mountains fifteen miles is close.

                        MAX
            Shh, here he comes, I'll tell you more
            later.

Shepard walks from the house with a teaset.

                        SHEPARD
            Well, are you going to join me? Sit
            down. We are going to have thirty-six
            devoted bees sweeten our cups of tea.

                        SUE
            Sir Shepard, I see you have a wedding
            ring. You're married?

                        SHEPARD
            Yes. Well, I was. Well I guess I still
            am. But that was many moons ago.

                        SUE
            She's not alive?

                        SHEPARD
            Ohh yes, she's still alive, alright.
            Very much alive. With all due respect,
            she's just a little messed up in the
            head.

                        SUE
            What do you mean?

Max looks at Sue with sternly.

                        MAX
            That's alright, Shepard, you don't
            have to share. You know how nosy
            girls can get about other females
            and marriage and all that stuff.

Sue stares at Max, eyes popping.

                        SHEPARD
            No, no, it's quite alright, Max. I
            don't mind sharing.

Shepard leans into Sue.

                    SHEPARD (CONT'D)
A long time ago, when I was fresh
out of college, I married my
childhood sweetheart, Rosemary. We
both had the mindset of getting
married and starting a family. We
had a lot in common, we were
hippies from the "then" generation,
we were into nature, plants,
animals, the great outdoors,
exploration travel, writing, music,
weed.

                    SUE
        (interrupting)
Weed? Well, there's a surprise!

                    MAX
Sue?

                    SHEPARD
She was half-Sioux Indian and half-
French. The love of my life.

                    SUE
What happened to her? Did you have
children?

                    SHEPARD
Yes, we have a son. Named him Verdun
after my brother.

                    SUE
Why didn't you tell us that the other
day when you were talking about your
brother?

                    SHEPARD
Because, you didn't ask. Well,
since I missed my brother so much I
named my son after him, Verdun, the
brother I never had. As for my
wife, she lost her marbles. I think
she ate one of the rare plants we
were smuggling from Mexico or
Nepal. She was always experimenting
with edibles. Anyway, one day she
turned around. I guess her brain
snapped and she thought she was a
witch, making potions and doing
crazy witchy things. I thought it
was a phase so I humored her for
years. Then..
                    (MORE)

                    SHEPARD (CONT'D)
I think it was maybe the eighth
time we went to Salem,
Massachusetts? She just...
disappeared.

                    SUE
Disappeared? Like in, abducted?

                    SHEPARD
No, like, got up from the seance table
and just disappeared. I was in the pub
at the time having a few pints with
some friends when this woman came
running in with little Verdun. She
said, "She's gone, Rosemary's gone."
It was a crazy time. How could a woman
get up and just vanish? We looked all
over for her for days. Everyone was
looking for her, even the mayor, but
she was nowhere to be found. Just up
and vanished. I thought she would
eventually come home, but she never
did. I waited and waited but she never
came home.

Shepard is on the verge of tears.

                    SUE
What about your child? How old was he?
What happened to him?

                    SHEPARD
Verdun? He was about eight at the
time. He lives in the city now with
his wife. So about, I would say,
fifteen years later after the
disappearance act, an old friend calls
me up and says they found my wife. So,
I raced up to Salem and sure enough
someone found her and put her in a nut
house.

                    SUE
Oh my. Really? Why?

                    SHEPARD
Well, as the story goes, she was
dressed like a gypsy witch, chanting,
throwing red paint at people
pretending it was fire, and burning
the demons out of them.

                    SUE
Red paint? Why red paint? I don't get
it!

                    SHEPARD
Well, when she was a little girl she
was told to never play with matches,
so, she didn't ever, in her life, play
with matches. In her witchy mind, red
paint was the antidote for fire, I
guess.

                    SUE
Then what happened?

                    SHEPARD
Well, while in the nut house, she
thought that the older part of the
hospital was possessed by witches and
demons. Which it probably was, being
that it was built in the 1800s and had
a notorious reputation for lobotomy
and torture. So, anyway, she decided
to burn down the whole wing of the
hospital. I heard that when the fire
department went into the hospital with
their hoses, Rosemary and another
friend were just standing in the
hallway, staring at the flames. The
firemen said it was so hot and intense
that no one could stand fifty feet
from those flames. But yet, those two
woman just stood there mesmerized, ten
feet away, staring like they were at a
campfire ready to cook marshmallows.

                    SUE
I thought she didn't play with
matches! How did she burn the hospital
down?

                    SHEPARD
It wasn't the whole hospital, it was
just the wing. So, she actually didn't
light the matches herself. She
convinced or hypnotized or whatever
the other patient to light the matches
and burn the hospital wing down.

                    SUE
So then what happened?

                    SHEPARD
So, the authorities didn't blame her
for the fire because the other woman
admitted to lighting the matches. But,
they still kept her in resident
therapy for being a self-proclaimed
witch and an assistant pyromaniac not
fit for society. When they were
finally ready to release her after a
long while, she didn't want to leave.
She just wouldn't go. The outside
world scared her, I guess. She was
institutionalized for so long that
that was home for her.

                    SUE
Wow that is some story. Have you seen
her after the fire?

                    SHEPARD
Ohh yeah, every month before the full
moon, like clockwork. I'd make the
drive to Massachusetts and bring her a
few jars of Magic, twenty boxes of
honey cookies, and fifty pounds of
wax. In her witch mind, she believed
that I was her good neighbor bringing
her gifts for the full moon party.

                    SUE
Wax? What does she do with all that
wax?

                    SHEPARD
Well, it may sound funny and I think
it's very ironic since she doesn't
play with matches, but she takes the
wax to make candles.

                    SUE
Candles?

                    SHEPARD
Yep candles! Big ones, small ones,
colored ones, ones with designs, ones
with small stones. Hundreds of candles
every month. And I had to supply the
wax. Some months I didn't have the
wax, so I would go and get it from
another apiary. But, she knew the
difference, the texture, the smell.
She is brilliant when it comes to wax
and honey.

                    MAX
Why didn't you take some of your wax
and mix it with the other wax to mask
the smell and texture?

                    SHEPARD
I didn't want to disturb the bees'
Magic-making process. Besides, she
would have known. You can't fool her.

                    SUE
What does she do with all those
candles she makes?

                    SHEPARD
She gave them away to people in the
hospital - and to me, of course. I
would light a candle for her every
night hoping she would come back home
with her mind put back together. She
even started a candle making class in
the hospital, but she only taught the
class on the full moon. She thought it
was spiritual. So I would have to
bring her a wax delivery two days
prior to make sure it was fresh.

                    SUE
A candle class? That's nice.

                    SHEPARD
Oh, you have no idea, candle making is
a very serious business, no joke. If
you even cracked a smile in class, let
alone a joke, the stare down would be
so intense you would just up and leave
the class in fear. I've seen it
happen.

                    SUE
Wow, that is some story.

                    MAX
Yeah, I got choked up hearing that
story.

                    SHEPARD
It's really a fun story, I like
telling it. That's just the tip of the
iceberg, would you like more tea?

                              FADE TO BLACK.

INT. APARTMENT - MORNING

Max and Sue laying in bed.

                    SUE
          Max, why didn't you tell me the truth
          about Shepard earlier? About the ghost
          fright and his craziness? Why did I
          have to wait so long to get the
          details little by little? If we're
          going to have a relationship that's
          going to work, you need to be honest
          with me.

                    MAX
          My dear, if I had told you all the
          facts that I knew beforehand, do you
          really think you would have even left
          the apartment? Shepard's not the kind
          of person that you hype up to people
          and expect them to go running to the
          Catskills to embrace. Besides, I learn
          new facts about him every time I see
          him. The other day was a real learning
          experience, I didn't know he had a
          brother or son named Verdun.

                    SUE
          You've known him for how long, and you
          didn't know he had a brother or son
          named Verdun?

                    MAX
          Well, I kinda knew he had a brother,
          but I didn't know his name was Verdun.
          When I asked him once about his family
          he started to get all emotional, so I
          changed the subject.

                    SUE
          Just be honest with me, Max. That's
          all I ask.

                    MAX
          I'm trying.

                    SUE
          I had some crazy dreams last night. I
          dreamt that witches were chasing you
          screaming, "He has fire down his
          pants!" Meanwhile, I'm chasing the
          witches to leave you alone. It was
          scary.
                    (MORE)

SUE (CONT'D)
Also, you were walking around like a
zombie scaring the shit out of me. You
wouldn't leave the place or the
hospital. You kept calling it the joke
factory, but I wasn't laughing.

MAX
You told me to be honest with you.
Just for the record, I do have fire in
my pants, right now.

SUE
No, you have the joke factory down
your pants.

MAX
No, it's fire.

SUE
No, it's a joke factory this morning
Max, because I'm not playing with
fire! I feel bloated, you know how I
get. But that was a crazy dream. I
still can't believe the story Shepard
told us about his wife. Her brain
snapped and she turned into a witch,
and then she disappeared for years,
leaving him to take care of the child.
She burned down hospital.

MAX
She didn't burn down the hospital, it
was just the wing of the hospital.

SUE
The wing, the hospital, like it really
makes a fucking difference. Also, he
drives up to Massachusetts once a
month to see her and bring her
gifts... that is true love. She makes
him candles. She must deep down love
him, as well, especially if he lights
a candle for her every night. If she
would only just leave that stupid
hospital he would take her back in a
second. You can see he has love for
that woman. I want to go to
Massachusetts and meet her, I need to
see what this woman looks like. Maybe
he has pictures.

MAX
Don't ask him, you see how emotional
he gets when he speaks about her!

                    SUE
I'm just curious what she looks like!
The dancing totem, the three hundred
year-old cemetery, what you told me
about him seeing ghosts when he was a
kid and his hair turning bleach
white... he had a tough life and yet
he graduated Yale, lives in a
fairytale setting, traveled around the
world, and was the director for one of
the most prestigious botanical gardens
in the world.

                    MAX
Don't forget that he's inventor of
Royal Magic. Like I said, he's an
interesting man, but he has a few
quirks about him.

                    SUE
A few? To say the least. I really am
having a hard time putting this puzzle
together about this man's life.

                    MAX
Don't think top hard, we might see
some smoke. I'm going to jump in the
shower and put out this fire down my
pants.

                    SUE
Max, that's all you ever think about.
I'm trying to share feelings with you
and the only feelings you have are at
the joke factory down your pants. Let
me use the bathroom first, Max, I have
to get ready for work.

                    MAX
Now all of a sudden she has to get to
work.

INT. APARTMENT - LATER

Max bangs on the bathroom door, Sue still inside.

                    MAX
Sue!

                    SUE (V.O.)
I will be out in a second.

                    MAX
          Are you done, toots? Can I have my way
          with the bathroom please?

Sue opens the door and stands in the entrance with a towel.

                    SUE
          Max? I hope you love me like Shepard
          loves his wife.

                    MAX
          Sometimes.
               (pause)
          I'm kidding, of course I do.

                    SUE
          I love you, Max. Come here, I'll put
          out your fire.

Sue drops the towel and pulls Max into the bathroom.

                    MAX
          I thought you had to go to work!

                                        FADE OUT.

EXT. GARDEN - DAY

Shepard tends to his bees. Max and Sue enter.

                    SHEPARD
          Well hello, strangers, long time no
          see.

                    MAX
          Hey Shep, did you know there are other
          apiaries and beekeepers that claim to
          have Royal Magic production?

                    SHEPARD
          Yes, I heard. I had about six hives
          swarm. They were from a good stock and
          strain. I looked all over for them,
          but nowhere to be found. Those were
          some of my best crops, but deep down,
          I'm glad. Now they can harvest pollen
          from other areas while still making
          their signature Royal Magic. My
          thoughts are to go globally with bee
          production. This way the whole world
          can have the benefits of Royal Magic
          while pollinating the flowers
          globally.
                    (MORE)

SHEPARD (CONT'D)

If I had it my way, I would have Royal
Magic manufactured on other planets
and universes.

                    SUE
Well, you have a great start right
here, how many hives do you have? It
looks like hundreds.

                    SHEPARD
There are exactly ninety-six full
working hives. If I fix up the hives
in the shed and split a few colonies,
I could potentially have over a
hundred.

                    SUE
Wow, that's a lot. What's the deal
with the two beehives on that massive
rock platform? Why is that so special
looking?

                    SHEPARD
I had my friends, Kate the stone lady
and Ben Magic the honey hippie build
it for me. Those were the first
beehives I ever owned. Those are the
original bees. Well thirtieth
generation. Believe it or not, those
colonies went through fourteen queens
throughout its existence and it's
still running strong. That gene pool
is purer then pure. At one time, I had
over two hundred and fifty bee hives
split from those two hives.

                    MAX
Ben Magic the honey hippie.. does he
have anything to do with Royal Magic?

                    SHEPARD
Well, sort of. You see Ben was my
caretaker when I was traveling. He
would take care of the bees, the
flowers, the dogs the property. One
day when he was dipping in the honey
he noticed it made his lethargic mood
come alive. He swore it was magical
due to the bees pollinating the
cannabis. I tested that honey back and
forth, up and down and there was
negative cannabis receptors. You know
those hippies, cannabis is the
creative cure for everything.
                    (MORE)

SHEPARD (CONT'D)
So, to humor him, I called my honey,
Royal Magic, the name stuck.

MAX
I like that name, Ben Magic the Honey
Hippie. Where is the Honey Hippie now?

SHEPARD
Ben? He lives in Woodstock, playing
guitar on the streets, and organizing
Full Moon Parties. He pops by now and
again.

MAX
What about Kate the stone lady, what's
her deal? Does she still come around,
as well.

SHEPARD
No, no, the stone lady, Crazy Kate,
had a meltdown. She was throwing rocks
at her clients' windows so the
authorities locked her up in Pine
Grove. When she gets out, I really
don't want her around. She upsets the
bees.

SUE
Sir Shepard, how long does a Queen
typically live?

SHEPARD
Well, in a healthy hive, a Queen can
live for up to five years. Typically
the bees or the beekeeper will change
the Queen after three years, but my
Queens can live past seven years
because they are eating the highly
nutritious Royal Magic. Did you know
that the Indian tribes, like the Aztec
and Mayans, would have the same bee
colony for hundreds of years?

SUE
Hundreds of years? How do bees live
for hundreds of years?

SHEPARD
Not the same bees, just the same gene
pool, their bees don't have a stinger,
they're called Melipona. The Egyptian
records indicate that they have had
the same bee colony for thousands of
years. Thousands of years!
(MORE)

SHEPARD (CONT'D)
This creature is as old as the
dinosaur. When King Tut was
discovered, he had edible honey in his
tomb. Of course, it wasn't Royal
Magic, but the honey survived over two
thousand years. That's magic in
itself.

                    MAX
Why do you smoke out the bees?

                    SHEPARD
Keeps the bees calm. You see, I fill
the smoker with cannabis. It gets the
bees really stoned so when I take
their Royal Magic they're not all
pissed off at me.

                    MAX
Really? Let me take a smell, not a big
one, it makes me paranoid.

                    SHEPARD
You want to behave like the bees?

Shepard looks up, imitating a stoned bee.

                    SHEPARD (CONT'D)
Yooo, bee dude, the guy with the
white costume is taking the roof
off our house again. Here comes the
smoke. Wow, I'm feeling light
headed. Now he's taking the Royal!
No way, that is so trippy. I can't
feel my wings. That royal honey
looks so good, now I have the
munchies. Ohh wow, the queen's
looking. Ah, now I'm all paranoid.

Max and Shepard start laughing.

                    SUE
You two are pathetic. Shepard, I
bought myself a bee outfit to go in
the hives and help you harvest honey,
but I don't want to talk to stoned
bees.

Sue holds up a pink bee suit.

                    SHEPARD
A pink bee suit?

                    SUE
Yeah, with matching gloves. What's
wronq with that? Pink's my favorite
color. Right Max?

                    MAX
That's an understatement.

                    SHEPARD
Bees don't like pink. They're going to
fly away.Do you know what you're going
to do to those poor bees if you walk
up to their hive in that thing?

                    SUE
What? What's the matter?

                    SHEPARD
And you call me pathetic? Nevermind.
Put that thing away, we'll finish this
conversation another day. I have to
get back to work.

                                FADE TO BLACK.

INT. DELRIDGE LOBBY - EVENING

Shepard walks into the lobby. Nurse shuffles papers. Mrs. Jo
shouting from back room.

                    SHEPARD
Hey Nurse, is the Doc around?

                    NURSE
Yeah, he's in the back trying to be a
scientist.

                    SHEPARD
Is my sweet, precious, Buttercup
around?

                    NURSE
There you go again, with those crazy
adjectives! She went to sleep early,
she was worn out from picking on Mr.
Stricklin. Please don't wake her, it's
finally quiet around here.

                    MRS. JO (V.O.)
Why don't we have any Royal in this
place? What's the delivery boy on,
vacation?

                         SHEPARD
          We spoke too soon. I'm going to the
          lab, don't tell her I'm here.

Shepard runs through the doors as Mrs. Jo comes from the back.

                         MRS. JO
          Who were you talking to?

                         NURSE
          No one, I was talking to myself.

                         MRS. JO
          Well you sound like a fucking man. Why
          don't we have any Royal in this place?

                         NURSE
          Calm down Mrs. Jo, did you ever think
          that maybe the bees can't crap that
          stuff out quick enough for you to
          smear on your little pouting lips?

                         MRS. JO
          Keep it up! I'll get even. slow
          torture.

                         NURSE
          So that's what you call it, when you
          speak to me? Mrs. Jo, go to bed. I'm
          tired, I have to make my rounds, I
          have no time for nonsense.

                         MRS. JO
          Rounds, of what? There's no one here.
          You're boring the crap out of me, I'm
          going to bed.

                                        FADE OUT.

INT. LAB ROOM - LATER

Doc and Shepard have cocktails.

                         DOC
          Vodka and tonic Shep?

                         SHEPARD
          Sure, but no lime. I was thinking,
          Doc... this world needs to be
          educated on how important the bees
          are to our existence.
                         (MORE)

SHEPARD (CONT'D)
I can't do it alone, I'm just a
washed up botanist beekeeper living
a secluded life in the mountains.
You, on the other hand, are a
prominent doctor, running a
facility that gives you the world.
I was thinking maybe you can have a
word with your board members. Maybe
they can go have lunch with
congressmen and senators to change
or make a few laws.

          DOC
I'd help if I could. What kind of
laws? I'm not too sure I'm with you on
this one... make... bee laws?

          SHEPARD
Exactly, bee laws. For instance,
people cannot kill the dandelions in
the spring. That's the first food the
bees eat after a long winter. Outlaw
the use of pesticides altogether. All
cell towers must have a porcelain
conductor on every hundred feet of
wire to reduce the hum in the wires.
You really don't know how this hum
drives the bees crazy. It also messes
with their honey-making process.

          DOC
I didn't know that. This all sounds
pretty good while we're drinking
vodka. I'm taking mental notes though,
what else?

          SHEPARD
We could start a national or
international apiary society. Make it
mandatory for every town and/or city
to have at least two public hives. We
can put them on top of the Post
Office, City Hall, or the Rec Center.
The honey from the public hives can be
given to the homeless. Every school
would have a small apiary where the
kids would get an education on the
importance of bees and beekeeping.
They can consume the honey in the
cafeteria.

          DOC
Every kid would get stung.

                    SHEPARD
That could happen, as well. It would
toughen them up! Also I would
personally make sure every hive was
manufacturing your RM-35. Every
household would have a hive and by
having a hive the tax-paying people
would get a tax incentive. This could
be big. I'm not looking to be famous,
I'm looking to help the planet.
Remember when you and I were kids, we
vowed to be doctors to help people in
life.

                    DOC
Yeah, yeah, yeah.

                    SHEPARD
I kind of strayed off of that path,
took to plants and animals. But you on
the other hand kept your word and are
still helping people. Now we can help
mankind by saving the bees, which are
in complete decay.

                    DOC
I read in the New York Times that if
you are a beekeeper, you're going to
need a renewable license with the
state or the local municipality every
year.

                    SHEPARD
That's what I'm talking about, Doc. We
need to change or make some laws and
do it quick. Can you imagine that?
Needing a license to raise bees and
having to renew it every year? What a
nightmare.

                    DOC
That would totally suck.

                    SHEPARD
So, you have to renew your driver's
license, your dog license, your
fishing license, your pilot license,
and now, you would have to renew your
beekeeping license. Did you ever
notice, you don't have to renew your
marriage license?
          (gesturing)
                (MORE)

SHEPARD (CONT'D)
Hey babe, we're going on our fourth
year. Our license is up for
renewal, you better be nice to me.

Both men start laughing.

                    DOC
Shep, I'm really liking these ideas.
Besides it will keep my mind's
creative juices flowing. What we need
to do is research what is already law,
how to change it, and how it will
benefit society as a whole. Then, we
need to figure out the new laws, how
to implement them, and how it will
impact or benefit society as a whole.

                    SHEPARD
Doc, I am so glad you are interested
in this project. I am way ahead of
you, I have been working two months on
this project. I have spent endless
hours on the computer researching laws
and bi-laws. I called a good friend of
mine from Harvard, he let me access
the law library.

Shepard hands Doc an envelope.

                    SHEPARD (CONT'D)
I wrote up all the new and old laws
that need to be addressed, it just
needs your seal of approval. Then,
it needs your letterhead.

                    DOC
You have been a busy bee. I like that,
you always were a go getter. I'll look
at this over the weekend when I'm on
the boat with my girl. If I have any
questions, I'll give you a call.

                    SHEPARD
On the first page I included the
access code to the law library, just
in case.

                    DOC
Cool, I'm very excited, I'll call up
my lawyer friend to get involved, as
well. His mother stayed here for three
weeks and of course was miraculously
healed, he says he owes me big time.

                    SHEPARD
That's good. We will definitely need
some legal council on this one. I
already spoke to the Indian Elders of
Council about protecting the bees. I
explained to them about my property,
with the hives and cemetery, they all
agreed to help with the cause. Get
this, when I told them that I had a
dancing totem on my property they all
bowed down to me, like I was a king.
Made me feel real special.

                    DOC
They weren't angry or curious how you
obtained the totem?

                    SHEPARD
No, not at all. They respect me cause
I'm American-Indian and now they
respect me even more cause I have a
dancing totem. I took a weekend trip
to Canada and spoke to the Canadian
Elders Council. They said they were
already doing their part and would
join in on the crusade. I gave them
the same copy of the proposed laws
that I drafted. They said they would
review the documents and see if they
can incorporate them into Canadian
law.

                    DOC
That's great news. Canada's
involvement can open doors for our
government, as well as introducing
these new laws globally.

                    SHEPARD
They were already talking about this
spreading from Nova Scotia to
Vancouver and beyond. There is a lot
of positive interest in this project
already and it just started. Just
think of how this is going to benefit
society as a whole. The flowers will
be more plentiful, same with the
fruits and vegetables.

                    DOC
Don't forget the massive abundance of
RM-35 society could draw from.

                    SHEPARD
          Also the schools. Giving our future
          taxpayers a fine education on bees
          while keeping them healthy.

                    DOC
          What about the prison system? Those
          guys are just sitting around reading
          books all day. Let's give them an
          education on beekeeping while they
          harvest wax and honey.

                    SHEPARD
          That's a great idea, think of all the
          wax there would be floating around.
          Everyone could light candles instead
          of expensive electricity. A win-win
          for all. Doc, I know a lot of these
          bills and laws that I drafted might
          not come to fruition but you don't
          know until you try. Like Neil
          Armstrong said: "one small step for
          man, one giant leap for beekind".

Doc stares at Shepard with admiration.

                    DOC
          Sir Shepard, that's clever. Now I'm
          impressed. You have impressed me in
          the past, but now I am truly
          impressed.

                    SHEPARD
          Doc, my brother. You getting involved
          puts a smile on my face.

                    DOC
          And a smile on mine, as well. Another
          drink you mad genius?

                    SHEPARD
          No, I have to drive, I reached my
          legal limit.

                    DOC
          Come on, one more. You can stay in one
          of the empty rooms. Maybe Mrs. Jo will
          stay out of Mr. Stricklin's room and
          hang in yours!

                    SHEPARD
          Forget Mrs. Jo, maybe your Nurse can
          sneak in my room and change my bed
          pan. Just kidding.

                    DOC
You dirty dog. Come on, just one more
drink.

                    SHEPARD
No really, thanks, I appreciate the
offer. I have the dogs to feed in the
morning and the kids said they would
help me in the garden. Can't pass up
free help. I have a case of Royal in
my car. Didn't want to pull it out in
front of Mrs. Jo and the staff. Meet
me at the back door, I'll pull my car
around. Doc, thanks for being
understanding and human, this is what
it means to be a real person.

                                        FADE OUT.

EXT. GARDEN - MORNING

Max and Sue walk up the garden path. Shepard weeds the garden,
talking to himself.

                    MAX
Your gardeners have arrived!

                    SUE
We can also be your beekeepers.

                    SHEPARD
No beekeeping today, but thanks for
the helping hand with gardening. Do
you realize that this is nearly a full
time job? I start weeding at this end
of the property, slowly making my way
down towards the stream. When I think
I'm all done, BAM, I have to start all
over again. It's tough tending to all
these flowers, but the bees rely on
it. If we have a drought, then forget
about it, I'm working morning, noon,
and night trying to keep the garden
alive. Thank god it's the summer of
Avery.

Max and Sue stare at each other.

                    MAX AND SUE
No problem.

                    SHEPARD
Hey Max?

                    MAX
          Yeah.

Shepard holds up some pulled weeds.

                    SHEPARD
          Do you want some weed?

                    MAX
          No thanks. I told you, it makes me
          paranoid.

                    SHEPARD
          Max, you know something?

                    MAX
          No, what?

                    SHEPARD
          If I had all the money right now in my
          hands that I ever spent on weed as a
          youngster... all the money right now,
          in my hands...

                    MAX
          Yeah!

                    SHEPARD
          I could buy a lot of weed. My brother
          Verdun would always say that to me.

Giggling, Sue rolls her eyes.

                    SHEPARD
          Hey Max, do you know anything about
          basketball?

                    MAX
          No, not really.

                    SHEPARD
          Good, neither do I! Hey Sue?

                    SUE
          Yeah, Shep.

                    SHEPARD
          You know if we keep working this hard
          in the garden...

                    SUE
          Yeah?

                    SHEPARD
          We're going to get really tired.

                    SUE
          No shit.

Max and Shepard laugh.

                    SHEPARD
          I love working with you people in my
          garden, you're a lot of fun. Normally
          I talk to the flowers and the bees,
          but they're not as funny as you two.
          All kidding aside, what do you want to
          be, when you're ready to conquer the
          world, Max?

                    MAX
          I want to be a botanist!

                    SHEPARD
          A botanist is a tough gig. When you're
          done with all that expensive fancy
          schooling, you could end up in a
          flower shop as the local florist.
          Although that's not a bad gig either.
          What if the botanist thing doesn't pan
          out? Then what?

                    MAX
          Then I want to work for the New York
          State roads department making
          potholes.

                    SHEPARD
          I'm sorry? You mean, fixing potholes?
          On the street?

                    MAX
          No, making potholes because somebody
          keeps making those little bastards
          that keep fucking up my front end.

Shepard and Max start laughing while Sue rolls her eyes.

                    SHEPARD
          Keep rolling your eyes, you might find
          some brains.

Shepard goes to the shed and comes back with clippers. He starts
clearing an area.

                    SHEPARD
Wow, holy shit. This is crazy! Look at
this.

                    SUE
What is it now?

                    SHEPARD
Come look at this, this is a very rare
and extinct orchid. I gave it its last
living rites many many moons ago. I
thought it had perished forever. Look,
there's more! Holy fuck, there's
thousands of them. Sue, run up to the
shed and grab me four small pots and a
hand shovel, please. We just made
history Max, my boy. This orchid was
one of the last surviving orchids from
Tulum, Mexico. The small beetle that
looks like the ladybug wiped out this
population years ago.

                    SUE
Here you go, sir, exactly what the
doctor ordered.

                    MAX
What are you going to do?

                    SHEPARD
I'm going to dig up some samples and
show the world. First, I'm going to
bring two samples to the New York
Botanical Garden. They'll clone these
back into population. They will also
put the originals on display for the
public to see. It will be all over the
papers - big news in the botanist
world!

                    MAX
What about the other two?

                    SHEPARD
One I'm going to put under the
microscope with Doc at the Delridge,
see if this is the flower with Magic
power. And the third one I'm going to
give to my loving wife. This should
bring her fond memories of our past.
Did you know this flower has
medicinal, hallucinogenic, and
poisonous properties? This is a very
helpful and destructive flower.
                  (MORE)

SHEPARD (CONT'D)

Not many plants on this earth have so
much good and evil in the same flower,
this flower is one of a kind. This
might very well be the flower that
made my wife go crazy.

SUE

You're going to drive that flower all
the way to Massachusetts to give to
your wife? That is so beautiful and
romantic.

SHEPARD

Drive to Massachusetts? No! I'm going
to drive two mountains over to deliver
this flower to my loving bride. I
thought you knew, my wife was
transferred to Delridge so she can be
closer. My friend, the good doctor,
keeps an eye on her for me. I would
never had been able to do it without
the gravity pull of the full moon and,
of course, the good doctor.

SUE

You never told us she was transferred.

SHEPARD

Well, you never asked.

SUE

How am I supposed to ask about
something I didn't know existed?

SHEPARD

I don't know. You're a woman, you know
everything.

MAX

We were there recently dropping off
some Magic, but the place was empty.
There was hardly anybody there except
Doc, the Nurse, Mrs. Jo, and-
    (pausing in shock)
No way, do you mean to tell me Mrs.
Jo is your wife?

SHEPARD

She sure is, the one and only.

SUE

Get the fuck out of here.

                    MAX
But she is so much older then you. How
could it be?

                    SUE
I never saw the connection. I never
saw that coming.

                    SHEPARD
We're the same age. She didn't age
very well with the hospital stress and
the drugs she took throughout the
years. But she is one hundred percent
my precious bride.

                    SUE
That can't be! It doesn't make sense.
She doesn't seem like a witch.

                    SHEPARD
Well, she's not a witch anymore, she
is a screen and stage actress to be
exact. You see, when she was seeing
her nut doctor in Massachusetts, he
convinced her that since she was a
witch she could put a spell on herself
and no longer be a witch. Child
psychology, if you will. So she made
up a spell and a potion and turned
herself from a witch into an actress.
But not just any old actress, a stage
and screen actress from the 1940s.

                    MAX
You never told me that. That is so
fucking bizarre. Mrs. Jo is your wife?
The lady blowing me kisses, taking her
clothes off in the window?

                    SHEPARD
That's her, the one and only. Part
actress, part stripper, I guess. You
see, I never told you Max because you
never asked. Another thing I never
mentioned is that her real name is
Rosemary Silender.

                    SUE
Wow, I am blown away. Doesn't that
bother you in so many ways?

                    SHEPARD
What? That she's a screen and stage
actress? Or her name is Rosemary?

SUE
No, that she is... I don't know, all
messed up?

SHEPARD
No, not at all. You see, it could be a
lot worse. She could be confined to a
wheelchair or lying in a bed the rest
of her life with atrophy. If I had to
visit, I would be very sad to see her
that way, knowing she might be
suffering. But instead, she has all
her faculties and functionalities. She
can walk, talk, see, hear, touch,
taste. The only problem is that she
can't remember her past. She is mad,
crazy as a loon, and a little flirty,
as well. I think I can live with that.
Frankly, it's not even a problem at
all. What's really funny is that she
thinks I'm one of her groupies or
followers that brings her gifts. I
think it's quite comical.

MAX
Wow, Mrs. Jo? Rosemary? I'm blown
away.

SHEPARD
You see, when she was a witch, she
thought I was her friendly, caring
neighbor. Now that she is an actress,
she thinks I'm her friendly, caring
groupie. So with this woman I went
from being a childhood friend to a
childhood sweetheart to a lover to a
husband to a father to a neighbor to a
groupie all in the span of about sixty
years. I would say that's a pretty
good resume and a lifetime of
achievements, wouldn't you?

MAX
I guess, but... Mrs. Jo?

SHEPARD
The kicker of it all, when she
looks in the mirror, she sees a
thirty-something-year-old woman,
not an old wrinkly woman. To her
I'm just a washed up groupie that
admires her and brings her gifts.
                (MORE)

SHEPARD (CONT'D)
Like I said, she remembers nothing
of her past, not even recently
being a a witch or bearing a child
thirty-something years ago. She has
complete memory loss. Or selective
memory, who's to say.

MAX
I can't believe it. Mrs. Jo?

SHEPARD
Yep, I still love her.

DISSOLVE TO:

INT. DELRIDGE LOBBY - NOON

Mrs. Jo speaks with RECEPTIONIST. Doc and Nurse go through
files.

MRS. JO
You're new here?

RECEPTIONIST
Yes, today's my first day. And who do
I have the pleasure of speaking with?

MRS. JO
Everyone calls me Mrs. Jo, but my real
name is Jasmin Johanson. Have you
heard of me?

NURSE
(interrupting)
That sounds like a porn star name.

MRS. JO
You can shut your jaw flapper right
now or the doctor and I will prescribe
you something so strong that you will
forget your name for a month. Right
Doc?

DOC
Enough, Mrs. Jo.

MRS JO
By the way Nurse, what is your name?
(beat)
You hear that Doc, she said
nothing, she just stares. She
doesn't even know her name!
(MORE)

                    MRS JO (CONT'D)
And we didn't even prescribe her
anything ha ha-
          (pause)
Unless you prescribed her something
behind my back? That would be
messed up. Working behind my back
Doc, that's a dirty trick. Are you
working behind my back?

                    DOC
I'm not working behind or in front of
your back, I'm not working with you at
all, ever. Enough is enough Mrs. Jo.
Go to your room and I mean now. I
can't concentrate.

Mrs. Jo marches away, still talking.

                    MRS. JO
This whole place is fucked up, they
don't even know who I am! They're
prescribing medicine behind my back.
I'm calling the FAA or the FCC... or
is it the FDA? Whatever the fuck it's
called.

                    DOC
Nurse, hold all my calls, keep an eye
on the place. I'll be in my lab for a
few hours.

Mrs. Jo marches back.

                    MRS. JO
Where's the Doc? I want to give him a
piece of my mind.

                    NURSE
That's physically impossible you can't
give him a piece if you only have a
piece left. Nevermind, he went to his
lab for a few hours. He's not to be
disturbed.

                    MRS. JO
Good. He's a pain in the ass, isn't
he? We should stick together! We have
to do something about him he's trying
to take over, run this place like he
owns the joint. I don't know who he
thinks he is or how he became a
doctor! He doesn't even have doctor-to-
doctor courtesy.

                    NURSE
Why would he listen to you? You're not
a doctor, you're just a patient, a
resident of his nightmare.

                    MRS. JO
I heard just about all I want to hear
out of you. You keep this up and I
will make it my mission to make sure
you spend the rest of your working
life changing bed pans - in an animal
hospital. Do you get the visual?

                    NURSE
Mrs. Jo! Go to your room! Ohh wait!
Now I have a visual... you are on the
back of someone's motorcycle doing
sixty and you fell off, you lost your
mind, but you lived. Did you get a
visual? You see, my visuals have a
happy ending: you lived, now go to
your room.

                    MRS. JO
I can't talk to you, you're so lucky I
was heading to my room anyway to fix
myself up. There you go again being
jealous.

Shepard pulls up on a motorcycle, with two plants.

                    NURSE
Looks like your ride just pulled up.
Looks like now I'm getting a visual,
make sure you forget your helmet!

                    MRS. JO
Ohh shit, the fucking groupie's here,
why does he keep following me? He
should have called first. Did you tell
him I was here? Nevermind, I gotta go
and fix my hair. Ohh, how sweet, he
brought me two flowers. You see Nurse?
One plant isn't good enough for this
groupie, he brought me two, how sweet.
Don't get jealous or try to get even,
either. Maybe I'll share if you're
nice to me and you get me an extra
teaspoon of Royal Magic in my tea to
make my button feel good.

                    NURSE
We'll see, we'll see, now go to your
room.

68.

                    MRS. JO
          Don't rat me out that I've been with
          Mr. Stiff One, bitch, or I'll push you
          off the stage at the next rehearsal.
          Here he comes, I gotta go fix my hair
          and put on makeup before he sees me.
          It's not easy being me.

                    NURSE
          I've been saying that for the longest
          time! I don't know how you find it so
          easy being you. I don't even know how
          you can find you!

Mrs. Jo stares then leaves.

                    SHEPARD
          Hello Nurse is the Doctor around?
          Where is my little starlet?

                    NURSE
          Good afternoon Mr. Excitement. The
          scientist is out back in the lab
          trying to be a scientist. Your little
          starfish is in her dressing room
          putting on hooker makeup, getting
          ready to greet her fans and sign
          autographs before her big performance.
          It just so happens that you are the
          first arrival. The line will start
          here and probably wrap around to the
          inside of O Reilly's pub next door.
          Thank God you got here early, there
          are limited tickets to be had, you
          might have missed all the excitement!
          Just an FYI, I would have let you in
          line anyway because I like you.

Mrs. Jo enters.

                    SHEPARD
          Hello princess, you look ravishing.

Nurse rolls her eyes.

                    NURSE
          That's the adjective you want to use?
          Suit yourself it's your prerogative. I
          would have used ridiculous or
          revolting.

Nurse walks away. Everyone ignores her.

                    MRS. JO
         Well hello, Mr. Groupie. Wow, two
         plants for me? I'm honored. You
         shouldn't have. You should have just
         brought me one.

Mrs. Jo grabs both plants

                    SHEPARD
         No, I'm sorry only one plant is for
         you. The other is for the good old
         Doctor, for research. Does this plant
         look familiar to you?

Thinking it's a hidden camera, she starts posing.

                    MRS. JO
         You paparazzi, think you're so clever,
         hiding your cameras in a plant. What
         will they think of next? It's
         disguised so good though, you can
         barely tell. But I can tell cause I'm
         a professional.

Max and Sue walk in.

                    MAX AND SUE
         Hey Shepard.

                    SHEPARD
         Madam Johanson, these are my friends
         Max and Sue.

Mrs. Jo walks up to Max.

                    MRS. JO
         Who are you? My understudy?

She turns to Shepard.

                    MRS. JO
         I don't think he's going to fit in
         my costumes! Could you have gotten
         someone that was a little more in
         shape? I mean please, I'm repulsed.

She turns back to Max.

                    MRS. JO (CONT'D)
         Can you even fit in my shoes?

                    MAX
         No Ma'am, I don't think I can fill
         your shoes.

                    MRS. JO
          Then, what are you doing here? Wasting
          my time? Ok, ok, wait, stick around
          Cupcake. I might get you to do my
          wardrobe as long as you're not a
          creeper stealing my panties. Are you a
          creeper?

                    MAX
          No ma'am.

                    MRS. JO
          I don't trust you with those beady
          eyes, so I'll put you on makeup so I
          can keep an eye on you. Now, I don't
          want too much makeup to look like a
          whore - unless I'm playing a whore,
          then that's ok. I really look good in
          lingerie. Right, sweet cheeks?

Mrs. Jo keeps winking.

                    MAX
          I don't know what you're talking about
          ma'am.

Mrs. Jo walks up to Sue.

                    MRS. JO
          I have to perform with this? She
          doesn't even look like she has talent.
          It looks like everyone is trying to
          throw this project together on a
          budget and I'm not standing for it.

Mrs. Jo turns to Shepard.

                    MRS. JO
          I tell you right now! I'm not
          putting my name on this project if
          you people aren't going to take
          this seriously. I'm a
          professional.

Mrs. Jo walks away shaking her head.

                    MAX AND SUE
          It was nice meeting you!

Mrs. Jo holds up her hands in the air in disgust.

                    SHEPARD
          I told you what she was like! A
          dramatic actress.

                    SUE
I'm in shock. That's all I can say,
I'm in shock. Just for the record, I
do have talent. I played lead roles in
my high school plays.

                    MAX
Ok Sue, we have to go. Where do you
want us to drop the boxes of Magic and
potting soil?

                    SHEPARD
I'll meet you around back by the lab.

                                   FADE TO BLACK.

INT. LAB ROOM - LATER

Shepard enters the lab, scaring Doc.

                    SHEPARD
     What's up Doc?

The two men hug.

                    DOC
If it isn't Mr. Shepard, the growing
organism? How's the Dancing Totem
doing? It was a full moon last night,
where did she dance to now? Is it
doing the twist? The Electric Slide?

                    SHEPARD
Don't make fun, have you ever thought
that the sacred totem might have a
spiritual vindictive side? I don't
think you'll gain momentum being on
her bad side. Yes, she did move last
night, she's sitting next to my house.
I gave up on trying to figure out the
science behind mystery and the mystery
behind science.

                    DOC
Next full moon, she'll have crept in
your bed giving you wood.

                    SHEPARD
This conversation has just expired. On
that note... surprise, surprise take a
gander at what I posses!

                    DOC
An orchid? And?

                    SHEPARD
This is not just any old orchid! Do
you remember the Tulum trip? Flower
smuggling?

                    DOC
Mexico? Of course, I remember Mexico!
How could anyone forget that trip!

Doc looks at the flower, shocked.

                    DOC (CONT'D)
No way, no way! That's the
forbidden plant? But where? How?
Really? All the botanists on the
planet calculated this as an
endangered species. You did a press
conference regarding its demise at
the Botanical Gardens: "The Lost
Species, But Not Forgotten."

                    SHEPARD
Well, as you know, when the last known
survivor died twenty-some-odd years
ago, I gave it a proper burial on my
property - thinking this plant was
lost forever, extinct, never to be
known to mankind ever again. But when
I was gardening with my friends, I
pulled back some weeds, and there she
was looking me straight in the eyes,
smiling at me. When I looked closer,
there were hundreds of babies staring
me right in the eyes.

                    DOC
You never noticed them before?

                    SHEPARD
I must have weeded that flowerbed a
thousand times and never noticed one
little sprout. I speculate that she
must have had that last little
surviving microorganism still living
deep down in her stem cell tissue to
rejuvenate the molecular structure and
come alive. Almost like Frankenstein,
if you will.
                    (MORE)

SHEPARD (CONT'D)
I also didn't realize that its
elongated root system and vine-like
body structure was the perfect
specimen for an all-terrain, all-
temperature type environment.

DOC
But a jungle species living in a four
season climate like the Catskills?
Some winters the thermometer dropped
to the negative teens. I would have
never thought there would have ever
been any type of lasting survival
rate. What about those hundreds of
other tropical plants that died on
your property or on your window sill?

SHEPARD
I'm speculating that the roots must
have dug so deep and firm into the
earth - below the frost line - that it
went dormant in the winter and sprang
to life in the summer. Every year she
kept coming back until she became a
hearty, healthy northeastern
perennial. Not many jungle plants have
the adaptability to endure a cryogenic
experience with any lasting survival
rate. Yet there are hundreds of these
beauties on my property, maybe even
thousands.

DOC
Wow, with the complex, snake-like root
system it makes a lot of sense for her
imminent survival rate.

Doc holds the orchid in the air.

DOC
I d remember this flower rather
well. This was my first and last
smuggling experience with you. The
Mayans were eating this flower and
getting high. But if one was to
consume too much, they would die.
If a person was to ingest just
enough before the dosage of death
they would lose their mind forever.
Hence the reason why the Mexican
government was trying to eradicate
this beauty.
(MORE)

                    DOC (CONT'D)
If you were caught with this very
plant in your possession, the
Mexican government would
incarcerate you for a very long
time. That is the very reason why I
never accompanied you on another
one of your adventurous excursions
ever again.

                    SHEPARD
That's why it was such a danger to the
Mexican people, no one knew the
proportionate measurements to consume
for recreational or medicinal.

                    DOC
They also didn't know the
proportionate measurement for death
either. It was rarer than some
truffles. Nearly impossible to find.

                    SHEPARD
I personally think that this is the
very plant that Rosemary - I mean Mrs.
Jo, lost her mind on. She would eat
anything and everything to get off.
She always had that oral fixation.
Like a little kid she had to put
everything in her mouth.

                    DOC
Is that what attracted you to her? The
oral fixation?

                    SHEPARD
Let's just say it was an added
attribute.

                    DOC
You might be right. This plant could
be the genesis of Rosemary - I mean
Mrs. Jo's - mind-altering state.
Didn't the Mayans swear that this
flower had all the medicinal
properties to cure every malady on the
planet? To actually get high one can
only eat the pink side of the flower,
the yellow side is poisonous. How did
the translated saying go? Pink is pure
it has the cure. The other side yellow
will kill a fellow.

                    SHEPARD
          Wow, I'm impressed, you have a great
          memory.

                    DOC
          You forget, I was in grad school at
          the time. I didn't go crazy partying
          like you two. You know, come to think
          of it, Rosemary was not quite right
          after that Mexico trip. That was a
          very crazy time. I remember when you
          were mixing this flower with other
          plants and flowers thinking no one at
          the customs and border would notice.
          The night before you were in the hotel
          room - if you can call it a hotel,
          more like a shack - painting the
          petals with ink from butterfly wings
          to disguise its appearance. I have to
          admit you were the James Bond of the
          plant world.

                    SHEPARD
          Well I had to make it look like the
          Nongke orchid to get through customs.

                    DOC
          Yeah, when we got to the airport the
          customs agents saw you with all those
          plants and called the minister of
          agriculture. It took him an hour to
          get there while they were holding the
          plane for us.

                    SHEPARD
          Yeah, we were drinking beers and
          tequila waiting for the creep.

                    DOC
          When the minister finally got there he
          rolled up in that old banged up,
          outdated limo which he claimed used to
          be owned by The Beach Boys.

                    SHEPARD
          Yeah right, The Beach Boys!

                    DOC
          The Minister studied your credentials,
          studied your plant collection, and
          then he got to this beauty.

Doc holds the plant in the air again.

                    DOC (CONT'D)
He stared at her for at least five
minutes. I thought we were going to
jail right then and there. The
entire time, the customs officers
were just staring at you with your
pure white hair and your pasty
skin.

                    SHEPARD
Nothing's changed, I still have my
white hair and my snow white tan.

                    DOC
Meanwhile, Rosemary...

                    SHEPARD
        (laughing)
Mrs. Jo, as she likes to be
addressed.

                    DOC
Yes, Mrs. Jo, Rose, or whatever, was
flying out of her mind. High as a kite
trying on the custom agents' hats and
uniforms while trying to take their
guns. The whole time everyone kept
staring at your white hair in
amazement. There must have been
fifteen of them. They couldn't believe
someone like you actually existed.
Remember the one agent kept wanting to
touch your hair?

                    SHEPARD
Yeah, when I turned around really
quick and went boo they all started
running.

                    DOC
That was funny, the one guy was so
scared he pissed his pants.

                    SHEPARD
Ohh yeah, I forgot about that. After
about fifteen minutes the minister
grabbed his briefcase, turned around
and just left. Didn't even say a word,
just walked away. We looked at each
other like, now what? So I grabbed my
credentials and the plants and we just
started walking toward the plane. No
one said a word they just stared. It
was fucking creepy.

                    DOC
Yeah that was really bizarre, when we
got on the plane everyone stared at
us, as well.

                    SHEPARD
Yeah, Rosemary was still wearing the
customs agent's hat. No one said
anything to us, the plane was silent
for over three hours. That was a very
bizarre and surreal experience. You
know, come to think of it, I still
have that hat somewhere.

                    DOC
How memorable was that Mexico trip? I
still think of that trip from time to
time.

                    SHEPARD
Oh yeah, I remember that trip like it
was yesterday.

                    DOC
Yeah, those were fun days. Remember we
met those three amigos? You kept
calling them the three amoebas, the
twins from New York.

                    SHEPARD
Dave and Chucky and the Gloucesterman
Pepe Loco.

                    DOC
Wow, those were the funniest guys I
ever met, they should do standup. We
told them to swim to the reef and get
us fish. For every fish they brought
back we would give them five bucks.

                    SHEPARD
Yeah, and they brought back so much
fish we gave them a hundred to stop
fishing. Later that night they came
back with steaks, beer, wine, guitars,
and six Mayan chicks. Now that was a
beach party.

                    DOC
The three amigos also brought that
powder, what was it? Dried sap from a
jungle plant? That stuff was good, it
was like the high from weed with the
zing from coke.

                         SHEPARD
          Yeah, I didn't care for that, made me
          paranoid. But, Rosemary on the other
          hand, loved that stuff. She emptied
          out all of her makeup and compressed
          the powder to look like makeup. At the
          airport while the customs officers
          were dealing with my plant dilemma the
          other officers kept asking her why her
          makeup had no color. She explained
          that gringos only use white makeup to
          match the color of their skin. They
          actually believed her! She was such a
          great bullshitter, the whole time she
          was flying out of her skin.

                         DOC
          We wouldn't have gotten away with half
          that stuff at the airport if it hadn't
          been for your credentials.
              (in an English accent)
          Shepard the botanist from the New
          York Botanical Garden.

                         SHEPARD
          Yeah I loved that job, had a lot of
          travel perks. It also opened a lot of
          doors for teaching.

Doc looks at the plant.

                         DOC
          So let's get busy. I know you
          didn't bring me this orchid to
          reminisce about almost doing time
          in Mexico. You're a curious mind.
          You want to see what's inside,
          right? Let's get a closer look
          under my new microscope I just
          received from God knows where. This
          facility is bizarre, Shep. I'll
          tell you the latest over a beer.

Doc begins dissecting the plant.

                         SHEPARD
          All kidding aside, how's my wife? Is
          she too much of a burden on you and
          your staff?

                    DOC
No, no, no not at all. She's fine. She
does need to keep her clothes on and
her mouth closed, but other than that
she's fine. I mean, she tells everyone
she owns the place. And threatens
everyone with prescribing them
medication if they don't behave. Other
than that, she's controllable. She's
fine, just fine. I mean as long as she
doesn't burn down my facility, she's
fine. I wouldn't know how to explain
that to the board members... a crazy
old actress burned the wing of our
convalescent home.

                    SHEPARD
They'd probably buy you a new wing
anyway. They love you, can't you tell?
Besides, as you know, she doesn't play
with matches.

                    DOC
Well, that just lifted thirty years of
stress off my shoulders and stopped my
heart from pounding.

                    SHEPARD
You know Doc, I still love her after
all these years. For better or worse
as the saying goes. She still has all
her faculties, she's smart as a whip.
        (reminiscing)
When she was in the witch and
candlemaking stage of her life, she
explained to her class the dynamics
of Icarus not being able to fly out
of Crete with his wax wings. She
explained how one pound of dry wax
has the volume weight of only
twenty ounces, which means Icarus'
wings would have weighed nearly
nine hundred pounds. Without jet
propulsion or some motorized
mechanism, Icarus would never have
taken flight.

                    DOC
That is quite perceptive.

                    SHEPARD
Not only that, she also explained the
fact that wax softens at 110 degrees,
starts melting at 300, and boils at
698 degrees. While explaining that
Icarus himself would have melted
before his wings had gotten soft.
People don't just make up science and
math equations like that, they are
taught it.

                    DOC
You're absolutely right.

                    SHEPARD
This is something that she had learned
in University and still retained in
her memory bank. She just doesn't
remember the mundane, the simple
things... like who you and I are and
her past life. It's almost like her
memory bank has been erased. I'd do
anything to turn that around. Maybe
this flower has the genetic reversal,
the key components to make her better.
Truthfully Doc, I do really love that
woman, she's my everything.

                    DOC
As long as she remembers not to play
with matches and burn my facility
down, I'll do anything to help her.
She can reside here for as long as
it's in my power.

                    SHEPARD
I'm really glad she's here. She's much
closer to home now. I can keep an eye
on her, as well. Like I've said
before, if I had it my way I would
take her home and take care of her
myself, but she thinks I'm her groupie
not her husband. I know she's in good
hands. She's safe. That's all that
matters to me. By the way, I brought
you another case of Royal Magic, the
kids dropped it off in back.

                    DOC
Thank you old pal. I'm doing my best.
Now, let's get started on the inside
of this plant.

                                    FADE TO BLACK.

INT. DELRIDGE LOBBY - DAY

Doc walks in front door. EMILY, a young child with bruised arms plays. Nurse walks towards the door.

                    DOC
          Nurse, why are all these kids running
          around? Where did they come from?
          Where did all these people come from?

                    NURSE
          Doc, we had a crazy influx of people
          last night. The Presbyterian Hospital
          sent us two buses full of people
          around midnight. The night nurse
          called all nurses to do emergency
          around the clock shifts. It has been a
          zoo here for the last twelve hours.

                    DOC
          Why didn't anyone call me? I'm the
          resident doctor here. I need to know
          what is going on in my facility! I
          have board members I have to answer
          to. In the future if a fucking ant
          walks into this building I want to
          know about it. Now get me the charts
          on every living and dead thing in this
          building and I want it, stat!

                    NURSE
          Yes Doc, right away. By the way, Doc?

                    DOC
          Yes, Nurse?

                    NURSE
          You look very sexy when you're angry.
          Don't let Mrs. Jo see you this way,
          she might hump your ankles like a
          rabid dog in heat.

Doctor stares at Nurse until she leaves. He looks around.

                    DOC
          Hello? Little girl, come over here for
          a moment, please.

                    EMILY
          Yes, Mr. Doctor, I didn't do anything!
          I'll keep quiet.

                    DOC
          What is your name, my dear?

                         EMILY
          Emily! What is your name?

                         DOC
          You can call me Doc.

                         EMILY
          Well, that's obvious. Hello Doc.

                         DOC
          Hello Emily, what is this
          discoloration on your arms?

                         EMILY
          Ohh, it's nothing! The doctor in
          Australia called it melanoma. It's ok,
          I can't give it to the other kids.

                         DOC
          Australia? You got this in Australia?

                         EMILY
          Yeah, they say there's a hole in the
          sky and the sun is no good for you.

                         DOC
          I would really like to look at this in
          my lab.

                         EMILY
          Well, if you want to see what's on
          these arms you should really look at
          my mommy. She has it over her whole
          body.

                         DOC
          Your mommy? Where is your mommy now?

Nurse arrives with a cart.

                         NURSE
          Doctor, here are the files you
          requested! The little girl's mother is
          in room 111.
                  (whispering)
          The records show her mother is on her
          deathbed. She's been in and out of
          consciousness for six weeks. Her chart
          is on top.

Doc looks at the chart.

                         DOC
          Emily, where is your father?

                    EMILY
          He's in Australia, he'll be here next
          month.

                    DOC
          Emily, this is important. We will
          visit your mother a little bit later.
          Will you accompany me and the nurse to
          my lab? I need to take a better look
          at your arms, please.

They all walk towards the lab.

                    EMILY
          Sure thing, do you think you can stop
          the itching and burning? It hurts so
          much!

                    NURSE
          Emily, if anyone can fix you up, it's
          the good old doctor. Just don't get
          him angry, he'll bite your ankles off.

Doc turns around.

                    EMILY
          If he's that good, can he fix my mommy
          instead of me? She needs it more than
          me. I can live with the itching,
          burning, and purple arms, but my mommy
          really needs help. Can we bring her
          here instead? I'm almost used to the
          itching and burning. See? I'm not even
          scratching. I can also wear long
          sleeves so no one sees my arms. No one
          will even know.

Doc opens the door.

                    DOC
          Don't worry Emily, we'll fix your
          mommy next. Step into my lab.

                                        FADE OUT.

INT. LAB ROOM - LATER

Emily sits on the table. Nurse pulls up chair. Doc grabs
equipment.

                    NURSE
Emily, did you ever see the movie The
Color Purple? Or hear the song Purple
Rain?

                    DOC
Nurse, enough, I'll take it from here.
Ok Emily, this is not going to hurt.
I'm going to take samples of your arm
and do a few tests.

Doc puts samples in a vial and shakes vigorously.

                 DOC (CONT'D)
This will take about fifteen minutes
before I can look under the
microscope. Emily, tell me what
happened that gave you purple skin.

                    EMILY
Well, me and my mommy were driving
through the desert to see Grandma and
Grandpa and the car broke down.

                    DOC
      (interrupting)
In Australia?

                    EMILY
Yeah, in Australia. That's where my
daddy's from. They all talk like
pirates over there.

                    NURSE
That's because Australia is where the
English sent their prisoners and most
of them were pirates. Is your dad a
pirate? Or a prisoner?

                    DOC
That's not funny, Nurse. Go on Emily.

                    EMILY
Well, our car broke down. So we stayed
in the car for two days and nobody
came to get us, so my mommy and me
started walking and walking and
walking. After a full day of walking
and the sun burning us, we sat down to
rest for a while. That's when my mommy
got bit in the leg by a snake and
fainted.

                    DOC
Oh my goodness, what did you do?

                    EMILY
I grabbed my mommy and dragged her
away from the rock where the snake
was. So we waited there all night
while my mommy was sleeping.
      (seriously)
That was a very cold night. I kept
hugging my mommy to keep warm. In
the middle of the night, this brown
boy walked up talking like a pirate
and he asked if he could help us. I
don't even know where he came from.
The desert went on for hundreds,
maybe thousands of miles.

                    DOC
Keep going.

                    EMILY
So, the brown boy named Nano was an
Aboriginal Indian. He took one look at
my mommy and he knew exactly what to
do. He ripped his shirt off, tied it
around my mommy's leg, and he started
kissing where the snake bit her. Then
he ran into the desert and came back
with these plants. He started smashing
them on the stones. When they were all
mushy he put them on my mommy's leg.
Then he took these two sticks and
rubbed them really hard and made a
fire for us. Thank God we met Nano
cause it was cold that night.

                    NURSE
Yeah temperature drops in the desert.
You're lucky you're not a popsicle.
Maybe that would explain your purple
skin.

                    DOC
Nurse, enough. Continue Emily.

                    EMILY
I asked him what he was doing in the
middle of the desert. He told me that
he was doing a walk-about. For him to
be a man he had to live in the bushes
for one month by himself.
                (MORE)

EMILY (CONT'D)
When he gets back home, his family
will have a party because walking in
the desert and sleeping in the bushes
makes him a man. One month in the
bushes, that's strange.

NURSE
It's the bush, not the bushes. He was
living in the bush.

EMILY
Anyway, the next morning my mommy was
looking better, but was still
sleeping. So Nano tied all these
sticks together with trees and made a
bed for her. Me and Nano dragged her
across the desert for about four days
and nights with no stopping.

DOC
What did you eat and drink? You didn't
sleep?

EMILY
Nano was killing snakes and desert
rabbits and cooking them on the fire.
We drank this cactus stuff but I
didn't like it. He made me drink it
anyway. He said it would keep me
alive. He put drops in my mommy's
mouth all the time. We also ate some
roots from a tree. We had them
sticking out of our mouths like
cigars. Those roots were sweet, I
liked them. They don't make you sleep.

NURSE
She was probably tripping on peyote
cactus, that trippy little hippie.

DOC
Nurse, not another peep out of you!
That's a fascinating and courageous
story, Emily.

NURSE
Yeah, psychedelic and mind blowing.

EMILY
Nano is very smart, he knew everything
about the desert. What you can eat,
what is medicine, what is poison. He
is totally smart about nature.
(MORE)

                    EMILY (CONT'D)
What he didn't know was that white
people's skin is different and can't
take the sun like his. So being in the
sun the whole time made my arms purple
and my mommy's face, neck, and legs
purple.

                    DOC
Emily, how did you get out of the
desert?

                    EMILY
So, this big airplane came down, I
forgot the name.

                    NURSE
     (rolling eyes and yelling)
Helicopter!

                    EMILY
Yeah that's it. So the helicopter came
down with my daddy and picked me and
mommy up, but they couldn't pick up
Nano because he still had two weeks
more of sleeping in the bushes before
he could go home. The weird thing was
that when we got in the air and saw
how big the desert was, I saw mommy's
car. It was really small and really
close to where we were picked up. I
thought we were walking for days, I
guess not. I also saw Nano walking far
away, he looked all alone.

                    NURSE
You thought you were walking for days
because you were tripping. You were
probably walking in circles. Wow that
cactus looks familiar.

                    DOC
Like I said Emily, that is a very
fascinating story and you are a very
heroic woman.

                    EMILY
I only turned a woman three months
ago, but this happened over two years
ago and my mommy has been in pain ever
since.

                    DOC
Regardless, you and your mommy are
very brave women.
                    (MORE)

                    DOC (CONT'D)
You should write this down on paper
and make a book. Emily, I'm going to
do some tests on these samples to help
you and your mommy. Why don't you go
with the nurse and play with the other
children while I get to work.

                    EMILY
The other kids don't want to play with
me cause I'm different. I have purple
arms. But I'm getting used to my
purple arms. My Uncle Jack has colored
arms and he says that my arms look
cool. He said that when I'm older, I
can drive his motorcycle and my arms
will look really normal and I can be
part of his club.

                    NURSE
Ok easy rider, let's let the Doc get
to work. I'll get you a pen and paper
so you can start writing your
psychedelic memoirs. When you're done
with your story you can start writing
about Mrs. Jo. That should keep you
busy till you get your motorcycle
license. Come to think of it, you can
take Mrs. Jo for a ride on the back of
your motorcycle with no helmet - do
you get the visual?

Doc stares at Nurse.

                    NURSE (CONT'D)
I'm going, I'm going.

                                        FADE OUT.

EXT. GARDEN - MORNING

Shepard is in a bee suit. Max and Sue enter the garden.

                    SHEPARD
Thanks for coming on such quick
notice.

                    MAX AND SUE
No problem.

                    MAX
So what's the emergency?

                    SHEPARD
The Nurse called from Delridge. She
just had a busload of people arrive
last night, and Mrs. Jo ate all the
Royal Magic. I need to harvest at
lease two hundred and fifty pounds
ASAP.

                    MAX
No problem, Shep, where do we start?
Let me suit up.

                    SHEPARD
Go in the shed I have a few bee suits
hanging in the back.

                    SUE
I'll get mine out of the trunk.

EXT. GARDEN - LATER

Sue walks like a zombie in a pink bee suit. Max walks from the
shed in a normal bee suit. Shepard works in the bee hive.

                    SHEPARD
What the hell are you wearing?

                    SUE
What? What's wrong? You've seen this
before! Remember? My favorite color is
pink!

                    SHEPARD
What are you, picking strawberries? Do
I really have to work with you looking
like that?

                    SUE
If you're gonna make fun of me all day
I can go home! I am a volunteer, you
know.

                    MAX
Calm down, calm down, Shepard's only
kidding!

                    SHEPARD
No I'm not. That suit is hideous it
goes against all principles of bee
keeping.
     (pause)
I'm only kidding. Ok kids, let's
start collecting frames.
                  (MORE)

SHEPARD (CONT'D)
Don't forget: two frames per hive,
no more, no less.

SUE
Ouch, I just got stung.

SHEPARD
You see? The bees think you're a
flower, they want to peel back your
petals.

SUE
Shit, I just got stung again and now I
have ladybugs all over me, what the
fuck?

SHEPARD
Maybe they like Chinese food!

SUE
I told you, I'm Korean. Maybe they
like Kimchi.

SHEPARD
Are you having your period?

SUE
Are you being a wise ass? Cause you're
not funny!

SHEPARD
No I'm serious! Are you having your
period?

SUE
I really don't think that is any
business of yours.

SHEPARD
Well, as science has it, when a woman
is menstruating, she gives off a lot
of estrogen. Like sixty percent more
than when they're horny. So the
estrogen, being a natural chemical
imbalance, attracts the opposite sex,
even in the animal world. That's why
you got stung - you are attracting
male bees and when you didn't give any
up, they stung you. Don't forget only
male bees have a stinger.

He holds his finger near his crotch.

As for the ladybugs, they aren't
ladies at all. They are
transvestites.

Shepard starts laughing.

                    SUE
This conversation is over. I can't
take you seriously. Besides, I don't
want to talk about my biological clock
anymore. Please keep in mind all hives
have a queen, not a king!

                    MAX
That's because the queen was going
through menopause and the king said
I'm out of here. Of course, the queen
ends up with his house and all his
belongings, like the Royal Magic. The
king? What does he get? Nothing,
absolutely nothing.

                    SUE
Really Max? I'll talk to you when we
get home.

                    SHEPARD
Wow Max, I've said some fucked up shit
before, but I would have never said
that. That was pretty stupid.

Shepard grabs Max's right hand.

                    SHEPARD (CONT'D)
Let me see this right hand of
yours! Yep, just as I thought! You
will be giving this a work out for
the next few days.

                    SUE
Pathetic. Both of you are pathetic.

Sue walks away.

                    SHEPARD
Hey Max.

                    MAX
Yeah.

                    SHEPARD
Did you ever notice women and life
always blame men? Think about it, Menopause, Men-strual/cycle, Men-tal.

                              MAX
          When you go to a restaurant the waiter
          hands you a menu because the man has
          to pay, why don't they call it a wo-
          menu?

Both men laugh.

                                        FADE TO BLACK.

INT. DELRIDGE - MORNING

Doc walks in the lobby. Emily laughs hysterically. Nurse flips
papers.

                              DOC
          Emily, what's going on over there?

                              EMILY
          Doc, Doc, get them off me they tickle,
          they tickle!

                              DOC
          That's just a few ladybugs, they don't
          mean any harm. They're good luck.

                              EMILY
          I don't care, please, they tickle me
          so much, I'm gonna wet my pants.

Doc removes the ladybugs.

                              DOC
          They are on you because ladybugs
          are attracted to ladies. Blow on
          them and make a wish so a farmer
          can put food on our dish.

                              EMILY
          I never heard that.

Doc looks at Nurse.

                              DOC
          How can such a small creature
          tickle such a big girl? There are
          so many ladybugs flying around
          lately, I wonder why that is.

                              NURSE
          Shepard - the one that lives in a bee
          hive and calls the crazy one living
          here, precious!
                              (MORE)

                    NURSE (CONT'D)
- he said the reason for the abundance
of ladybugs is due to the Summer of
Avery.

                    DOC
Yeah, he has mentioned that before.

                    NURSE
I don't even know what that means. I
never heard it before.

                    DOC
It's a science term. I'm gonna put
this ladybug under the microscope!
I'll be back, watch the fort.

                    NURSE
There he goes, trying to be a
scientist again. Why don't you put
Mrs. Jo under your microscope? Maybe
you'll find some brains! Or maybe
you'll see air, you'll be the first
scientist to actually see air.

                                        FADE OUT.

INT. DELRIDGE - LATER

Doc rushes in the lobby. Nurse drinks coffee. Emily plays.

                    DOC
          (excitedly)
Nurse, please get Shepard on the
phone right away and keep ringing
till he picks up. Emily, come over
here for a moment please.

                    EMILY
Yes Doc, what's up?

Doc grabs Emily's arms.

                    DOC
Your arms are a light purple, I
didn't see that before. It looks
like it's fading.

                    EMILY
I know! You and Mrs. Jo are making me
and mommy better.

                    DOC
Mrs. Jo? Where's your mother? I went
to her room yesterday and she wasn't
there. I thought she took a stroll in
the garden.

                    EMILY
Mrs. Jo put my mommy in Mr. Stiff
One's room. She said he was done, he
went home. She wanted my mommy closer
to her room so she can treat her with
medicine. She's a great doctor.

                    DOC
Emily, Mrs. Jo is not a doctor! She is-
just a helper.

                    EMILY
She feeds my mommy RM-35 all day and
night. She puts the empty jars in the
closet, and there's a lot of empty
jars in the closet. She gives it to me
too, but after I eat a few teaspoons I
feel funny inside. It's a weird
feeling, I'm not sure if I like that
feeling. But it did stop the burning
itch and made the color purple go
away.

                    NURSE
Doc, there's no answer at the Shepard
residence!

                    DOC
Keep trying. Tell him to get over here
stat- Never mind hang up the phone, I
got an idea. Emily come with me to my
lab. I need to do a quick test.

                    NURSE
Make up your mind. Run here, run
there, do this, do that. I guess now
I'm escorting Emily to your lab!

                    DOC
Nurse, I think I have it, it's the
honey with the oils-

Doc's cell phone rings.

                                   FADE TO BLACK.

INT. LAB ROOM - LATER

Doc and Nurse tend to Emily. Max walks in the room.

                    DOC
          Emily, sit on the table. I'm going to
          test your arms again.

Doc examines her arm.

                    EMILY
          Test what? I told you, the purple is
          almost gone. After the Doctor puts RM-
          35 on my arms she scrubs it off with a
          brush to get rid of the purple. Then
          she makes me eat two teaspoons of it.
          I told you it really makes me feel
          funny inside.

                    NURSE
          Doctor? She? What doctor? What doctor
          named she?

                    EMILY
          Mrs. Jo.

                    NURSE
          Ohh, now Mrs. Jo has graduated to
          doctor? Doctor Frankenstein!

                    DOC
          She transferred Emily's mother to Mr.
          Stricklin's room and Mr. Stricklin
          just up and left. Do you know anything
          about this transfer and Mr.
          Stricklin's departure?

                    NURSE
          I heard about Mr. Stricklin's
          departure, but I didn't hear about
          Emily's mother's transfer. Just for
          the record, I don't take care of that
          wing. I found Mrs. Jo reworking all
          the nurses' schedules behind my back.

                    DOC
          Ok, ok, I'll take care of Mrs. Jo
          later. Nurse, take Emily back to her
          mother's room. I need to do one more
          test on this sample. Emily, tell your
          mom I will see her later to do some
          tests on her, as well.

                    EMILY
You better hurry because we are
leaving tonight.

                    DOC
Leaving tonight? Where are you going?
Nurse, why wasn't I informed of this?

                    NURSE
This is the first time I'm hearing of
it, Doc. Where you going little girl,
to be a hippy in Woodstock?

                    DOC
Emily, where are you going? Why are
you leaving so soon?

                    EMILY
My daddy is coming early to pick us
up. We're going to our new house in
Vermont. My daddy says the sky up
there is better for our skin.

                    DOC
You and your mom have to speak to me.
I have forms your mom has to fill out.
You can't leave without seeing me.

                    EMILY
We can't sign out, we were told not
to. We heard that if we sign out that
you wouldn't get your money to run
this hospital. So if we just left,
then there are no papers, and your
hospital can keep saving people's
lives.

                    DOC
Who told you that?

                    EMILY
The bus driver told mommy.

                    DOC
What bus driver?

                    EMILY
The bus driver that brought us here,
Mr. Verdun.

                    DOC
The bus driver Verdun? Nurse take
Emily back to her mother's room and
get Shepard on the phone stat.

                    NURSE
Now I'm back on the phone, trying to
reach a man who only has a landline
but lives in a beehive. Maybe he
should get a landline in the beehive.

                    DOC
Emily, please don't leave your
mother's room until your mommy and
daddy see me. Nurse, put a lockdown on
this building. Nobody in or out
without my permission.

                    NURSE
What if Mrs. Jo wants to leave
forever, can I let her out?

                    DOC
Nurse, please. I don't have time for
games.

                    NURSE
Just a dream, I was getting a visual.
How come everyone is disappearing from
this facility forever, except Mrs. Jo?

                    EMILY
Doc, please hurry. My mommy and me are
excited to move to Vermont, you can
come visit anytime.

Max knocks and walks in.

                    MAX
Did someone say Vermont? I love
Vermont, I ski there all the time.

                    EMILY
Yes, I have a new house in Vermont! We
move in tomorrow, I'm so excited. The
name of the mountain is Sugarbush. My
father says the mountain is so sweet
it looks like sugar on the trees when
it snows.

                    MAX
That's my favorite mountain in
Vermont! I ski there all the time!

                    EMILY
Maybe you can teach me to ski! What's
your name?

                    MAX
Max, Max Silo, at your service.

                    EMILY
Well I'm Emily, Emily Brixton, at your
service.

                    MAX
Hey Doc, I'm going to Shepard's. Just
passing by. You need anything?

                    DOC
Yeah, sure, whatever Shep can spare.
Tell him Mrs. Jo ate everything and
tell him I need to speak to him ASAP.

                    MAX
Will do, Doc.

                    DOC
Now, if you guys will let me be,
please, I have a lot of work to do.

                    MAX
Emily, come out to my car. I want to
introduce you to my girlfriend Sue.
She loves skiing as well.

                    DOC
Remember Nurse, no one in or out with
out my approval.

                    NURSE
What about Max? Ok, ok, we're leaving.

Doc looks through microscope, talking to himself.

                    DOC
Same compounds as the RM-35, that's
good. Looks like the cannabis plant
from college -
     (keeps looking in
      microscope)
Wow everything is moving! I would
need at least a week to do more
extensive testing. Never saw
anything like this before. The
bacteria is consuming the host.
     (pause, then)
It has some of the characteristics
of Royal but all the DNA of a plant
and a living organism.

                                        FADE OUT.

INT. DELRIDGE - LATER

Doc and Nurse enter the room. Mrs. Jo and Emily are feeding
EMILY'S MOM. Shepard strolls in. Doc waves the construction sign
in the air.

                    DOC
          Why is this on the door?

                    MRS. JO
          What are you doing here? This is a
          quarantined area. You must leave, you
          might infect the patient. Nurse Emily,
          get me another jar of RM-35, stat.

Emily looks at Doc.

                    EMILY
          She calls me nurse, but I'm not a
          nurse.

                    MRS. JO
          Yes you are. Now do as I say, it's for
          your mother's health. Don't you want
          your mother to get better so she can
          drive a race car?

Emily looks at Doc, confused.

                    EMILY
          Drive a race car? My mom's car broke
          down.

                    DOC
          It's ok Emily, go get Mrs. Jo what she
          needs.

                    EMILY
          Ok, Doctor Jasmine, I'll be right
          back.

                    NURSE
          Doctor Jasmine? Sounds like a tea for
          diarrhea.

Nurse turns to Doc.

                    NURSE (CONT'D)
          Doctor Jasmine? You better not be
          humoring this little girl!

                    DOC
          What are you looking at me for?

                    NURSE
Now Mrs. Jo is a doctor? She has a
nurse? I knew I should have given her
some arsenic, or a salad bowl for a
motorcycle helmet.

                    MRS. JO
Doc, that's right I needed a nurse.
Better than that useless thing you're
paying, she doesn't even know how to
schedule nurses. My nurse works for RM-
35.

                    NURSE
You thought your lips were puffy
before? I'm gonna make Mick Jagger
jealous when I get through with you.

Emily runs back into the room.

                    EMILY
Who's Mick Jagger?

                    DOC
So that's the reason for my
diminishing stock... how many bottles
have you used?

                    EMILY
Every time she gives mommy one
spoon, she eats two. I've been to
the stock room three times today.
All the empty bottles are in the
closet.

                    MRS. JO
Shut up you little narc, I knew I
should have never trusted you. I
can put the purple back on your
arms, you know. You want to work in
a circus the rest of your life?

Doc turns to Emily's Mom.

                    DOC
I'm so glad you're doing better. Every
time I went to check on you, you were
either strolling in the garden or they
switched your room. I didn't know
where you were at times.

                    EMILY'S MOM
Thanks for everything Doc. My daughter
talks about you all the time.

                    EMILY
Doc, look what Mrs. Jo gave me! A book
about bees!

                    MRS. JO
Excuse me, remember what I told you?
Address me proper. Say it, say it.

                    EMILY
Oh yes, I'm sorry - Dr. Jasmine gave
me this book.

                    NURSE
Dr. Jasmine? Sounds like a tea for the
sick. In the mind.

Shepard walks in.

                    SHEPARD
Why does the door look like a
construction site?

                    MRS. JO
Who invited the groupie? Nurse Emily,
when I'm treating a patient I want no
interruptions. Now get these people
out of this room stat-

                    DOC
Don't listen to her Emily. What's up
Shep?

                    MRS. JO
Well, since you're my boss -

                    SHEPARD
Doc, we are going to Washington. The
attorney called about our new
draconian laws.

                    DOC
That is monumental news! I have some
epic news, as well: RM-35 can aptly be
renamed to RM-1-35. We were missing
the one component - the living
organism!

                    SHEPARD
I'm confused. What living organism?
The species from Mexico?

                    DOC
When I show you in the lab, then,
you'll understand-

                    NURSE
Now I guess I'm escorting everyone to
the lab. Come on Doctor Emily, we're
going to the lab. And bring the
science project that gave you the bee
book. Good old Doc wants to see air
under his microscope.

                              FADE TO BLACK.

EXT. CAMPFIRE CIRCLE - NIGHT - TWENTY YEARS LATER

                    GIRL STUDENT
I really liked all those stories
today, Sir. Do you live here in the
Catskills?

                    MAX
No, I live in Vermont.

                    GIRL STUDENT
Do you have beehives in Vermont?

                    MAX
Yes, my wife Emily has about sixty
hives. She teaches entomology and
horticulture at the University of
Vermont. She also has three dozen
hives at the University.

                    GIRL STUDENT
Very nice, I would love to meet her
and maybe attend her classes one day.

                    MAX
You would love her, she has really
honed her craft, making the finest RM-
35 ever manufactured. Currently, she
is using bee stingers and bee venom
paste to treat people with joint and
muscle pain and arthritis. It's a
really fascinating technique. The
medical journals can't keep up with
her never-ending, over the top,
controversial healing processes.

                    GIRL STUDENT
Wow, she is a woman with many talents.

                    MAX
Many talents to say the least. Last
year she wrote a book on bees that
held the number one best seller spot
for three weeks in a row. She is
currently working on an out of the
blue story about the disappearing
bats. I really don't know where she
gets the time or energy. She's like a
machine.

                ALL STUDENTS
Wowwww.

                    MAX
I'll make sure everyone gets a copy of
her latest at the end of this trip.

                GIRL STUDENT
Make sure you don't forget!

                BOY STUDENT
Professor, I have a quick question,
off topic.

                    MAX
Please, call me Max.

                BOY STUDENT
Right, Max. So, Sir Shepard was
actually knighted? But he wasn't
British, so how can he be knighted, if
he was not a Brit?

                    MAX
Yes, good question. He was the only
American Indian to ever be knighted
and legally allowed to use the prefix
Sir before his name. When you are a
foreign national receiving an honorary
knighthood from the UK you may not use
the prefix. Sir Shepard was allowed
because he not only won a Nobel Peace
Prize, but also because he saved
mankind from many deadly diseases.

                BOY STUDENT
Wow, that is so fascinating.

                    MAX
Well, Sir Shepard was a very
fascinating man.

                    GIRL STUDENT
                 (interrupting)
         When and how did Shepard pass?

                    MAX
         He left this world due to
         loneliness. After his wife passed
         away, he started planning for his
         new future with her. He spoke to
         the Elders of the Indian council
         and made arrangements for him and
         his wife to be buried on his
         property next to the three-hundred-
         year-old chiefs. He thought that
         was the highest honor he could ever
         receive on this planet. Having his
         wife buried in an all-male cemetery
         was proof enough for him that he
         was well revered in the tribal
         community.

                    GIRL STUDENT
         So, you explained that Shepard was
         your teacher. How come you two became
         so friendly towards each other? He was
         really only your teacher in
         retrospect. What was the magnetic
         draw?

Max looks up with a smile.

                    ALL STUDENTS
                 (shouting)
         Yeah, yeah, yeah, good question.

                    MAX
         Well, we both took a shine to each
         other right away. We could be goofy,
         funny, and silly, while neither one
         would judge the other. I really loved
         his adventure stories, but when he
         found out I was part American Indian,
         that's what sealed the deal. We both
         had American Indian blood, that was
         the real bond, I guess. Once an
         American Indian, always an American
         Indian, as he would say. Later on in
         life, when I needed the RM-35 for
         friends and family, he was the go-to
         guy. He liked the fact that we made
         everyone around us healthy. We liked
         the fact that it had a great side
         effect. It made us feel randy.
                    (MORE)

                    MAX (CONT"D)
My girlfriend Sue, really loved that
aspect.

                    GIRL STUDENT
Randy? As in horny?

                    MAX
Yes, exactly. We're all adults here.
The word is horny. Besides, Sue and I
were really fascinated with his rare
flower garden and his massive apiary.
Shepard really liked us around, as
well. We loved the fact that he was a
true humanitarian. Not too many
humanitarians in this world would go
above and beyond for people like good
old Shepard.

                    GIRL STUDENT
What happened to Sue? Do you still
keep in touch? Does your wife know
about Sue?

                    MAX
Yes, of course. Emily and I keep in
touch with Sue all the time.

                    GIRL STUDENT
Really? That's cool.

                    MAX
Sue and I parted ways when she went to
Korea to help her ailing grandmother.
She ended up staying longer than both
of us thought, and we kind of grew
apart after the move. I went to Korea
a few times. The friendship was still
there, but the spark was lost.

                    GIRL STUDENT
Ohh, I'm sorry to bring it up.

                    MAX
No, no worries. I'm glad I had the
opportunity to meet and experience
such a brilliant woman and still keep
in touch.

                    GIRL STUDENT
What does Sue do in Korea?

                    MAX
Sue created the World Bee Awareness
organization in Asia.
                    (MORE)

MAX (CONT'D)
Everywhere in Asia that has a bee hive
or apiaries, Sue is the brain child.
Everyone in Asia has a mandatory
obligation to plant flowers that
attract bees. All because of Sue.

                    BOY STUDENT
What kind of flowers attract bees?

                    MAX
Didn't you have that on your midterm?

                    BOY STUDENT
Yes, but are the flowers the same or
different in Asia?

                    MAX
Oh, yes, I see, you're right.
Depending on the part of Asia, the
typical flowers are sunflower,
lavender, mint, oregano, sage, and
cosmos to name a few. These flowers
grow all over the world.

                    GIRL STUDENT
Good for Sue, you go girl!

                    MAX
That's just the tip of the iceberg.
Sue received huge grants and donations
for her efforts, so she developed
special wings - no pun intended - at
various Asian universities dedicated
to bees and wildflowers. Sue won the
equivalent of a Nobel Peace Prize in
Asia. That's the highest honor you can
receive in Asia without being royalty.
The last I heard, Sue was breaking
ground on a new university in Moscow:
The Susan Parker University of
Entomology and Horticulture.

                    GIRL STUDENT
I heard of The Parker University of
science. The one in Moscow is
currently open, as well as two in
Thailand, and one in Vietnam. The main
University is in Korea, of course. I
think North Korea is even entertaining
the idea of a Parker University. I
really can't believe Sue progressed
that much in such a short period of
time.

                    MAX
Me neither. She refined the RM-35 down
to a drop having the same potency as a
teaspoon - all natural of course. She
learned everything from Shepard. She
would pick his brain day and night.
Sue asked so many questions Shepard
would have sensory overload and send
her home. Shepard created the RM-35
and Sue perfected it.

                    GIRL STUDENT
So, Shepard is the real hero. In more
ways than one. Creating the RM-35 and
getting all those sick people better.
Also teaching Sue all of his secrets
so she can share her knowledge around
Asia and the world. Between Sue and
Emily, these girls can conquer the
world, thanks to Shepard. That's what
you call the three musketeers.

                    MAX
Well, I guess. But it wasn't Shepard
alone that discovered this
breakthrough natural cure. He had help
from his friend Doc at Delridge. Doc
was the one that named the Royal Magic
RM-35. The thirty-five was the
quantity of pollen count he saw under
the microscope. Doc was going to add a
one to the formula's name, which would
have made it RM-1-35. The one being
for the one microbe inside the
ladybugs' oily skin. But he thought it
was too long. Besides, he liked the
mystery value behind the name.

Max stares at the fire.

                    MAX (CONT'D)
Come to think of it... after all
these years, I never did learn the
doctor's real name. Everyone always
called him Doc.

                    GIRL STUDENT
What happened to Doc?

                    MAX
Ironically, he passed away from a rare
blood disorder shortly after the new
bee laws were put in place.

                    BOY STUDENT
Why didn't Doc use the RM-35 on
himself?

                    MAX
He did, but it didn't work. After
handling it and consuming it everyday
for so many years, he thought his body
became immune. It didn't work as a
serum on him. It is said that the RM-
35 only works if you are already sick -
it's not a preventative, it's the
cure.

                    GIRL STUDENT
But how are we to know it doesn't have
a preventative value if we are using
it and not getting sick?

                    MAX
Maybe it is working. I guess we'll
never know with RM-35 if it's
preventative or a cure. One thing's
for sure: Doc was very skeptical with
the big pharmaceutical meds, so he
never took medicine for his illness.

                    GIRL STUDENT
That is so sad, I'm sorry to hear.

                    MAX
That's ok, he had a great life. He was
happy. They both were happy knowing
that they helped eradicate ninety-nine
percent of those nasty diseases. It
just so happened that Doc was the one
percent that didn't make it. Doc and
Shepard devoted their life to helping
mankind and they did just that while
helping to save the bees and the
ladybugs in the process. Doc and
Shepard were the creators of "Save the
Bee Day", which as you know is
globally recognized as April 25th. So
on this day in April, the entire
planet plants a flower to feed the
bees - in Doc and Shepard's honor.
That is a monumental achievement in
itself.

                    GIRL STUDENT
Wow, that's harmonious, a real honor.

                    MAX
The Doc singlehandedly enacted a law
that forbade the cutting or poisoning
of dandelions in springtime. As you
know, they are the first food the bees
can get after a long, cold winter.
What's really ironic is that
dandelions, being the archnemesis of
suburbia for years, is now a global
welcoming of spring. The people of the
suburbs now have competitions to see
who can grow the most dandelions on
their lawns. The upscale neighborhoods
import wild dandelions to make their
whole lawn yellow. It's really a sight
to see.

                    BOY STUDENT
Yes, it is amazing and ironic - the
suburbs wanting the yellow dandelion
in their yards instead of their nice
green manicured lawns.

                    MAX
Doc and Shepard also, collectively,
started the National Apiary Society,
which donated one standard bee hive to
every big and small town in the U.S.
Doc also convinced all the schools and
prison systems to have apiaries on
their roofs run by the students and
prisoners. Now all the harvested RM-35
can be consumed by the institution's
attendees. Doc really had some major
achievements before his passing. When
he was laid to rest he actually had a
smile on his face. He looked peaceful
and happy. He also received a Nobel
Peace Prize posthumously. Maybe that
explains why he had a smile on his
face in the end.

                    GIRL STUDENT
That's actually a happy story. So now
I kind of understand the story about
the bees, Shepard, Doc, and you. But
what about the ladybugs? How did the
ladybugs get their big debut while
saving the planet?

                    MAX
Well, the ladybugs didn't actually
save the planet on their own.
                    (MORE)

MAX (CONT'D)
They were a contributing factor to the
enhancement of the honey. You see, Sir
Shepard planted these exotic flowers
from around the world for the bees to
feed on, which in the end helped the
bees make a high grade honey, or Royal
Magic.

                    GIRL STUDENT
In my mind I thought the ladybugs were
the real hero and that's why tomorrow
morning we will be up at the crack of
dawn collecting ladybugs!

                    MAX
Like I said, the ladybugs are a
contributing factor. You see, the
ladybugs killed the deadly varroa
mites that were decimating flowers and
apiaries around the world. In essence,
they were the cleaning crew for the
bees. So the ladybugs have a very
powerful oily enzyme in their body.
When in contact with the high pollen
count in the honey, the two would make
an epic cocktail called RM-1-35 which
eradicates most cancers and viruses.

                    GIRL STUDENT
I get it, so why do we collect
thirteen ladybugs? That's an unlucky
number.

                    MAX
Because, as you know, we ship the
ladybug packages around the world to
people with beehives to protect their
bees from the deadly varroa mite.
Also, the ladybug cleaning crew will
help facilitate the manufacturing of
foreign countries' versions of RM-1-
35.

                    GIRL STUDENT
I get it. But that doesn't explain the
quantity thirteen.

                    MAX
So, it goes like this. The recipient
of the ladybug package will insert 12
ladybugs in their hive. The thirteenth
ladybug will be released into the wild
to propagate the area for generations
to come.
                 (MORE)

MAX (CONT'D)

Plus, traditionally the recipient will
hold the last ladybug, number
thirteen, in the air and make a wish.
"Free a ladybug make a wish, let the
farmer put food on your dish", as the
saying goes.

BOY STUDENT

What if the recipient of the package
has more then one hive? Like your
wife, for instance. The recipients
have to buy a package for each hive?

MAX

No, a package of twelve, or shall I
say thirteen, can be dispersed into
three hives, provided these hives are
less then ten yards away from each
other. The ladybugs are very
territorial. Each group has a specific
scent to attract their breeding
partners and resume propagation.

GIRL STUDENT

So, the ladybug was not a close
descendant to the varroa mite after
all? Instead, they were a similar
looking species but the true
eradicator of the nasty mite.

MAX

Correct. You see, everyone thought
that the ladybug delivered the mite to
the bees or that the ladybug was a
version of mite or tick because not
all have the traditional polka-dot
coloring. Did you know there are over
a thousand different types of
ladybugs? When you look at the
characteristics of a non-traditional
ladybug, they have similar features to
the tick or mite. Small head, larger
body, almost identical. They were mis-
categorized in the world of entomology
for a long time.

GIRL STUDENT

This is such a cool story. Whereabouts
did the research take place?

MAX

Like I said before, the research came
from the Delridge Nursing Home right
here in the Catskills.
                    (MORE)

MAX (CONT'D)
This was the kind of place, where
people of all ages and walks of life
would spend their last living days, to
pass in peace. You see, Mrs. Jo-

                GIRL STUDENT
            (interrupting)
        Shepard's wife?

                MAX
Yes, Shepard's wife. Doctor Jasmine as
the drollery went, would take all the
RM-35 and feed it to the patients in
mass quantities. She was a little
messy with her half-empty bottles,
leaving them exposed. So, the ladybugs
had a field day on the sweet nectar.
With the pure oily enzyme in the
ladybug and the high potency of RM-35
on their feet and bodies, the ladybugs
were able to cure people just by
landing on them. It seemed like the
high concentration of the two made it
a natural topical for skin cancer. The
testimonial was there. It helped my
wife, Emily, and my mother-in-law.
This is the reason for the miracle in
the Catskills. All because of this
highly potent honey and the ladybug.

                BOY STUDENT
The facility is still there?

                MAX
Yes, the facility is still there. It
was put together anonymously by
Shepard's brother, the artist and
philanthropist Verdun Grey.

                BOY STUDENT
Verdun Grey the artist? I know his
work! Very idealistic, very macabre.

                MAX
That's the one. A bit of a genius, a
bit of a recluse, a bit of a mad man.
That's where Grey's Anatomy came from.

                GIRL STUDENT
Really!? Wow, that is so interesting.

MAX
I'm only kidding. Henry Gray wrote the popular anatomy textbook in the early 1900s. Obviously not the same person.

GIRL STUDENT
Why are you always playing around like that? I'm not sure if you're serious or kidding anymore.

MAX
I was taught by the best, Sir Shepard himself. He said that if you take life too seriously, serious life won't give you any pleasure. Even though Sir Shepard was serious with his bees and flowers, he always tried to have fun everyday. I truly miss that man. Anyway, forgive me, while I ramble with more details.

GIRL STUDENT
Yes, please tell us more.

MAX
As I said before, I hate repeating myself. In the beginning of summer when the ladybugs are full grown and the bees honeycombs are fully stocked, that's when the miracle would happen. While cleaning the hives and garden flowers from unwanted pests, the ladybugs would unknowingly excrete a natural oil enzyme on everything they touched. This enzyme mixed with the honey and pollen to create the famous RM-35. This process would start at the beginning of summer, nationally known as the Summer of Avery, which would go well into the middle of fall. The real magic is the Summer of Avery and the full moon combination.

BOY STUDENT
So which insects are more important, the ladybugs or the bees?

MAX
So, you see, the bees are a very important part of our human existence, they pollinate all the flowers for everything we consume. But, it was the ladybug who was the real queen of the bug world.
(MORE)

                    MAX (CONT'D)
They had that special enzyme in
their bodies to enhance the honey
which would eradicate diseases.

                    GIRL STUDENT
Yeah, of course the ladies save the
day again. Keep in mind, boys, that
there are only queens in the hive, no
kings.

                    MAX
That is so true, that's because-
        (pause)
nevermind. I was in trouble in the
past with my childish comments.
Anyway, that's why we have a Ladybug
Hunt.

                    GIRL STUDENT
Well, you wont be disappointed with my
hunting performance. Your stories are
real motivators.

                    ALL STUDENTS
No disappointment here, either. Me
neither.

                    MAX
Some more interesting facts: Did you
know that all Indian burial grounds
are required by Indian law to have at
least one beehive in the graveyard?
The wild animals never touch the hives
for they instinctively know they are
sacred. During the time of the Colony
Collapse Disorder, rumor had it that
the Indian Chiefs in the
Catskills started eating the very
rare toxic Rhododendron honey which
would make them fall into eternal
sleep.

                    GIRL STUDENT
Toxic honey?

                    MAX
Yes, toxic honey. Only from the
Rhododendron trees. The chiefs were
consuming this on every mountain:
Slide Mountain, Pantherkill,
Peekamoose, Overlook, even
Tripp Mountain.
                    (MORE)

MAX (CONT"D)

By doing so, wherever their bodies
were laid to rest would be hallowed
ground, instantly becoming a sacred
Indian burial site. Then, the
Indian tribes would donate their
burial sites to the National Parks
Department for the people, the
animals, the flowers, and of
course, the honey bees. By doing
this, they pretty much started a
trend that saved the world from
extinction. As you know, no bees,
no trees, no fruits, no vegetables,
no animals, no humans.

BOY STUDENT
Wow, that takes a lot of courage to
sacrifice yourself for other people
and animals.

MAX
It sure does. Within a month's time
the trend spread like wildfire, like a
domino effect. The rest of the
American Indian chiefs followed suit.
Indians from around the world joined
in and were sacrificing themselves for
the existence of the honey bee. The
Mayans, Incas, African Tribes,
Thailand, Vietnam, Borneo,
Scandinavia... all over the planet!
They did this so the land would never
be compromised by government, big
business, or cell towers. Did you know
cell towers are very bad for the bees
existence? It disorients their flying
patterns, so they would instinctively
fly under the cell signal so as not to
disrupt their honey making process.
Tomorrow, ladies and gentlemen, all
cell phones must be turned off for the
duration of the hunt unless an extreme
emergency arises. Or if you need to
call for a pizza delivery. Just
kidding.

BOY STUDENT
Wow, that's interesting, Professor - I
mean Max.

MAX
Ok, ladies and gentlemen, I am
officially going to bed.
We have a big day tomorrow.
(MORE)

                    MAX (CONT'D)
We only have a forty-eight hour
window to catch as many ladybugs as
possible for this hunting season.

                    GIRL STUDENT
Quick question, please! Why is it that
we only have a forty-eight hour
window? Why was it so hard for our
class to get these hunting permits?

                    MAX
Because only American Indians and
scientists with tribal permits can
legally capture the ladybug at the
start of the Avery's first full moon.
Thus, the forty-eight hour window:
twenty-four hours before the moon
peaks and twenty-four hours after the
moon peaks. So, you folks being
students of entomology obtained your
permits through an American Indian,
which happens to be me. If you haven't
noticed, I am your sponsor and guide.

                    GIRL STUDENT
Yes, we did notice. We all thank you
for this experience.

                    MAX
Also, ladies and gentleman, a quick
reminder. We can only capture thirteen
ladybugs from the same species within
ten-yard ratios. So, we need to keep
that in mind. We cannot disrupt the
breeding order of these mountains. Our
task tomorrow will be extremely
tedious and exhausting. By the way, we
have a very talented and experienced
Indian tracker accompanying us
tomorrow at 6:00 am. So be ready, and
get some rest. He is never late.

                    BOY STUDENT
What's his name?

                    MAX
Verdun.

                    BOY STUDENT
Verdun Grey? The artist? Shepard's
brother?

                         MAX
          No, Shepard's son, Verdun. Also the
          big surprise, which I was going to
          save till tomorrow, but... Verdun is
          allowing us on his property for the
          last leg of the hunt. So, after our
          first long day of hunting we will pack
          up and go to Verdun's property where
          it all started. We get to see
          Shepard's house, the hives, the rare
          flowers, the old Indian cemetery where
          Shepard and his wife are buried. But
          the real treat, as I mentioned
          earlier: the dancing totem. As you
          know, it will be a full moon tomorrow
          so we never know what we'll see. Maybe
          some chanting Indian spirits, maybe a
          dancing totem. I think I am more
          excited about the totem than I am
          about the hunt tomorrow.

                     ALL STUDENTS
                 (talking to each other)
          I'm gonna watch that totem all
          night. Me too, I'm not taking my
          eyes off it, I'm drinking two
          energy drinks.

                         MAX
                  (looking around)
          I need some rest! Which tent is
          mine?

The students laugh.

                     GIRL STUDENT
          Sir, it's the one with the Indian
          statue and the ladybug flags.

                                  FADE TO BLACK.

EXT. ENGLISH COUNTRY FARM - MORNING

DELIVERY LADY with cockney accent walks up a driveway. KID runs
out of farm house.

                     DELIVERY LADY
          It's here! The package you've been
          asking about for the past three bloody
          weeks.

                         KID
          Thank you, thank you, thank you.

                    DELIVERY LADY
May I ask, what's in that parcel that
is so important? I can see the words
"Fragile" and "Alive." What is it? A
mouse?

                    KID
Wow, it even has an American
Agricultural stamp on it. I'm gonna
keep this box forever. These are my
ladybugs! My father said that when I
get my "ladybug security team", as he
calls it, he would give me my first
beehive. Now I finally have my own
bees! I won't disappoint him. Without
the bees the world would be doomed.

                    DELIVERY LADY
I thought this world was already
doomed, with the people we elected for
government office.

                    KID
With responsibilities like this, I am
finally a man, I'm going to save the
world with my version of RM-35. Thanks
again for the delivery. When I make my
wish, I'll think of you, as well. Free
a ladybug make a wish, let a farmer's
best friend put food on your dish.
I'll also say let the mail lady have a
brighter day on this gloomy English
countryside.

                                FADE TO BLACK.

A
JOURNEY
HOME

BY

GLENN TRIPP

INT. AIRPORT LOUNGE - DAY

SKIPPER, a young man talks with his best friend, RODGER, over a few farewell cocktails.

                    SKIPPER
          Rodger, you have time for one more?

Rodger looks at his phone.

                    RODGER
          I'm checking my flight now. Well...
               (pause)
          I guess I do have time! Delayed two
          more hours!

                    SKIPPER
          That's great, that will put you in the
          same flight time as me. I love a
          drinking partner. Another Jack and
          Coke?

                    RODGER
          Sure, what else am I gonna do? While
          you're up, grab some snacks, please.

Skipper gets drinks. Rodger stares at his phone, leg shaking.

                    SKIPPER
          Here you go brother, extra strong.
          What's with the nervous leg?

Hands Rodger a drink, throws snacks on the table.

                    RODGER
          Thanks, Skip. Nothing much, a bit on
          my mind.

                    SKIPPER
          You know, you don't have to go through
          with this. We can walk out of this
          airport and never look back.

                    RODGER
          I'm cool, I've done this a hundred
          times. Besides everything is in my
          checked bags.

                    SKIPPER
          Ok, my friend. Just letting you know,
          there's always a plan B.

Skipper opens a bag of chips.

                    RODGER
          You know something Skip... I'm
          thinking of settling down. I have a
          girl, Grace, who treats me like a
          king. I'm pretty set financially. I
          think this might be my last trip to
          Asia.

                    SKIPPER
          Go with your heart brother, you've
          always made some great decisions in
          life. If you really want to change
          your life, you can move to New Zealand
          and be my neighbor.

Rodger's phone buzzes and flashes on the table.

                    RODGER
          What the fuck, these incompetent
          airlines. Skip I have to run, they
          just assigned us a gate, we're
          boarding now, no warning, no nothing.
                    (reading aloud)
          Please proceed to gate sixty-four,
          which is at the other end of the
          fucking terminal.

                    SKIPPER
          Don't sweat it brother, they'll wait
          for you. They don't have a choice, you
          bought a ticket. They're waiting for
          you as we speak.

Rodger hugs Skipper, grabs his backpack, chugs his drink.

                    RODGER
          I'll chat you when I get home, let you
          know how I made out. Send my love to
          your family.

                    SKIPPER
          And you do the same. It'll all work
          out, don't be nervous. In twenty-four
          hours you'll be home, walking easy
          street.

                    RODGER
          I hope, wish me luck.

Rodger runs down the terminal. Skipper sips his drink, watching through the lounge window.

                                        DISSOLVE TO:

INT. AIRPOT TERMINAL - MOMENTS LATER

Rodger reaches the gate out of breath. AIRLINE AGENT checks tickets while THREE POLICE OFFICERS stand next to the gate entrance.

                    RODGER
          You really don't give your passengers
          much notice.

                    AIRLINE AGENT
          Ticket and passport please.

Rodger hands his documents to the agent.

                    RODGER
          I hope you're serving dinner early.
          I built up an appetite running
          through your mile long airport.
          Couldn't you have made the gate
          closer to the lounge? After all,
          frequent flyers are your best
          passengers.

                    AIRLINE AGENT
          You are Mr. Rodger Ridgeway? With your
          final destination being JFK
          International Airport in New York?

                    RODGER
          That's what the documents say, loud
          and clear.

Three police officers walk up to Rodger.

                    POLICE OFFICER
          Mr. Ridgeway, would you please come
          with us? We need to have a word with
          you.

                    RODGER
          What! A word!? I don't have time for
          words, I'm about to board my plane.

                    POLICE OFFICER
          Please, Mr. Ridgeway. Come with us.

Two police officers grab Rodger's arms.

                    RODGER
          No, no, where are you taking me? I
          can't miss this flight, I have a
          business meeting tomorrow. Please,
          stop grabbing my arms, you're hurting
          me. Do you know who I am?

                    POLICE OFFICER
          Yes, Mr. Ridgeway, we are trying to
          figure that out. Now, if you stop
          resisting we won't be forced to add
          pressure on you.

                    RODGER
          I need to be on that plane.

                    POLICE OFFICER
          No worries, Mr.Ridgeway, we are
          holding your plane until further
          notice. Let's make this as quick as
          possible so your plane can get in the
          air in a timely fashion.

                    RODGER
          I don't trust you, I want the American
          Embassy, I've seen those locked up
          abroad movies.

The police officers and Rodger walk through double doors.

                    POLICE OFFICER
          No need to worry, Mr.Ridgeway. Your
          embassy has been notified.

                                        DISSOLVE TO:

INT. AIRPLANE - LATER

Rodger sits in business class. STEWARDESS walks over as CAPTAIN
makes announcement.

                    STEWARDESS
          Sir, would you like a glass of
          champagne before we take off?

                    RODGER
          No, thank you. I'm tired, I need to
          rest my eyes for a spell. Please
          wake me when dinner's being served.

                         STEWARDESS
          No problem sir. Buckle up, enjoy your
          rest. I'll be sure to wake you for
          dinner.

                         CAPTAIN (V.O.)
          Flight crew, please prepare the cabin
          and take your seats.

                                        FADE OUT.

INT. AIRPLANE - LATER

Rodger wakes up to the Captain's emergency announcement over
loud speaker and the stewardess yelling. People in the
background are screaming, saying prayers, crying, yelling.

                         CAPTAIN (V.O.)
          Flight crew, code red, code red.
          Ladies and gentlemen this is not a
          drill. I repeat, this is not a drill.
          Everyone take your seats immediately.
          Buckle up and prepare for impact. I
          repeat: buckle up and prepare for
          impact. This is not a drill.

                         STEWARDESS
               (screaming)
          Sit down, sit down now, this is an
          emergency.

                                        FADE TO BLACK.

EXT. PLANE OVER FOREST - LATER

Plane flies over forest on its descent, hitting tops of trees.
It lands successfully in the forest, with trees and brush
cushioning the landing.

                                        FADE OUT.

INT. AIRPLANE - LATER

Captain walks out of the cockpit and hugs Stewardess. PASSENGERS
cheer, scream, cry, moan with pain.

                         STEWARDESS
               (crying and screaming with
                joy)
          We're alive, we're alive, thank
          you, thank you, thank you Captain.

                    CAPTAIN
          Yes we're alive. Thank god. Are you
          ok?

                    STEWARDESS
          Shaken up, but I'll be ok.

The captain grabs the intercom.

                    CAPTAIN
          Ladies and gentlemen, sorry for the
          impromptu landing. I hope
          everyone's ok. I will personally be
          talking to each and every one of
          you to address your needs and
          concerns. Help is on its way.
          Please relax and be patient.

                    PASSENGER 1
               (shouting)
          Captain, was this a terrorist
          attack?

                    CAPTAIN
          Ladies and gentlemen, I want to
          make it very clear that this
          unfortunate incident was not a
          terrorist attack. I repeat this was
          NOT a terrorist attack. This
          aircraft started losing oil
          pressure and then the left engine
          seized up. It was a mechanical
          malfunction. Folks, make yourself
          as comfortable as possible. We have
          a rescue team on its way. Everyone
          needs to be patient, it might take
          a while for the extraction. Thank
          you for your understanding and
          patience.

The captain hangs up the intercom.

                    STEWARDESS
               (whispering)
          Captain, what do you need us flight
          attendants to do?

                    CAPTAIN
          Make the passengers as comfortable as
          possible. Hand out blankets, pillows,
          magazines, food, and water. Please be
          sparing with the food and water, we
          might be here for a while.

                    STEWARDESS
          You got it. Anything you need please,
          let me know. Captain, how long do you
          think until we're rescued?

                    CAPTAIN
          It's hard to say, the local FAA are
          aware of our emergency landing and the
          black box beacon has been
          automatically activated so... only
          time will tell.

                    STEWARDESS
          I'm patient, I just hope the
          passengers are.

                    CAPTAIN
          Just keep reassuring everyone help is
          on its way. Again, make everyone feel
          as comfortable as possible. We'll get
          through this.

                    STEWARDESS
          You got it.

Captain walks down the aisle, talking to passengers.

                    CAPTAIN
          Are you ok? Are you ok, are you ok?

                    PASSENGER 1
          Captain, I hit my head and I'm not
          feeling well.

                    CAPTAIN
               (screaming over the
                chatter of people)
          Is there a Doctor or a nurse among
          us?

                    PASSENGER 2
          I'm a nurse!

                    PASSENGER 3
          I'm a nurse, as well!

                    CAPTAIN
          Ok great, can you two nurses give a
          hand with some medical assistance? We
          have first aid kits throughout the
          aircraft. Stewardess, assist these two
          nurses, please.

The captain gets on the intercom.

                    CAPTAIN (CONT'D)
          Ladies and gentlemen, please: if you
          do not have to use the lavatories,
          please stay seated. It is necessary to
          have the aisles free for staff to
          assist the people in need. Thank you
          for your cooperation.

INT. AIRPLANE - LATER

Now that the passengers have settled down, the plane has a
somber mood. Captain and Stewardess walk up and down the aisle
helping people. Rodger turns to passenger, GRACE, sitting across
from him.

                    RODGER
          That was a scary landing. Are you ok?

                    GRACE
          I'm fine, just a little shaken up. How
          about yourself?

                    RODGER
          I'm great, I guess! I went from dead
          sleep to emergency landing in a matter
          of seconds... real eye opener.

                    GRACE
          I was looking out the window watching
          the trees getting closer and closer,
          that's when I knew something was
          definitely wrong.

                    RODGER
          Well, thank god we're alive. I have a
          bottle of whiskey from duty free.
          Would you like to have a celebratory
          landing drink with me?

                    GRACE
          I'm not a big whiskey fan, but, today,
          I'd celebrate with a drink of urine.

Grace and Rodger start laughing. Rodger opens the bottle of
whiskey, pours two glasses.

                    RODGER
          You're funny, I like you. What's
          your name? Where are you from?

                    GRACE
     My name is Grace. I'm originally from
     Japan, but I live in New York. And
     you?

                    RODGER
     I'm Rodger, I live in New York as
     well. Upper West Side, Seventy-Ninth
     and Broadway.

                    GRACE
     Rodger, we're neighbors! Seventy-sixth
     and Broadway.

They both hold up drinks.

                    RODGER
     To neighbors, cheers.

                    GRACE
     To alive neighbors, cheers.

                    RODGER
     What kind of work do you do, neighbor?

                    GRACE
     I'm an artist, everything from makeup
     to oil on canvas. And you?

                    RODGER
     I'm a writer.. short stories, screen
     plays, adventure travel.

                    GRACE
     Well, this flight just wrote a great
     adventure travel story for you.

                    RODGER
     I guess, I typically don't write
     action packed, suspenseful, horrifying
     thrillers.

                    GRACE
     Which of your writing makes you a
     living?

                    RODGER
     Adventure travel is my main staple.
     Short stories and screenplays are just
     a hobby for now.
         (pausing)
     I was actually hoping you were a
     producer so I can give you one of
     my screenplays.

                    GRACE
          Sorry, I'm not a producer, not even
          close. But I would love to read one of
          your scripts.

                    RODGER
          Really? Ok, I would be honored if you
          read my work. I'll tell you what: when
          we get through this mess, I'll give
          you my latest story. After you're done
          perusing through it, I'll take you out
          to dinner and we can talk about it
          over a bottle of wine. I'm always
          looking for constructive criticism.

                    GRACE
               (holds out her hand)
          You got a deal.

                    RODGER
          Deal.

Grace and Rodger shake hands.

                    RODGER (CONT'D)
          Grace, another drink?

                    GRACE
          Not for me, thanks. I'm a light
          weight, this one made me sleepy. I'm
          gonna rest for a bit. Wake me up when
          the rescue ship comes.

                    RODGER
          Will do. I'm getting a bit groggy
          myself. I'm gonna finish that sleep I
          was abruptly woken from. Wake me up if
          the rescue ship hits you first.

                                        DISSOLVE TO:

INT. AIRPLANE - LATER

Rodger wakes up to passenger chatter. Grace is still sleeping as
the Captain and Stewardess walk by.

                    RODGER
          Excuse me Captain. I want to
          personally thank you for the
          outstanding landing.

                    CAPTAIN
Thank you very much, sir. I did the
best I could, with the short notice I
was given. What is your name, sir?

                    RODGER
Rodger Ridgeway, sir, but you can call
me Rodger.

                    CAPTAIN
Pleased to meet you Rodger.

                    RODGER
Believe me Captain, the pleasure is
all mine. You are truly a miracle man.

                    CAPTAIN
Just doing my job, son, just doing my
job.

                    RODGER
     (whispering)
Captain, I gotta tell you
something.. I need to get off this
plane. We've been sitting here for
over eighteen hours.

                    CAPTAIN
I'm sorry son, I can't allow that.
When I called in my emergency landing,
I received strict orders from my
superiors to not let anyone leave the
aircraft.

                    RODGER
With all due respect, Captain, I need
to get off this aircraft. Not only am
I claustrophobic, but I'm not a big
fan of crowds.

                    CAPTAIN
Sorry son, there's nothing I can do.
You are my responsibility for the
moment. I received strict orders from
my superiors, I'm also under contract
with the airline. At the moment there
is nothing I can do.

                    RODGER
Captain, I had a contract with your
airline. Your airline promised me that
if I gave them fifteen hundred dollars
they would get me from point A to
point B.
                    (MORE)

RODGER (CONT'D)
Your airline broke their contract with me. As far as your superiors, they are not my superiors. So please open that door and let me leave this aircraft.

CAPTAIN
Rodger, I know how you feel, I want to help you, but I can't.

RODGER
Captain, I overheard you talking about the two dead bodies in the back of the plane. This plane currently has no operable ventilation system. I'm not a doctor or a mortician but, I do know what happens to dead bodies if they're not properly taken care of.

CAPTAIN
I know Rodger, I know. Unfortunately-

RODGER
(interrupting)
You don't know, bacteria starts setting in the soft tissue of the eyes, nose, mouth, ears and lower extremities. The good air has already been consumed by the two hundred plus passengers. It's only a matter of time until this vessel becomes a toxic cesspool. I beg you, please, let me off this aircraft, I beg you.

CAPTAIN
Did you look outside? We are in the middle of a forest. I know what's out there, I flew the plane. There's nothing for hundreds of miles, if the mosquitoes don't eat you alive the wild animals will.

RODGER
(desperately)
Captain, I'll take my chances. I'm an experienced survivalist with a first hand knowledge of adapting to my surroundings no matter how minimal or bleak they may be. I just can't adapt to these toxic claustrophobic surroundings.

Grace stands up and whispers to the Captain.

                    GRACE
          I've been listening to your
          conversation and I want off the plane
          as well. I want to be with Rodger in
          the forest, not on this toxic vessel.

Rodger smiles, grabs Grace by the hand.

                    RODGER
          You see Captain, it's two against one.
          Now, please let us slip out the side
          door and know one will be the wiser.

                    CAPTAIN
          Ok, I can't stand here arguing all
          day. All I ask is that you stay close.
          When the rescue team comes, we don't
          want to spend more time trying to
          rescue you two.

                    RODGER
          You have my word, Captain.

                    GRACE
          And my word too.

                    RODGER
          I looked out the right side of the
          plane and I saw a river. We're gonna
          set up camp there and patiently wait
          for the rescue team.

                    CAPTAIN
          Ok, stay close.

                    RODGER
          Captain, can I ask you something? Do
          you happen to have a knife and some
          matches by chance? It would make the
          survival experience that much more
          enjoyable.

                    CAPTAIN
             (hesitating)
          I understand, give me a moment.

Captain goes to the cockpit and returns with a leather satchel.

                    CAPTAIN (CONT'D)
          Here is a survival kit. Everything you
          need to survive in the wilderness:
          fishing gear, fire starter, knife,
          machete, first aid kit, and a bunch of
          other goodies.
                    (MORE)

14.

                    CAPTAIN (CONT'D)
          Use it and enjoy, but when we get
          rescued, I want it back. I got this as
          a gift thirty-five years ago. I stared
          at it every day, hoping I would never
          need to use it.

                    RODGER
          Thank you, Captain, you just made our
          world a whole lot easier. I promise I
          will respect it and return it exactly
          the way we received it.

                    GRACE
          I'll make sure he does Captain. By the
          way, my name is Grace.

                    CAPTAIN
          Pleased to meet you Grace. So, both of
          you collect your personal belongings
          and be ready. When I have the front
          exit disarmed, I'll call you to the
          front door. Let's be quiet about this,
          I don't want to alert the other
          passengers.

                    RODGER
          They won't even know we exist.

                    GRACE
          Captain, what about our checked bags?
          Do we have access to them, as well, by
          chance?

                    CAPTAIN
          Sorry Grace, that access port is on
          the exterior of the plane and judging
          by the looks of the plane's position,
          we are a bit too high to access that
          port. Don't worry though, the rescue
          team will be collecting everything in
          the baggage compartment as well.

                                        FADE TO BLACK.

EXT. RIVER BANK - DAY

Rodger fishes. Grace sits next to the river with a raging fire.

                    GRACE
          This is a much better option than
          sitting on that stuffy old plane.

                    RODGER
          You can say that again.
               (excitedly)
          I got a fish, I got one, look at
          the size of that beauty! We're
          gonna eat good tonight.

Rodger reels in the fish, pulls out a knife, and cleans it on
the river's edge.

                    GRACE
          Did I happen to mention, I'm
          impressed! You are in survival mode.

                    RODGER
               (looks up at Grace)
          Grace, I want you to understand,
          the reality is, we'll be sleeping
          out here tonight. I don't think
          rescue will be here before
          nightfall. Are you cool with this?

                    GRACE
          I kinda got that feeling. I really
          couldn't spend another moment on that
          plane, too many emotions running high.
          I'm definitely cool with this. After
          all we're neighbors, remember?

                    RODGER
          Yes, I remember. We can do this. See
          that indent in the side of the rocks?

                    GRACE
          Yes, it looks like a shallow cave.
          That's home?

                    RODGER
          Yes, I'm gonna make it home. I'll cut
          some small tree limbs, stand them up
          against the cave and support the base
          with heavy stones, that should keep
          any unwanted animals out. I'll also
          line the floor with spruce bows to
          give it a softer sleep.

                    GRACE
          Well, what are you waiting for? Get
          started! While you're doing that, I'll
          collect more firewood and start
          cooking this fish.
                    (MORE)

                         GRACE (CONT'D)
          Wait, before you start your Home Depot
          project, can you cut me a long stick
          to put through the fish and two sticks
          in a Y shape, please? I need to make a
          spit.

                         RODGER
          You got it.

                                             FADE TO:

EXT. RIVER BANK - LATER

Rodger works feverishly cutting down small pine saplings with a
machete. Grace scurries around picking up firewood while tending
to the fish on the fire. In no time, a simple lean-to is made
and dinner is ready.

                                             FADE TO:

EXT. RIVER BANK - LATER

Grace turns the fish as Rodger puts finishing touches on the
lean-to.

                         GRACE
          How you making out?

                         RODGER
                   (standing like a
                    presenter)
          So this is home, come take a look.

                         GRACE
          Rodger, you have impressed me again.
          Where did you learn all these skills?

                         RODGER
                   (bragging)
          Did a lot of camping as a kid. I
          never met anyone that was more
          skilled in survival than me.

                         GRACE
          I'm amazed. Well, good timing. The
          fish is done. Do you have any more of
          that whiskey left?

Rodger reaches into his backpack, unwraps blankets.

                    RODGER
          Sure do, I even smuggled out the
          two glasses in the blankets as well
          as salt and pepper shakers and real
          cutlery. One of the nice benefits
          of being in business class.

                    GRACE
          You can say that again. You thought of
          everything didn't you!?

                    RODGER
          I never thought I'd be spending this
          time in the forest with someone like
          you, that's for sure.

                    GRACE
          Me neither. This has been a big
          surprise for the both of us. Can you
          help me take the fish off the spit,
          please? It's quite heavy.

                    RODGER
          Sure, give me a moment. I saw a flat
          stone by the river, we can put it on
          that.

Rodger goes to the stream, grabs a flat stone.

                                        FADE TO:

EXT. RIVER BANK - LATER

Rodger and Grace by the fire, pouring drinks, eating fish,
talking, laughing.

                    GRACE
          That was good, I'm full.

                    RODGER
          Full! There's still a whole other side
          that hasn't been touched. Whatever we
          don't eat we need to throw in the
          river! Don't want any bears looking
          for a free meal.

                    GRACE
               (moves closer to Rodger)
          You eat it, I can't fit another
          bite. Or throw it in the river, I
          don't care.
               (shyly)
          But I will take some more whiskey.

                    RODGER
          I thought you didn't like whiskey..
          you were a light weight, one glass and
          you're done?

                    GRACE
          When you offered me whiskey before, it
          wasn't next to a raging river, a
          scented camp fire, and a beautiful
          sunset.

Rodger pours two more drinks.

                    RODGER
          Tomorrow morning I want to catch
          some fish and surprise the captain.
          A little thank you for loaning us
          his survival kit.

                    GRACE
          Ohh, that's nice, he'll love that.
          Heck you could probably catch enough
          fish to feed all the passengers,
          you're that good.

                    RODGER
          I don't know about that. Hey Grace, I
          have a little surprise for you. Close
          your eyes and hold out your hands.

                    GRACE
          What is it? What kind of surprise?
          This better not be creepy or I'm gonna
          kick your butt.

                    RODGER
          No, no, nothing like that, just close
          your eyes.

Grace closes her eyes, Rodger pulls a brick out of his backpack
and puts it in Grace's hand. Grace opens her eyes.

                    GRACE
          What is this? Is this what I think
          it is?

                    RODGER
          Well if you think it's gold, then
          you're right.

                    GRACE
          This is gold. Where did you get it?

                    RODGER
It's, not just one, there's eight of
them in total.

                    GRACE
Where did you get them?

                    RODGER
Well, earlier, when I was cutting the
saplings to make our shelter, I roamed
down the river bank and came across a
small little fishing shack. As my
curiosity got the best of me, I
entered the shack to find out it was a
gold smelting shack, not a fishing
shack.

                    GRACE
       (upset)
This is somebody's property, it's
stealing. I want no part of this.

                    RODGER
Grace, this shack is abandoned,
probably for fifty years or more. I'll
show you tomorrow. You'll see. That's
just one bar, there's seven more just
like it. I found them under old news
papers, some papers were Russian, some
were Chinese, dating back to the early
seventies.

                    GRACE
Wow, that's bizarre. What do you
suppose happened?

                    RODGER
Well, by the looks of it, they were
pulling gold out of the river, melting
it down and making these ingots. They
were probably doing some serious
manufacturing judging by the equipment
and molds they left behind.

                    GRACE
You don't think they'll come back for
their gold? People don't typically
leave behind a pile of hard earned
money.

                    RODGER
Not a chance. When I opened the front
door, it almost fell off the hinges.
                     (MORE)

RODGER (CONT'D)
I checked the wood stove and the door
was rusted shut. There's no way any
activity has been there in the last
ten years, let alone fifty.

                    GRACE
            (playing with the bar of
             gold)
That is so strange. I like the
weight this bar has, the color is
very pretty.

                    RODGER
I have another surprise for you.

                    GRACE
Another surprise? Better than this?
What is it?

                    RODGER
I have your rucksack, I put it in the
lean-to.

                    GRACE
My checked bag? It's here? Really?
Don't play me! How did you get that?

                    RODGER
Well, when I went for the piece of
metal from the plane...

                    GRACE
Yeah, I was gonna ask you what that
was for.

                    RODGER
It's for the fire in our lean-to to
contain and radiate the heat, while
keeping the bugs away.

                    GRACE
You are truly a survivalist.

                    RODGER
Anyway, when I was by the plane, I saw
the door for the luggage compartment
like the captain said. So, I thought
I'd give it a try. I climbed the tree,
turned the handle, lo and behold, it
opened. Twenty bags or so fell to the
ground and mine was right there on top
looking at me.

                         GRACE
          What about mine, how did you know it
          was mine?

                         RODGER
          Well you said earlier today, it was
          green and you always have a pink
          ribbon on top. It took me some digging
          but sure enough, there was a pink
          ribbon staring at me and attached was
          a green rucksack.

                         GRACE
          Now I can honestly say, you are my
          true hero. Now I can brush my teeth.

                         RODGER
          I also picked some wild citronella to
          keep the mosquitoes away tonight.

Grace stares at Rodger for a moment then passionately kisses him
on the lips.

                                        FADE OUT.

INT. LEAN TO - MORNING

Grace and Rodger wake up to the sounds of PARATROOPERS landing
on the river bank.

                         GRACE
          Rodger wake up, someone's outside. I
          think it's our rescue team.

                         RODGER
          What is it? Who's outside?

                         GRACE
          Shhh, what did they say?

A Paratrooper lands next to the lean-to with his parachute
covering it like a tent. Unknowingly he leans his gun and pack
next to the door of lean-to.

                         PARATROOPER 1 (V.O.)
          Fuck, I broke my leg. I broke my
          fucking leg.

                         PARATROOPER 2 (V.O.)
          Quiet, you imbecile. You're gonna ruin
          our surprise attack.

                    PARATROOPER 1 (V.O.)
          I'm sorry, but I broke my fucking leg
          on these rocks. I fucking can't move.

                    PARATROOPER 2 (V.O.)
          Now what are you gonna do? We have a
          mission to carry out! We can't have
          dead weight and I'm not carrying you
          out of the forest, we have over a
          hundred and fifty kilometers to hike.

                    PARATROOPER 1 (V.O.)
          What do I do? What do I do?

                    PARATROOPER 2 (V.O.)
          What do you do? You go to fucking
          sleep.

A gun shot is heard.

                    GRACE
               (whispering)
          He fucking shot him!

                    PARATROOPER 3 (V.O.)
          What the fuck have you done? Our
          mission is to kill the survivors on
          the plane, not our team members.

                    PARATROOPER 2 (V.O.)
          What the fuck were we supposed to do?
          Carry him out? He broke his fucking
          leg!

                    PARATROOPER 3 (V.O.)
          Ok, but you didn't have to kill him.

                    PARATROOPER 2 (V.O.)
          Sir, we have a three day hike out of
          the forest, we don't need dead weight
          bringing down our mission.

                    PARATROOPER 3 (V.O.)
          Ok, ok. Let's finish our mission and
          we'll deal with him later.

                    PARATROOPER 2 (V.O.)
          There's nothing to deal with. Take his
          body and throw it in the river.

                    PARATROOPER 3 (V.O.)
          No, we're gonna give him a proper
          burial.
                         (MORE)

Let's get on with the mission, then
we'll take care of this shit show.

The sound of footsteps in the background leaving the area.

                    GRACE
               (whispering)
He fucking shot him, he fucking
shot him. Now they're gonna kill
everyone on the plane. What do we
do? Next it will be us. We have to
do something.

                    RODGER
               (whispering)
Ok, ok, calm down. I heard exactly
what you heard. Let's get the heck
out of here. There's nothing we can
do.

                    GRACE
We should warn the people on the
plane.

                    RODGER
How are we gonna do that? That plane
is a hundred meters away, we would
never get there in time. Let's get out
of here while we're still breathing.

                    GRACE
Look, he left his pack and gun by the
door. Grab the gun and shoot those
fucking bastards.

                    RODGER
I'm not fucking playing Rambo in the
forest. There's about a dozen guys out
there, armed to the teeth. Let's slip
out of here as quickly and quietly as
possible.

                    GRACE
Give me that fucking gun, I'm gonna
kill those pieces of shit myself.

Gun shots and screaming are heard in the background. Rodger
grabs the gun.

                    RODGER
Listen to that, they're already at
the plane starting their carnage.
Let's get the fuck out of here NOW.

                    GRACE
          Isn't there anything we can do?

                    RODGER
               (angrily whispering)
          Yeah, we can get the fuck out of
          here with our lives.

                    GRACE
          Ok, ok, let's do it.

                    RODGER
          Let's skirt the river bank, grab the
          rest of the gold, and keep moving.

                    GRACE
          That's all you think about? The gold?

                    RODGER
          Enough, let's go.

Rodger and Grace grab their packs and gun and slip out the back
of the lean-to.

                                        FADE TO BLACK.

EXT. RIVER BANK - LATER

Rodger and Grace running along the river bank.

                    GRACE
          Rodger, slow down I need to catch my
          breath.

                    RODGER
          Ok, I think we have a bit of distance
          between us, but still, we must keep
          moving.

                    GRACE
          I feel horrible there was nothing we
          could do for those poor people. We
          actually knew what was gonna happen
          before it happened. I felt helpless.

                    RODGER
          There was nothing we could have done.
          Don't beat yourself up over it. If we
          got involved, we wouldn't be having
          this conversation, we'd be floating
          down that river.

                    GRACE
          I know, I know, I just wish-

A huge explosion is heard in the background. Rodger and Grace
stop and stare at each other.

                    RODGER
          Hear that?

                    GRACE
          They just blew up the fucking plane.

                    RODGER
          I would say, that's what it sounded
          like. You see, those guys weren't
          messing around with just guns, they
          have heavy artillery. Thank god I
          didn't pull a Rambo in the forest.
          Let's keep moving.

                    GRACE
          I still feel guilty that we didn't do
          something, anything. Maybe the dead
          guys had hand grenades in his pack.

                    RODGER
          I guess we'll never know. Everything
          happened so quick. I went from a dead
          sleep, you whispering in my face,
          people jumping out of airplanes,
          people getting shot, and a plane
          blowing up in a matter of ten minutes.

                    GRACE
          You're right! It all happened so
          quick. At least we're alive to tell
          the story. I told you this adventure
          is gonna make some good writing for
          you.

                    RODGER
          That's really funny! I wouldn't even
          know where to begin. How do you write
          something like this to make it, I
          don't know... make it believable?

                    GRACE
          Let's have a pact, not to mention the
          horror show to each other until we get
          back to civilization. It'll keep us
          focused.

                              RODGER
                    I'm good with that. Let's keep moving
                    before they start focusing on us.

                                        DISSOLVE TO:

EXT. FOREST - LATER

Rodger and Grace walking in the forest following the river.
HELGA, an older lady with a heavy accent, pops out from behind
the rocks. Rodger holds up the rifle.

                              RODGER
                    Holy shit, you scared the fuck out
                    of us. Who are you? What do you
                    want?

                              HELGA
                    Put that thing down, you're gonna hurt
                    yourself. Were you two on that plane?

                              GRACE
                    Yes, how did you know?

                              HELGA
                    Not many people walking around this
                    part of the world looking like you
                    two. Give me that rifle.

                              RODGER
                    No, I'm not giving up our only
                    protection.

                              HELGA
                    Take my handgun and give me that
                    rifle. If the military see you with
                    their equipment, they will kill you as
                    quick as look at you. Do you want to
                    live or die?

Helga hands Rodger a pistol and Rodger hands over the rifle.

                              RODGER
                    Who are you, where did you come from?

Helga plays with the rifle.

                              HELGA
                    I'm Helga. I came from my village
                    Prit, about forty kilometers from
                    here.
                              (MORE)

                    HELGA (CONT'D)
I've been walking all night to try
and warn any survivors about the
military ambush, but from the
sounds of it, I guess I'm a little
too late.

                    GRACE
Did you hear the explosion? They blew
up the fucking plane.

                    HELGA
Yeah I heard. Very tragic. how many
living people on the plane?

                    RODGER
Nearly all the passengers were alive
at landing except two.

                    HELGA
What happened to those two?

                    GRACE
I think heart attacks, they were both
old.

                    HELGA
So there were over two hundred people
on that plane.

                    GRACE
Yes, something like that.

                    HELGA
So tragic. Now, the million dollar
question: how did you two become the
only survivors of a plane crash and a
military ambush?

                    RODGER
Well, it's kinda strange.

                    HELGA
Try me.

                    RODGER
Well, I couldn't sit on that stuffy
plane anymore, so I told the captain I
wanted off. When Grace heard that, she
wanted to join me. By the way, my name
is Rodger, this is Grace.

                    HELGA
Pleased to meet both of you. And the
rifle? How did you end up with a
military grade weapon?

                    RODGER
Well, when the paratroopers landed,
one of the guys broke his leg, so the
other guy shot him.

                    HELGA
Yeah, because those lazy sons of
bitches would have to carry him out of
the forest, easier to kill him. So,
how did you get the gun?

                    RODGER
Well, the paratrooper that got shot
nearly landed on our lean-to. Before
he got shot he put all of his gear
against the door of our lean-to. Since
he was dead, we didn't think he would
need his gun.

                    HELGA
Very smart, but, very stupid. Does the
military know you two exist?

                    RODGER
We don't think so. The dead guy's
parachute was covering our lean-to so
no one saw us. Once we saw everything
going down the drain, we hightailed it
out of there.

                    HELGA
Well, when they remove the parachute,
see your cozy home and the soldier's
gun missing, the hunt will be on.

                    GRACE
Well, let's keep moving before we run
out of time.

                    HELGA
             (pointing with the rifle)
We need to get over to that
mountain before the soldiers creep
up on us. At that mountain, we'll
go west and they'll go east towards
Boarder Town. Follow me.

Everyone starts walking real fast.

                    GRACE
Helga, where we're heading.. is there
any internet?

                    HELGA
Where we're heading there's no
electricity.

                    RODGER
Quick question, why is some of the
river hot like a bath and some cold as
an ice cube?

                    HELGA
This is a special part of the world
you landed in. You see, we are located
directly in the Ring of Fire. Did you
ever hear of the Ring of Fire?

                    RODGER
Yeah, sure.

                    GRACE
I have, it's where the most seismic
activity in the world is. All the
underground and underwater volcanos
live there.

                    HELGA
Yeah, something like that. So, since
we're in the Ring of Fire, there are a
lot of heat thermals actively coming
out of the ground.

                    RODGER
It's like an instant jacuzzi.

                    HELGA
Without the odor of rotten eggs. When
we get to my village you may use our
heated cave pools to wash up.

                    GRACE
Helga, thank you so much for all your
help.

                    HELGA
Nothing for nothing. You have
something I really need.

                    RODGER
        (nervously)
What might that be?

                    HELGA
I need you to take my two daughters
with you when you cross the border.

                    RODGER
Take your two daughters? Where? Cross
what border?

                    HELGA
The closest border for you to be free
and clear would be Japan.

                    GRACE
That's perfect, that's where I'm from!

                    RODGER
So if my geography is correct we are
in China?

                    HELGA
Well kinda. China and Russia have been
fighting over this land for hundreds
of years. If you talk to a Chinese man
he swears you're in China, but if you
speak to a Russian, he'll say
different.

                    RODGER
        (whispers to Grace)
Hence the reason for the two
language newspapers in the mining
hut.

                    GRACE
Helga. Where do you want us to take
your daughters once we reach the
Japanese boarder?

                    HELGA
You take them to the border, they'll
cross on their own. Children never get
bothered at the border.

                    RODGER
Once they get across, then what?

                    HELGA
Take them to the nearest orphanage and
drop them off. I will give them enough
gold so they can get a great
education. The girls can't get ahead
in this part of the world, it's a
beautiful place but no room for
advancement.

                    GRACE
As a little girl I used to go to the
orphanage and play with the other
children. My father thought it would
give me a better understanding of
humanity. How old are your daughters?

                    HELGA
Ten and twelve. They are self-reliant,
very independent. It's important you
personally escort them to the
orphanage so they don't get picked up
by the traffickers.

                    GRACE
Helga, we will do the best we can.

                    RODGER
For sure. Thanks for helping us, we
will definitely return the favor.

                                        FADE OUT.

EXT. MOUNTAIN TRAIL - LATER

Rodger, Grace, and Helga walk on mountain ridge trail.

                    HELGA
          (panicking)
Step back, closer to the mountain.
Take a glance down the mountain.
Those are the soldiers walking back
from your crash site.

                    GRACE
Let's get the rifle and blow their
fucking heads off.

                    HELGA
Rodger, where did you get this one?
She's not too fucking bright.

                    RODGER
We're just pissed off the soldiers
didn't help the people, they just went
there to hurt them.

                    HELGA
Keep moving, walk while talking. Stay
away from the ridge or they might see
you.
          (pause, then)
                  (MORE)

                    HELGA (CONT'D)
So you two have a better
understanding: if the plane crash is a
wreckage, then there's not much
attention to the area. If the plane
crash is a rescue, then it will bring
a lot of attention to the area.

                    GRACE
That's stupid. If they saved the
people, they would have looked like
heroes instead of murderers.

                    HELGA
In good people's eyes, you are
absolutely correct. In bad people's
eyes, if no attention is brought to
the area there is no fighting over
land and natural resources. I don't
know if you know this, but there is a
lot of gold in this area.

                    RODGER
        (excitedly)
Really? Where exactly are we
located? What's the name of this
region?

                    HELGA
I'm not exactly sure. The mountain
range is call Adair, part of the
Himalayas. My town is called Prit.
What I do know is, a few hundred
kilometers south east of my village is
an island owned by Japan. And that's
all I know.

                    GRACE
That's exactly where we want to go.

                    HELGA
Don't get your hopes up too high.
Crossing that border is no easy task
even with your paperwork in order.

                    GRACE
Don't worry about that. Get us to the
border and I'll take it from there.

                                        FADE TO BLACK.

EXT. VILLAGE - LATER

Rodger, Grace, and Helga walk into a quiet village.

                    GRACE
So this is where you were brought up?

                    HELGA
The one and only, all my life. It
seamed like a longer walk to meet you
then it was coming back, but I'm glad
I'm home. I really didn't want to
sleep a night in the forest.

                    GRACE
Your village is lovely, very cozy.

                    HELGA
Thank you.

                    RODGER
You said earlier that you walked all
night to warn the passenger of the
military mission. How did you know
about the mission?

                    HELGA
I have a brother in the military, he
knows everything. I wish I was quicker
then the soldiers though.

                    GRACE
Me too. You would have ran into us
first and we could have made
arrangements. Maybe hide everyone in
the forest, or at least have done
something. Instead, we really felt
helpless and useless.

                    RODGER
Let's not look back, let's look
forward. Remember our pact.

They walk up to the last house in the village.

                    HELGA
So this is it, home sweet home.

                                        FADE OUT.

INT. HELGA HOUSE - LATER

Helga, Grace, and Rodger enter the house. They are greeted by
Helga's husband, ADRIAN.

                    ADRIAN
You are home quick, you made it to the
plane I see!

                    HELGA
Not exactly. This is Grace and Rodger,
they'll tell you the story at dinner.

                    RODGER
Pleased to meet you.

                    ADRIAN
Pleased to meet you as well, I'm
Adrian.

                    HELGA
Where are the two girls?

                    ADRIAN
Your sister took the girls this
morning to walk to the border.

                    HELGA
She did? What a blessing, thank god.
They're finally on their way. Did you
give them food?

                    ADRIAN
I sure did. I also gave them each two
kilos of gold. I figured that should
be plenty to get them moving.

                    HELGA
That is perfect, what a relief.
     (then, to Grace and
      Rodger)
I guess you're off the hook, my
sister took the girls to the
border.

                    GRACE
Wow, that's wonderful. I wish we could
have helped.

                    HELGA
You can, by helping me eat some
dinner.

                    ADRIAN
I'm making pasta and vegetables. I
need more time, I just started, I
thought you'd be back later.

                    HELGA
So did I, well, that's perfect. Do you
kids want to relax in the cave pools
before dinner?

                    GRACE
Yeah, sure.

                    RODGER
That sounds excellent.

                    HELGA
Go out the back door, there's towels
on your way out. It's the big metal
door on the side of the mountain. I'll
come get you in an hour or so.

                              FADE TO BLACK.

INT. CAVE POOLS - LATER

Rodger and Grace enter a sunlit cave with natural pools of hot
water.

                    RODGER
Wow, this place is beautiful. You feel
the heat coming from the ground, all
the pools are steaming.. this is
seriously the Ring of Fire.
        (singing)
I fell into a burning ring of fire,
I went down down down-

Grace looks at Rodger.

                    GRACE
The fire just got hotter, Mr. Cash.
Everybody's naked, close your eyes.

                    RODGER
        (looking around)
They are naked! You close your
eyes.

                    GRACE
Why? They're all girls, well.. most of
them, I don't really care anyway, the
human body is a piece of art.

                    RODGER
Looking around the cave, you can say
that again. We can still go in our
underwear as planned.

                    GRACE
          Don't be such a prude. When in Rome,
          let's do as the Romans.

Grace takes off her clothes and slips in the pool, and Rodger
follows her lead.

                    RODGER
               (looking around the cave
                in amazement)
          Look at that Buddha statue. If that
          was pure gold that would be
          priceless.

                    GRACE
          Did you see the gold cross? I thought
          China was Taoists or Buddhist, why the
          Catholic cross?

                    RODGER
          I think, I read somewhere that China
          recognizes five religions. Don't
          forget, Helga said depending on the
          person you speak to, it would
          determine the country of origin this
          place is located.

                    GRACE
          Yes, I do remember her saying that.
          You think the shiny stuff on the walls
          and ceiling is gold?

                    RODGER
          I didn't even notice that! You're
          right, wow. This place is a gold mine,
          literally.

                    GRACE
          Now we know why everyone wants to keep
          this place a secret.. there's gold
          everywhere.

                    RODGER
          Did you see the gold ornaments on the
          front door? I thought they were
          painted or leaf, but judging by the
          looks of this place, it's probably
          solid.

                    GRACE
          I think gold has a soothing energy on
          people. It does on me.

                    RODGER
          Gold gives me an exciting energy -
          that's why they say gold fever.

Grace slides closer to Rodger.

                    GRACE
          Come here, let me feel, are you
          excited now?

                    RODGER
          Stop, don't look now, here comes
          Helga. With all due respect, I hope
          she's not getting naked and jumping in
          with us.

                    HELGA
               (motions to the girls in
                the other pool)
          Girls get in this pool and give our
          guests massages.

                    RODGER
          Helga, that's not necessary. We're
          fine, really, the hot water is very
          soothing.

A few girls get in the pool and start massaging Grace and
Rodger. Helga leaves the cave.

                    HELGA
          I'll call you when dinners ready.

                    GRACE
          Thank you, Helga.
               (then, to Rodger)
          Well, aren't you enjoying life with
          two naked girls massaging you? One
          of the perks of being a Westerner.
          I'm kinda enjoying this myself. I
          can't get over how good a foot
          massage feels right now after that
          long walk.

                    RODGER
               (flustered)
          A two girl massage is always nice,
          especially when they're naked!

                    GRACE
          Are you getting excited? Let me feel.

                    RODGER
          I'm getting excited for the gold, not
          the girls. Well, actually, I'm getting
          excited looking at you!

                    GRACE
          Good answer. Well, I'm getting excited
          looking at you too.

                    RODGER
          Grace, this girl keeps rubbing my
          crotch.

                    GRACE
          This one is doing the same to me.

                    RODGER
          Shouldn't we say something? Tell them
          to stop?

                    GRACE
          Why? If it feels good, let it ride. I
          don't mind if you don't mind. After
          all, it's just another part of your
          body being massaged, right?

                    RODGER
          Well, I guess, I don't mind if you
          don't mind, besides, it does feel very
          nice. Like you said, when in Rome...

Grace closes her eyes.

                    GRACE
          Shh, silence please. Just relax,
          enjoy the experience. I know I am.

Rodger closes his eyes.

                                        FADE OUT.

INT. CAVE POOLS - LATER

Rodger and Grace sleep in cave pools with girls massaging them.
Helga enters the cave.

                    HELGA
          Grace, Rodger, dinner's ready.

                    GRACE
          Ok, we're coming.

                    RODGER
That was an hour? That was the
quickest hour I ever experienced.

                    GRACE
Well it goes quick when you have two
girls rubbing you into a coma.

                    RODGER
That it does, that it does. Now, I'm
very relaxed.

Rodger and Grace exit the pool, wave to the girls, and the girls
wave back.

                    GRACE
Goodnight.

                    RODGER
I feel I should tip them or something.

                    GRACE
Why don't you give them one of the
bars of gold you found by the river?

                    RODGER
What! Are crazy? That massage wasn't
that great.

                    GRACE
I thought you'd say that. I'll give
you a massage later, you'll be begging
me to take all the gold.

Rodger and Grace laugh.

                                        FADE OUT.

INT. DINING ROOM- LATER

Rodger, Grace, Helga, and Adrian sit around the dinner table.

                    RODGER
That was a great meal, I am stuffed.

                    GRACE
Me as well, thank you. You're both
great cooks.

                    HELGA
It sure is quiet without the girls
around.

                    ADRIAN
          Honey, we spoke about this. We were
          all prepared for the girls to move on
          with life. They'll be fine, they'll be
          back to visit.

                    HELGA
          I know, I'm just saying.

Grace points to the shelf.

                    GRACE
          Is that a photo of your girls?

                    HELGA
          Yes. They are my everything, Prim and
          Zane. I hope they make out well on
          their new journey.

                    RODGER
          I'm a bit tired after the big day we
          had - and the delicious meal. Helga,
          where are our sleeping quarters,
          please? I think we're probably ready
          to turn in.

                    ADRIAN
          Upstairs. I made up the girls' room.
          The restroom is to the right. Help
          yourself to anything you need.

                    GRACE
          Thank you Helga, thank you Adrian,
          you've been very gracious hosts.

                    RODGER
          Yes, thank you very much for
          everything.

Rodger and Grace grab their rucksacks and walk towards the
stairs.

                    ADRIAN
          I'll have breakfast around eight, then
          you can hit the cave pool.

                    RODGER
          Ok, we'll see you in the morning.

                    GRACE
          Thanks again, good night.

                                        FADE TO BLACK.

INT. BEDROOM - LATER

Rodger and Grace lie in bed.

                    GRACE
          I was thinking about the crash.

                    RODGER
          Remember our pact.

                    GRACE
          I know, I know, this has been a crazy
          forty-eight hours.

                    RODGER
          It really has. From the crash, to the
          gold find, to the paratroopers, to
          finding Helga, to the village of gold,
          to a relaxing exotic massage, to a
          great dinner, in a cozy bed in a
          country we know nothing about.

                    GRACE
          I was thinking, did you ever have a
          dream while you were half asleep and
          it seams so real.. but nothing really
          makes sense? But, you keep moving
          forward with the dream because you
          want to see the final outcome?

                    RODGER
          Yes, of course.

                    GRACE
          That's the way my life feels right
          now. Like, I'm living a dream or a
          nightmare. I'm not sure what it is
          yet, but I hope it has a happy ending.

                    RODGER
          Me, as well, I know exactly what you
          mean. I almost want to say it could be
          worse, but we don't know what the
          future has in store with our journey.

                    GRACE
          Well, one thing I have to say, thank
          god we don't have to travel with the
          two daughters. I really didn't want
          that responsibility.

                    RODGER
Me neither. So, what's our game plan?
What's the next leg of this crazy
journey?

                    GRACE
I think Helga said we have a 60K walk
to the border village. From there we
still have to trek another 100
kilometers or so to the Japanese
border. Why don't we see if we can
stick around for a few days before we
move on?

                    RODGER
That's a really great idea. Helga said
she would escort us to the border
village, and she probably needs a
rest, as well. Let's take it as it
comes and see what happens.

                    GRACE
That's fine, We're not in a rush to
take on this long journey. I just wish
I had internet so I could let my
family know I'm safe and alive.

                    RODGER
Yeah, me as well. At least we have
each other.

                    GRACE
So true. Come closer and hold me
tight. I need a good hug.

                    RODGER
                (hugging Grace,
                 whispering)
You said in the cave earlier that
you would give me a massage I
wouldn't forget.

                    GRACE
                (whispering back)
Do you have the gold? Are you
getting excited for the gold or me?
Let me feel.

                                        FADE OUT.

INT. DINING ROOM - MORNING

Rodger and Grace walk downstairs, greeted by Helga and Adrian.

                    ADRIAN
Did you have a well rested sleep?

                    GRACE
We sure did.

                    RODGER
Something smells really good.

                    ADRIAN
Breakfast is almost ready, hungry?

                    RODGER
Sure am.

                    HELGA
Two coffees? Cream and honey ok?

                    GRACE
Sounds great, please!

                    RODGER
Adrian, how far is the border village
from here? We're trying to figure out
our game plan.

                    ADRIAN
It's roughly sixty kilometers. But,
stay a few days, rest up. You're gonna
need the energy for the long trek.

                    RODGER
We appreciate that, we just don't want
to be a bother. You and Helga have
been very helpful, we want to respect
your privacy.

                    HELGA
Don't be silly. The girls are gone, we
love the company. Besides, I could use
a rest before that long walk to the
border village.

                    GRACE
What two countries does the border
village sit on?

                    HELGA
It's not countries, it's provinces -
the Shen and the Arn provinces.

                    RODGER
It's China, then.

                    HELGA
          Remember what I said. It depends on
          who you ask.

                    RODGER
          Yes I remember. Just checking.

                    GRACE
          So, we like the prospect of sticking
          around for a few days. What can we
          help with around the house to keep
          busy?

                    ADRIAN
          Oh, you want to help? Great. We can
          harvest honey, pick vegetables, pick
          gold -

                    RODGER
               (interrupting)
          Picking gold? That's right up my
          alley, when do we start?

                    GRACE
          Rodger, maybe we should pick the honey
          and vegetables first before we go into
          gold prospecting.

                    HELGA
          Stay a few days and we can do all the
          above.

Everyone laughs.

                    ADRIAN
          Well, let's start the day with
          breakfast. Grab some plates.

                                        FADE OUT.

EXT. FRONT OF HOUSE - MORNING - FEW DAYS LATER

Adrian stands in the front door frame, saying goodbye to Helga,
Rodger, and Grace. Adrian kisses Helga.

                    ADRIAN
          Did you grab the gold set for
          market?

                    HELGA
          Yes, we only had twelve rings, two
          armbands-

                    RODGER
               (interrupting)
          You're selling rings? How much do
          you want for them?

                    ADRIAN
          We get three dollars per ring, five
          dollars per armband-

                    HELGA
               (interrupting)
          And one cross necklace which is
          seven dollars.

                    RODGER
          Why don't I buy all of them from you
          so you don't have to trouble yourself
          at market?

                    ADRIAN
          Really? That would be great. Then I
          can speak to the goldsmith this
          afternoon about molding the rest of
          the nuggets we've harvested.

Helga opens her crude leather purse and counts the gold pieces.
Rodger takes money out of his wallet and pays Adrian.

                    ADRIAN (CONT'D)
          Thank you, Rodger. This really helps
          us to expedite manufacturing more
          gold, as well as buying more
          groceries.

                    RODGER
          The pleasure's mine.

Grace stares at Rodger.

                    GRACE
          You really are obsessed with gold
          aren't you?

                    RODGER
          Just a little hobby you might say.
          Shall we get a move on while the sun
          is starting to shine?

                    GRACE
               (sarcastically)
          I guess that would be a great idea,
          Mr. Rodger Goldman!

Rodger gets on one knee, holds out a ring.

                    RODGER
          Grace, will you marry me?

                    GRACE
               (surprised)
          What? What did you say?

                    RODGER
          Will you marry me?

                    GRACE
          I don't even know you. We really just
          met, you're embarrassing me.

                    RODGER
          I don't care, I want to live for you
          and I can't live without you. I want
          your world to be my world.

                    GRACE
               (through tears)
          I can't believe this.
               (pause)
          Of course I will marry you. I never
          felt more comfortable with another
          partner before in my life, until I
          met you. Even if our relationship
          is only a few days old.

Grace jumps on Rodger, knocking him to the ground while kissing
him.

                    HELGA
          This is absolutely wonderful news, why
          don't you two get married in the cave
          pools? W'll invite the whole town. The
          priest would be more than happy to get
          you two married for a few gold pieces.

                    RODGER
          I was thinking the gold pieces would
          buy us a nice simple wedding in Border
          Village, but I guess we can do it
          here. It's up to you, Grace.

                    GRACE
          You amaze me every second I know you.

Grace turns to Helga.

                    GRACE (CONT'D)
We don't want a big ceremony,
something small, to exchange vows,
we don't want the word to get out
to the wrong people. This would be
a lovely place for a ceremony.

                    HELGA
Whatever you like.. big, small, as you
wish. I have my old wedding veil you
can use.

                    ADRIAN
     (to Helga)
Can we break out the honey mead?
I'll do the cooking!

                    HELGA
He's been wanting to break out that
honey mead for a long time. I guess
you're staying another night or two.

                    ADRIAN
Can I get out the honey mead now for a
pre-toast?

                    HELGA
It's morning!
     (pause)
But yes, my love. Also, take out some
cheese and biscuits for the pre-toast.
In the meantime, while you three are
toasting, I'll run over to the church
and see when the priest is available.

                    ADRIAN
I guess you're staying another day-

                    HELGA
Only if the priest is available today!
It might not be till tomorrow.

                    ADRIAN
Then you stay another two days, it
doesn't matter.

                    RODGER
We would love to stay as long as you
will have us. This is a great place to
exchange wedding vows and relax.

                    GRACE
Yes, so romantic and memorable, a
story book wedding.

                         RODGER
              A destination wedding.

                         ADRIAN
              A honey-mead-drinking wedding.

Everyone laughs.

                                        FADE OUT.

EXT. FOREST - MORNING - THE NEXT DAY

Rodger, Grace, and Helga walk through the forest towards Border
Village.

                         GRACE
                    (to Helga)
              Helga, thanks again for your and
              Adrian's generous hospitality. Our
              wedding memories will be a part of
              our lives forever.

                         RODGER
              Yeah, thanks so much. Actually, you
              should be a wedding planner. You
              pulled that off in less then twenty-
              four hours. The planners in New York
              would be jealous.

                         HELGA
              Everything was last minute, but I did
              the best with what I was given.

                         RODGER
              You and Adrian did an awesome job.
              Adrian is very funny when he starts
              drinking that mead.

                         HELGA
              Yeah, it's his one little pleasure so
              I let him behave as he will.

                                        FADE TO:

EXT. FOREST - LATER

Rodger, Grace and Helga walking through the forest towards the
Border Village.

                    GRACE
Helga, with the Border Village being
sixty kilometers away through the
forest, don't you ever get scared of
wild animals?

                    HELGA
No, not a chance, more like the
animals are afraid of me. Afraid I
might put them in a pot or on a grill.

                    RODGER
What about rabid animals! Or, even
bears.

                    HELGA
Rabid animals are killed instinctively
by the other animals, in fear of
spreading the deadly disease.

                    RODGER
Interesting. And bears?

                    HELGA
Bears are very territorial. The bears
in this territory have known me since
I was a little girl. I leave them
alone, they leave me alone.

                    GRACE
Well, that's a good thing.

                    HELGA
For the bears! Cause they know I would
put them in a pot.

                    RODGER
I noticed we're just randomly walking
through the forest. I was expecting
some kind of trail to follow. Do you
ever get lost? After all, sixty
kilometers is a long distance to
navigate through a dense forest
without a compass or a trail marker.

                    HELGA
We don't walk the same footprints
twice in fear of other people
stumbling on our village. I never get
lost. This is my migration path: my
ancestors have been traveling this way
for thousands of years.

                    GRACE
Why don't you use a compass?

                    HELGA
Because I don't have one and I don't
need one. Besides, compasses don't
work in this region.

                    RODGER
Compasses don't work in this region?
Why's that?

                    HELGA
Like I said we are in the Ring of
Fire. With all the precious metals in
these mountains, especially gold and
the molten lava below our feet, this
place turns into a magnet disorienter.

                    GRACE
Disorienter? I'm confused by that
word.

                    HELGA
It's not even a word, I think, but
it's the best way I can describe it.
You see, the compasses go crazy when
you get to the second mountain from
the Border Village. The hikers,
explorers and scientists get so turned
around backwards with their compasses
they end up back in Border Village
every time.

                    RODGER
They never reach your village?

                    HELGA
Never! Unless someone brings them
there. Besides, the forest is so dark
and scary to the foreign world,
they're afraid to venture. We have
lookouts twenty-four-seven for the
brave traveler who wants to wander
into our uncharted territory.

                    RODGER
What happens to the brave traveler
that breaches your security lookout?
How do they get deterred from
venturing onward, towards your
village?

                    HELGA
When the lookouts find a trespasser,
one notifies the village to bring out
more villagers, while the other heads
towards the trespasser.

                    GRACE
What does the one do when they reach
the trespasser?

                    HELGA
The lookout scares them into thinking
there's wild animals or the military
chasing them, and they run towards the
Border Village. It throws even the
most experienced tracker into a frenzy
for safety.

                    GRACE
Wow, that's amazing.

                    RODGER
What would have happened if the entire
plane full of people started walking
into the territory of your village?
What would your lookout have done
then?

                    HELGA
First of all that would have never
happened. As you saw, the military
takes immediate action on trespassers
in the outlying areas. Secondly, if it
did happen, I would have been on it
and like a good shepherd I would have
steered the sheep around our village
in the direction of the Border
Village.

                    RODGER
Why did you accept us into your
village? After all, we are complete
strangers.

                    HELGA
When I saw you with that military
grade weapon and that you two beat the
odds of death twice, I figured there
must be some good in those soles of
yours.

                    GRACE
Thank you for putting faith in us.

                    HELGA
          Besides, I figured if I saved your
          asses you would owe me one. So I was
          gonna have you take my girls to Japan
          to start their new lives. You got
          lucky on that one, my sister finally
          stepped up to the plate to make the
          journey.

                    RODGER
          Why doesn't the military occupy your
          village? It appears they are always on
          a mission and there's enough precious
          metal to make people greedy -
          especially military and governments.

                    HELGA
          Oh, they tried hundreds of times, but
          never with success. One time they
          dropped paratroopers on us and
          surrounded the mountains for twenty
          kilometers.

                    GRACE
          What did the villagers do?

                    HELGA
          Well, for the paratroopers, we were
          picking them off in the sky like
          target practice, clay pigeons. The
          ground troops we were picking off one
          by one. It took us twelve hours to
          slaughter 186 soldiers, not including
          the paratroopers.

                    RODGER
          How many casualties did your side
          endure?

Helga starts to cry.

                    HELGA
          One hero.. he was a little boy, his
          name was River-

Grace hugs Helga.

                    GRACE
          I'm so sorry to hear. Was it a
          stray bullet?

                    HELGA
          No. The soldiers executed him.

                    GRACE
Oh my god, that's horrible.

                    HELGA
You see, every time we killed their
soldier, River would scurry down the
mountain, grab the dead soldier's
weapon, and drag it back to our people
so we had more firepower. We killed
almost all the soldiers with their own
weapons.

                    RODGER
Wow, that is a real hero. How old was
the boy?

                    HELGA
He was six-

                    RODGER
     (interrupting)
Six? He was six?

                    HELGA
Yeah, a small little lad, but a
fearless worrier. We erected a statue
of River at the edge of town
overlooking the mountain.

                    RODGER
I did see that statue, but I couldn't
read the plaque.

                    HELGA
The inscription is in his native
tongue.

                    RODGER
Was that statue gold plated? It seemed
solid.

                    HELGA
Our townspeople would never disrespect
a warrior like River. That is 100%
solid gold. All the townsfolk chipped
in to create the monument. That statue
in the Western world would be
priceless - it weighs over nine
hundred kilo.

Rodger looks up to the sky.

                         RODGER
          That's almost a ton, that would be
          worth about...
                    (pause)
          fifty million dollars in the
          Western world.

                         HELGA
          Thank you for enlightening me on
          the price of the statue. It makes
          me feel happy that the warrior
          River has so much worth and value
          in his honor. I miss River. Does
          anyone want any berries or
          mushrooms to nibble on?

                                        FADE TO:

EXT. FOREST - LATER

Rodger, Grace, and Helga walk through the forest towards Border
Village. They stumble upon a little boy named SKY.

                         GRACE
          I hate to sound like a little kid,
          but.. are we there yet?

                         HELGA
          I told you. Sunrise to sunset, that's
          how long the trek is. Judging by where
          the sun is hitting, we have another
          few hours to go.

                         GRACE
          Can we take a rest, then? I'm tired.

                         HELGA
          No, we'll take a rest in a bit, but we
          must keep moving or we will be
          sleeping in the forest tonight, I
          really don't see that in my stars.

                         GRACE
                    (whispering to Rodger)
          She's a tough cookie, I used to
          have a gym teacher like her.

                         HELGA
          I heard that.

Rodger stares at Grace.

                         GRACE
          Sorry, I didn't mean anything by it,
          my gym teacher was actually a nice-

Helga stops quickly.

                         HELGA
                    (whispering)
          Quiet, stay still, get low.
          Someone's out there.

                         RODGER
                    (whispering to Grace)
          I didn't hear anything. Let's hope
          it's an animal.

                         GRACE
                    (whispering)
          Helga. Look over there, it's a
          deer. Wait - with a little boy.

                         HELGA
                    (relieved)
          Oh yeah I see them, that's Sky.

                         RODGER
          You know him?

Helga, Rodger, and Grace walk towards Sky.

                         HELGA
          Sky, what are you doing?

Sky drops his leather bag, gives two thumbs up, and runs to
hug Helga.

                         SKY
          Hello Aunty I'm happy to see you.

                         GRACE
          This is your nephew?

                         HELGA
          No, he just calls me Aunty because he
          lives near my Aunt in Border Village.
          So, I call my aunt Aunty, and he calls
          me Aunty.

                         GRACE
                    (to Sky)
          Were you petting that wild deer?

                    SKY
          Yeah. He's my new friend, he was
          keeping me company.

                    RODGER
          That's amazing.

                    HELGA
          Animals in this area love children.
               (then, to Sky)
          Where are your parents?

Sky stares at Rodger.

                    SKY
          They didn't make it.

                    HELGA
               (yelling)
          What do you mean they didn't make
          it! Where are they?

                    SKY
          They didn't make it. They fell down
          the ravine at the Great Pines and
          died.

                    HELGA
          They're lying down at the Great Pines,
          now?

Sky cries and hugs Helga.

                    SKY
          Yes Aunty, there was nothing I
          could do. It's not my fault.

                    HELGA
          It's ok, don't cry. How long ago did
          this happen?

                    SKY
          Well, I slept in the forest for I
          think five nights. I didn't know how
          to go home to get help.

                    HELGA
          Well, you're doing good, you're only a
          mountain away.

                    RODGER
          Let's go and see. Maybe they're still
          alive.

                    HELGA
No, there's no time. Great Pines is
fifteen kilometers west of here, we'll
never make it there and back before
nightfall. I'll send out the dog bikes
tomorrow early. They'll get there in
no time.

                    RODGER
Dog bikes? What are dog bikes?

                    HELGA
You heard of dog sleds? Or sled dogs?
Well, when there's no snow, the dogs
pull motor-less motorcycles. We call
them dog bikes.

                    RODGER
Well, that's a new one for me.

                    HELGA
It's pretty impressive watching the
dogs and the musher navigate through
the forest. The dogs know exactly the
width between the trees to navigate
for the musher.

                    SKY
My friend made a dog bike, he hooked
up his dog to his bicycle, it was a
lot of fun, but, he only had one dog
not three.

                    RODGER
        (to Helga)
Is there anything we can do right
now?

                    HELGA
What can we do? We have to keep
walking toward the border village and
deal with everything in the morning.

                    GRACE
        (to Helga)
I can't believe this little boy has
been walking in the forest for
almost a week! And he lost his
parents?

                    HELGA
That's what he says.

Rodger holds his hand to Sky.

                    RODGER
          By the way, my name is Rodger, and
          this is my wife, Grace.

Sky gives two thumbs up.

                    SKY
          Pleased to meet you, Rodger. Where
          do you come from?

                    RODGER
          Grace and I live in New York.

                    SKY
          Will you take me to New York? Let's go
          now. I've never been there.

                    RODGER
               (laughs)
          I'm afraid that's not possible Sky.
          We are traveling towards Japan
          right now.

Sky gives two thumbs up.

                    SKY
          I'll go with you, I like to hike.

                    GRACE
          Sky, you said you have been traveling
          in the forest for almost a week. What
          were you eating?

Sky picks up his leather bag and opens it.

                    SKY
          I have mushrooms, berries, onions,
          fiddle heads, ginger, truffles -

                    GRACE
          How do you know the mushrooms aren't
          poisonous?

                    HELGA
               (interrupting)
          He knows what to eat in this
          forest. He's been picking food for
          as long as he can remember. His
          parents are, or were, called the
          foragers. Why pay for food when
          it's free in the forest?

                    RODGER
               (to Grace)
          I thought I was a survivalist, but
          this kid has me beat hands down.

                    HELGA
          Ok folks, enough with the chitter
          chatter we're losing daylight! Let's
          keep moving. Talk while you walk, walk
          while you talk.

Sky holds out his hand.

                    SKY
          Rodger, can you hold my hand while
          we walk? I've never met a Western
          boy before.

                    RODGER
          Sure, Sky. I'll be like your big
          brother, Brother Rodger.

                    SKY
          I like that, Brother Rodger. When are
          we going to New York, Brother Rodger?

                    GRACE
          Try to get out of this one, Brother
          Rodger.

                    RODGER
          Let's talk about New York another
          time.

                    SKY
          Ok, we can talk about it on the way to
          Japan.

                    GRACE
          You have a lot of explaining to do
          Brother Rodger.

                                        FADE OUT.

EXT. MOUNTAIN TRAIL - LATER

Rodger, Grace, Helga, and Sky walk on the mountain trail towards
the Border Village.

                    HELGA
          Look, there's Border Village.

                    RODGER
I am supper tired, I can't believe I
actually walked sixty kilometers.
That's almost forty miles, that's
about three miles an hour.

                    HELGA
It was not actually sixty kilometers,
we just say that to throw everyone
off.

                    SKY
Finally home, but it's not gonna be
the same without mommy and daddy.

                    GRACE
        (crying)
It will be alright, Sky. The
motorcycle dogs are gonna get your
parents tomorrow and bring them
home.

                    HELGA
        (whispering to Grace)
Don't promise him that. They've
been in the forest for over a week.
Nothing good ever happens to hurt
people in this forest for a week.
Besides, when we hit Border
Village, he probably won't have a
home either.

                    GRACE
        (angry and upset)
What do you mean, he won't have a
home! Why not?

                    HELGA
Border Village is government land,
everyone who lives there are
squatters. When someone leaves their
dwelling for over twenty-four hours,
the villagers take their belongings
and new squatters move in.

                    GRACE
That's horrible. Well, we're gonna go
and kick the new squatters out. The
little boy might have lost his
parents, but he needs a home to live.

                    HELGA
It's the way of the land. Don't get
involved or the villagers will take
everything you got including those
bars of gold Rodger has in his
rucksack.

                    RODGER
How did you know I have bars of gold?

                    HELGA
I was wondering why you were
struggling with the weight of your
pack, so when you went into the cave
pools I took a peek.

                    RODGER
Just for the record, Grace and I were
gonna give you a bar at Border Village
for helping us out.

                    HELGA
That's ok, you're gonna need it to
barter your way across the border. How
many bars do you have anyway? I just
took a peek, I didn't do a count.

                    RODGER
Eight bars in total.

                    HELGA
Good, because you'll probably be
giving three away. Unless I can get
someone to cut them in half which
would give you more bargaining power
and less loss. Where did you acquire
them?

                    RODGER
        (hesitating)
Well, where the plane crashed, I
was wandering down the river and
came across an old fishing hut-

                    HELGA
        (interrupting)
Yeah, that was Yolanda and Peel's
shed. They've been dead for thirty
years. That place has been
ransacked a hundred times.

                    RODGER
I don't know about that, there were
gold molds, a cooker and a few other
things as well as these bars under
some newspapers. The papers were in
Chinese and Russian.

                    HELGA
Yeah, she was Russian and he was
Chinese. Well it looks like you got a
pretty good score from those two
bastards up the river. They were mean
as a rattlesnake, no one liked them.

                    GRACE
How did they die?

                    HELGA
Rumor has it they kept poisonous
snakes in their hut to keep thieves
away. One day they both got bit. The
end.

                    RODGER
I hate snakes, I'm glad I found that
out now and not before I went in the
hut.

                    GRACE
That's a shame.

                    HELGA
Not for everybody else.

                    GRACE
    (whispering to Helga)
So, where is Sky going to live if
he doesn't have a home?

                    HELGA
Well, tonight we'll all stay at my
Aunty's house, and then we'll figure
out future living situations in the
morning.

                    SKY
Anybody hungry? I have some tasty
mushrooms and berries.

                                        FADE OUT.

EXT. BORDER VILLAGE - LATER

Helga, Rodger, Grace, and Sky walking through Border Village
toward AUNTY VERA's house. A few of the VILLAGERS stare at them
like they have the plague. Sky gives two thumbs up.

                    SKY
          Hello Mrs. Linz, how's your day?

MRS. LINZ stands in a nearby doorway.

                    VILLAGER 1
          Go back to the forest where you
          belong forager boy!

Sky turns to a horrified Grace.

                    SKY
          She must be having a bad day.

                    RODGER
          Helga, why do I get the feeling we're
          not wanted here?

                    HELGA
          Cause you're probably not.

                    GRACE
          Where's Sky's house?

                    HELGA
          The red one with the people standing
          in the doorway. Don't say anything, or
          even look at them, just keep walking.
          Sky, be a big boy and keep your mouth
          shut. I'll figure everything out.

                    SKY
          Ok Aunty, I'm a big boy.

They arrive at Vera's house and knock on the door.

                    HELGA
          Aunty Vera, open up, it's me!

Vera opens the door, in shock.

                    VERA
          Helga how the heck are you? Where
          the heck did you get these
          Westerners? Hurry up get in the
          house.

                                        DISSOLVE TO:

INT. LIVING ROOM - LATER

Helga, Rodger, Grace, and Sky walk into Vera's one-bedroom home.

                    VERA
          (to Helga)
     Where did they come from? Are they
     from the plane crash?

                    RODGER
     Yes, hi my name is Rodger. This is my
     wife Grace.

                    VERA
     Not so pleased to meet you two. Where
     are you from?

                    RODGER
          (confused)
     We're both from New York.

Sky gives two thumbs up.

                    SKY
     Hello, Aunty Vera.

                    VERA
     Sky! What did I tell you about that!?
     I'm not your Aunty, I'm Vera, just
     call me Vera. Where're your parents?

                    SKY
     Oh yeah, I forgot, I'll remember next
     time.

                    VERA
          (to Helga)
     What the heck's going on here?
     Where's the boy's parents? The
     squatters ransacked their house and
     moved in, I could only hold them
     back for so long.

                    HELGA
     I can explain everything, put on a pot
     of tea.

                    VERA
     Good timing, I just started a fire.

                    HELGA
     Sky, go to Kail's house and tell him
     to get together three dog bikes for
     tomorrow morning. It's an emergency.

Sky gives two thumbs up and heads towards the front door.

                    SKY
          Will do Helga. See I didn't forget,
          I didn't say Aunty.

                    HELGA
          You're a good boy Sky, now get a move
          on.

                    RODGER
          I'll go with him.

                    VERA
               (screaming at Rodger)
          NO! Stay put, don't go anywhere.
          You're from the plane crash? The
          military have been snooping around
          looking for you. I don't know what
          you did, but they want you bad.

                    HELGA
          They stole their gun.

                    VERA
          Wow, that was fucking smart. Where's
          Sky's parents? And why do you need
          Kail and his dog bikes?

                    HELGA
          We ran into Sky roaming the forest. He
          said his parents fell down the ravine
          at Great Pines. We're assuming they're
          dead, but we won't know until we get
          Kail and his dog bikes out there.

                    VERA
          And these two from the plane crash,
          how did you come across them?

                    HELGA
          I bumped into them in the forest. I
          took their military gun away from
          them.

                    VERA
          Where's the gun now?

                    HELGA
          Under my house.

Vera pours tea.

                    VERA
          Good, no evidence. We need to get
          rid of these two. Fast.

                    GRACE
          We can leave right now if you'd like.

                    VERA
          You're not going anywhere. You get
          caught walking out of this house it's
          death for all of us. Sit down, let us
          think. The good thing is the military
          thinks it's only one person, she can
          mix in with the rest of us. Well,
          almost.

                    HELGA
          Let's change their Western clothes to
          something simple.

                    VERA
          He's a little tall, he needs to slouch
          down. He can wear the traditional
          cloak to fit in.

                    HELGA
          That's a good idea, they can both wear
          one. They also have those fancy
          rucksacks, we need to change them to
          leather-

                    VERA
               (interrupting)
          We could put a gunnysack over their
          rucksack. I have a few in the
          basement, no one would be the
          wiser.

                    HELGA
          Better idea.

Vera turns to Rodger and Grace.

                    VERA
          The only thing going in your favor
          is that the whole village hates the
          military, so... no one's gonna turn
          you in.

The front door opens up and Sky walks in. He gives two thumbs
up.

                    SKY
          I told Kail to get three dog bikes
          ready for tomorrow, he said they'll
          be here at seven.

                    HELGA
          You're a good boy, Sky.

                    GRACE
          Why does he always do the thumbs up?

                    HELGA
          That's the first thing he learned when
          he was young. He was told to do that
          when he's happy.

                    RODGER
          I guess he's always happy.

                    GRACE
          Vera, is there anywhere to get the
          internet? We want to let our families
          back home know we're ok.

                    VERA
          That's pretty presumptuous of you,
          wanting to tell people you're ok when
          you have half the military hunting
          your ass. The answer is: no internet,
          no electricity, and no promises.

                    HELGA
          We're all pretty tired from the long
          hike. What are the sleeping
          arrangements?

                    VERA
          Well, you can sleep on the couch, Sky
          can sleep with me, and the two
          fugitives can sleep in the basement.

                    RODGER
          Thanks Vera, you're a very gracious
          host.

                    GRACE
          Yes, thank you Vera and thanks again,
          Helga.

Sky hands Vera his leather bag.

                    SKY
          Vera, I'm going to bed, I'm so
          tired.
                    (MORE)

                        SKY (CONT'D)
          Here is some food for breakfast.
          Wake me up when the dog bikes get
          here.

                        VERA
          Sky, go in the hot pool in the
          backyard and wash up. You've been
          hiking all week.

                        SKY
          Ok, but I have no clean clothes to
          wear!

                        VERA
          Go on my dresser and grab a clean
          shirt and a towel. I'll wash your
          clothes later, they'll be dry by
          morning.

Sky leaves room, comes back moments later. He holds up sexy
lingerie.

                        SKY
          You want me to wear this one? It
          has all holes in it!

Everyone starts laughing.

                                        FADE TO BLACK.

EXT. FRONT OF HOUSE - NEXT DAY - MORNING

Helga and Vera standing in front of the house. KAIL, an Asian-
looking, middle-aged man, and two MUSHERS pull up with their dog
bikes.

                        HELGA
          Good morning Kail, how you been?

                        KAIL
          Good morning Helga, long time no see!
          How's Adrian?

                        HELGA
          Adrian's doing great, I'll let him
          know you asked about him.

                        VERA
          Hey Kail, thanks for stopping by.

                    KAIL
              (flirty)
          Hey Vera, you're looking as pretty
          as ever.

                    HELGA
          Knock it off Kail, that's my Aunty.

Everyone starts laughing.

                    KAIL
          Ok, sorry.

                    HELGA
          Kail, you need to take your guys over
          to the ravine at Great Pines and
          retrieve Sky's parents, they fell to
          the bottom.

                    KAIL
          Do they need medical treatment? Are
          they alive?

                    HELGA
          Not sure what you're up against, but
          they've been in the ravine five or six
          days. I don't think it's gonna be a
          good outcome.

                    KAIL
          Ok, ok, I'll take care of it. I'll
          drag two sleds with us and some
          medical equipment, just in case. Is it
          the front side of the ravine or the
          back side?

                    HELGA
          I'm not sure, but from what Sky told
          me, they were mushroom picking, so I'm
          guessing the front side.

                    KAIL
          Either way, we'll take care of it. Sky
          said he was going with us.

                    VERA
          No, Sky's not going with you. He'll be
          traumatized. Besides, he's still
          sleeping.

                    KAIL
          No problem, we'll take care of it.

                    VERA
          (whispering)
     Kail, I need to ask you of a
     personal favor.

                    KAIL
     Sure, Vera, what is it?

                    VERA
     You know the military has been
     snooping around for a few days?

                    KAIL
     Yeah, they we're looking for the plane
     crash survivor.

                    VERA
     Yeah, well the reason they're looking
     for the survivors is because they
     stole their weapon.

                    KAIL
     They? You mean there's more than one?

                    HELGA
     Yeah, there's two, a male and a
     female. They're in Vera's basement.

                    KAIL
     Wow, how exciting!

                    VERA
     We were thinking, if you can get these
     two on the dog bikes, and get them
     south of Border Village, they can walk
     towards the Japanese border and get
     off the military's radar.

                    KAIL
     Japan, I loved Japan. But, do you know
     how far that is?

                    VERA
     Yeah, that's not our problem. Just get
     them far enough away from Border
     Village-

                    HELGA
          (interrupting)
     For compensation, we would give you
     the military weapon that these two
     idiots stole.

                    KAIL
Sounds sweet.

                    HELGA
There's a little catch though. You
would have to pick up the weapon at my
house.

                    KAIL
Can I stay the night and drink mead
with Adrian?

                    HELGA
Of course you can, you never have to
ask. Adrian would love to get drunk
with you.

                    KAIL
Can I make moves on your Aunty?

                    HELGA
That's up to her, you have to charm
her on your own.
     (whispering)
To tell you the truth, I heard
she's easy.

                    VERA
Helga!

                    KAIL
Sounds like a lot of fun, count me in.
Let us get moving. First we pick up
Sky's parents, then we'll work out the
logistics of people smuggling.
     (to the Mushers)
Let's go guys, we got a big job
ahead of us. Let's go back to the
barn, get some sleds, and let's not
forget the tarps and rope.

Kail and the Mushers whistle and yell at the dogs.

                    KAIL (CONT'D)
Yeah. Come on.

                    VERA
     (shy, blushing)
Thanks Kail, be safe.

                    HELGA
Thanks, guys.

                                        FADE OUT.

INT. LIVING ROOM - LATER

Rodger and Grace watch as Vera and Helga walk towards the door.
Rodger stares out the window, talking to Grace. Sky wakes up
from the chatter.

                    RODGER
          So, those are the dog bikes? Very
          cool, very cool. I want to ride one
          of those.

Vera and Helga walk through the door.

                    GRACE
          That looks dangerous. If you crash and
          the dogs don't notice, they'll keep
          dragging you down the trail.

                    VERA
               (defensively)
          Kail is a professional, he never
          crashes.

                    RODGER
               (startled)
          I believe that, looks like he knows
          exactly what he's doing.

                    VERA
               (bragging)
          You're damn straight. He's won the
          dog bike competition three years in
          a row, all the girls go crazy for
          him -

                    HELGA
               (interrupting)
          No they don't, only Vera goes crazy
          for him. Who wants breakfast?

                    GRACE
          Coffee would be great.

                    RODGER
          Yes, coffee sounds great.

                    HELGA
          Sorry, Vera only drinks tea.

                    GRACE
          Oh, that's fine, whatever's easy.

73.

                    HELGA
          I'll put on the water and make eggs.
          Where's Sky?

                    GRACE
          He's still sleeping, I'll give you a
          hand with breakfast.

Vera rummages

                    VERA
          Rummaging through Sky's leather bag.

Helga, Sky has, mushrooms, wild onions and ginger for the
skillet. Ohh look, some wild mint, this sounds yummy.

                    RODGER
          How long will it take for the dog
          bikes to get back to town?

                    HELGA
          It's hard to say, they'll be back.
          Maybe by three or four.

                    RODGER
          I can give a hand with the burial.

                    VERA
          You stay in the house and keep away
          from those windows.

                    RODGER
          No problem, Vera. I'll help Helga and
          Grace with breakfast.

Sky walks into the living room.

                    VERA
          There's my precious package, you
          really slept hard.

                    SKY
          Did Kail come yet?

                    VERA
          He left, he was in a hurry.

                    SKY
          You should have woke me, I wanted to
          help Kail and ride on the dog bikes.

                         VERA
          They were on a mission. Too many
          people would slow the mission, the
          mission had to be quick.

                         SKY
          Ok, I understand. Do you want me to go
          in the yard and get some eggs?

                         VERA
          Helga, how many eggs do you have?

                         HELGA
          We can use a few more.

                         VERA
                    (lovingly, motherly.)
          Sky, that would be great if you can
          get your Aunty some eggs.

                         SKY
          Ok, but you told me not to call you
          Aunty!

                         VERA
          I changed my mind while you were
          sleeping. You can call me Aunty
          anytime you want.

                         SKY
          Ok Aunty, I like that much better than
          Vera. I'll be right back with some
          eggs.

Sky gives two thumbs up and gives Vera a big hug.

                                        FADE OUT.

INT. LIVING ROOM - LATER

Helga, Vera, and Grace have tea. Rodger looks at a magazine with
Sky. Kail enters the living room, knocking on the door and
whistling.

                         KAIL
          Vera.

                         HELGA
          I guess Kail's back.

Vera jumps to the door, excited.

                    VERA
          I'll get it.

Vera fixes her hair and dress, then opens the door.

                    VERA (CONT'D)
          Hey Kail, come in, I'll put some
          tea on for you.

                    KAIL
          Thank you, Vera. These are your
          fugitive guests? Hello, my name is
          Kail.

Rodger puts out his hand.

                    RODGER
          Pleased to meet you Kail, my name
          is Rodger, and this is my wife
          Grace. We heard a lot of good
          things about you and your dog
          bikes.

Grace holds out her hand.

                    GRACE
          Yes, Vera speaks very highly of
          you.

                    KAIL
          Pleased to meet both of you. Don't
          listen to those rumors about me,
          they're only rumors.
               (to Grace)
          You look familiar. Did anyone ever
          tell you, you look like the
          emperor's daughter? Of, Japan, of
          course.

                    GRACE
          Yes, I've heard that a few times, but
          unfortunately I don't have such luck.
          I'm an artist.

Kail stares, confused at Grace.

                    KAIL
          Well, it's still a pleasure.

                    HELGA
          How did you make out Kail?

Kail looks at Sky.

                    KAIL
          Umm, well.

                    VERA
          Sky! Go in the backyard and fetch some
          more eggs for dinner. Then go to the
          edge of the forest and find something
          to put in the eggs.

                    SKY
          Ok Aunty! See? I remembered not to
          call you Vera.

Sky gives two thumbs up.

                    SKY (CONT'D)
          Ohh wait, Aunty there's nothing at
          the edge of the forest, we picked
          that last week.

                    VERA
          Well, go in a kilometer. You should
          find something further out. Don't get
          lost.

                    SKY
          I don't get lost in one kilometer,
          it's twenty kilometers that confuses
          me.

                    VERA
          Ok, Sky, get a move on it.

                    SKY
          Where's my leather bag?

                    HELGA
          By the fire-

                    SKY
               (interrupting)
          Ohh, I see it. Be back in a bit.
          Kail, when I come back, can you
          take me for a ride on your dog
          bike?

                    KAIL
          Sure Sky, but hurry back with food.
          We're losing daylight and I'm getting
          hungry.

Sky exits through the back door and calls over his shoulder.

                    SKY
Sure thing.

                    HELGA
Kail, what's the good word? Talk to
me.

                    KAIL
Well, what Sky said was true, they
fell down the ravine. The bodies were
pretty decomposed and chewed up from
the animals. We fetched everything,
even their foraging bags.

                    VERA
So now what?

                    KAIL
Well, I didn't think we would have a
proper service being that Sky has no
money, so my guys are at the burial
grounds digging graves as we-

                    RODGER
          (interrupts, excited)
We have gold, we'll pay for the
service. We would be more then
happy to pay for all the services.

                    KAIL
It's a little late-

                    VERA
          (interrupting)
No, we don't want Sky to remember
more then he has to. We don't want
any elaborate service.

                    HELGA
Vera's right.

                    KAIL
That's very nice of you, Rodger. If
you can pay my two helpers for
retrieving the bodies and digging the
graves that would be a big help. It
would also help feed the dogs, which
is always a big deal.

                    RODGER
Sure thing-

                    HELGA
          (interrupting)
     Wait, Kail, I have a great idea.
     You still have that metal cutter?

                    KAIL
     Yeah, I sure do.

                    HELGA
     Rodger and Grace have a few gold bars
     that needs to be downsized into
     smaller pieces. Like they said, they
     can pay your mushers, as well as give
     you a little piece for your cutting
     troubles. They would also be able to
     pay you for smuggling them out of the
     area. Ain't that right fugitives?

                    RODGER
     Absolutely, we'll take care of you and
     your team for all your troubles.

                    KAIL
     I'm human smuggling and gold
     smuggling? This sounds exciting, count
     me in.

                    HELGA
     Can you bring your cutter here? We
     don't want these two roaming the town
     while the military is still doing
     their search.

                    KAIL
     Yeah, no problem. We can work here at
     the kitchen table, if that's ok with
     you, Vera?

                    VERA
          (winking)
     Kail, anything for you.

                    KAIL
     Great, tomorrow. It's a date. How many
     bars are we looking at?

                    RODGER
     We have eight bars in total, we would
     love it if you could cut all of them
     into quarters.

                    KAIL
     No problem at all. I'll bring an extra
     blade, just in case.

                    RODGER
Thanks Kail, we appreciate it. How
long have you been dog biking? I was
looking out the window, you handle
that thing really well.

                    KAIL
My grandfather invented it, it's been
a family tradition for over seventy
years. I won the dog bike competition
three years in a row. You should try
it sometime.

                    RODGER
I would love to, but I'm not gonna be
in town for long. As you know, we have
a few enemies looking for us.

                    KAIL
No problem, another time.

                    RODGER
How do you break and steer the dog
bike?

                    KAIL
The brakes are the same as on a
motorcycle: a disc brake with cable..
when I hit the brakes, the dogs feel
the resistance and slow down.. the
more resistance, the slower they get.

                    RODGER
And steering?

                    KAIL
The reigns are attached to the
handlebars. When I want to go left, I
jerk the handlebars left. The only
tricky thing is, when I want to turn,
I need to calculate the handlebar turn
earlier then my actual turn. I need to
always keep in mind that my lead dog
is approximately seven meters from the
handlebars, takes a lot of practice,
concentration and a little skill.

                    RODGER
I bet it does.

                    VERA
     (proudly)
I told you: Kail's a professional.

                    KAIL
          Vera loves to watch me race.

Sky walks through the back door.

                    VERA
          You're back already? You're quick!

                    SKY
          Aunty, I didn't have to go to the
          forest. I bumped into Lotus, and she
          gave me some pig meat and vegetables
          for dinner. Do you still want me to
          get some eggs?

                    VERA
          No that's ok, we have enough food for
          now. Lotus is a nice woman.

                    SKY
          She's a very happy woman, she gave me
          hugs and kisses all over my face. I
          think one kiss would have been just
          fine.

                    GRACE
          Sky, bring everything in the kitchen,
          I'll start prepping.

                    HELGA
          You better hurry or Grace is gonna
          start kissing you all over your face.

Sky gives Helga a dirty look.

                    SKY
          I can help prepare the food.

                    RODGER
          I'll give a hand, as well.

                    KAIL
          Sky, while dinner's being cooked,
          let's go on a quick dog bike ride
          around town.

                    SKY
          Oh yeah! Awesome! I'm ready, let's go.

                    GRACE
               (jokingly)
          I thought you were gonna help with
          dinner?

                    SKY
          Next time, Grace. We have man things
          to do.
                    (then, to Kail)
          Can we ride by the burial grounds?
          I want to have one last look at my
          parents' new home.

Everyone turns and looks at Sky.

                    KAIL
                    (hesitating)
          Sure, if that's what you want
          buddy.. your wish is my dogs'
          command.

Sky gives two thumbs up.

                    SKY
          I want to stop by the meadow first,
          pick some flowers.

                    KAIL
          Anything you want, today is the first
          day of your new life. Today is your
          day.

                    SKY
          Thanks Kail, you're like a big brother
          to me. Now I have two big brothers,
          you and Brother Rodger.

Sky gives two thumbs up, and everyone starts laughing.

                    GRACE
          Don't be long lover boy, dinner will
          be ready shortly.

Sky gives the evil eye, everyone still laughing.

                                        FADE OUT.

INT. LIVING ROOM - THE NEXT DAY

Helga, Vera, Grace, and Rodger eat. Sky comes in the back door,
and Kail comes knocks on the front door, whistling

                    KAIL
          Vera.

                    HELGA
          I guess Kail's back.

Vera jumps to the door, excited.

> VERA
> I'll get it.

Vera fixes her hair, then opens door.

> VERA
> Hey Kail, come in, do you need a
> hand with your cutter machine?

> KAIL
> No I got it, just clear the table,
> please.

Helga, Grace, and Rodger scurry to clear the table.

> HELGA
> Good timing, we just finished eating.

> RODGER
> That's a cool machine, how does it
> work?

> KAIL
> Pretty simple, pretty basic. I pour
> water in the back reservoir and I pump
> these two pedals, one pedal is for the
> movement of the blade, the other pedal
> is to keep the water moving over the
> metal. Very effective tool.

Helga fills a pitcher of water.

> RODGER
> Wow, so basic, and yet so effective.

> KAIL
> That it is.

> HELGA
> Here's your pitcher of water, Kail.

> KAIL
> Thanks Helga. So, where's the precious
> metal?

Grace goes into the rucksack, pulls out bars, hands them to
Rodger.

> RODGER
> So, Kail. Like we said yesterday, we
> would like each bar cut into quarters.
>   (MORE)

                    RODGER (CONT'D)
We can give each one of your mushers a
quarter bar and a half bar for you to
help us get out of town. Is that ok?

                    KAIL
That's great, very generous of you
two. I'll cut my bar last incase the
cutter craps out on us.

                    GRACE
That's perfect. Water's still hot,
should I make some tea for you while
you're working?

                    KAIL
That would be great.

                    VERA
          (excitedly)
I'll get it, I'll get it. Would you
like some honey in your tea Kail?

                    KAIL
That would be great, extra sweet
please.

                    VERA
          (flirty)
I will make it as sweet as you want
it, honey.

Helga rolls her eyes. Sky comes through the back door.

                    SKY
Hey Kail, what are you doing?

                    RODGER
Shh, he's concentrating, he's cutting
gold for us.

                    SKY
What for?

                    RODGER
So we have smaller pieces to sell and
bargain with.

                    SKY
Sell, who's gonna buy rocks?

                    RODGER
What do you mean? That's gold man!
That's twenty four karat gold.

                    SKY
          How can rocks be worth money?

                    RODGER
          That's not rock, that's metal. That's
          gold.

                    SKY
          There's plenty of yellow rocks in the
          hidden river. Much bigger than those.

                    VERA
          Here's your tea, Kail, just the way
          you like it.. HOT and SWEET.

Helga, in the background, rolls her eyes.

                    KAIL
          Thank you Vera.

                    HELGA
          Sky, you've seen this color before in
          the river? Where is the river located?
          Up by Great Pines?

                    SKY
          I can't tell you, my parents and I
          said we would take this secret place
          to our graves and they did.

                    HELGA
          Ok, we'll talk about it another time.

                    KAIL
          I would like to know as well, Sky.

                    SKY
          Sorry, it's a secret. Besides my
          parents said they were sacred rocks
          and should never be removed from the
          hidden river.

                    RODGER
             (pointing to the bars on
              the table)
          If you know where there's more of
          this, you will be a rich man. Do
          you know what those bars of metal
          are worth?

                    SKY
They have no worth! Food has worth!
Meat is worth more than fish, fish is
worth more than eggs, eggs are worth
more than vegetables, vegetables are
worth more than berries, berries are
worth more than nuts, nuts are worth
more than seeds.

                    RODGER
That's true but-

                    SKY
          (interrupting)
What's worth more than food is
water and the most precious worth
is people.

                    GRACE
You have an awesome way of looking at
life, Sky. What do you want to be when
you grow up?

                    SKY
I want to make people smile and feel
good about life. I also want to eat
really nice food that I grow and make
myself.

Sky gives two thumbs up.

                    GRACE
I think you're in the right direction.
Keep doing what you're doing,
everything will work out.

                    SKY
I'm a good cook, right Aunty?

                    VERA
You sure are Sky. One time, he brought
me over a mixed berry pie that was
truly out of this world.

                    SKY
          (proudly)
I picked the berries myself, except
the neighbor, Lotus, gave me some
blueberries to add in. I had so
much fruit, I made an extra pie for
Lotus.

                    GRACE
          I would love to try your cooking one
          day, Sky!

Sky gives two thumbs up.

                    SKY
          I'll cook for you anytime.

Kail stands up.

                    KAIL
          Finally, done! Vera where can I
          dump this water? Do you have an old
          shirt by chance? I want to sift the
          water for gold flakes.

                    SKY
          Don't use the one on her dresser, it
          has holes in it.

Everyone laughs.

                                        FADE TO BLACK.

INT. LIVING ROOM - LATER

Helga, Vera, Grace, Rodger, and Kail talk. Sky cleans the house,
sweeping the living room.

                    SKY
          Aunty, I just saw a mouse!

                    VERA
          Did you kill it?

                    SKY
          No, it was too quick. I'm gonna go to
          the forest and get some herbs to keep
          the mice away. I'll be back in a bit.

                    VERA
          That would be great, thanks Sky.

                    SKY
          I'll finish sweeping when I get back.

Sky leaves out the back door.

                    KAIL
              (to Helga and Vera)
     So, I was thinking, the quickest
     way to get these two out of town
     would naturally be the dog bikes.
     Since no one knows that we buried
     Sky's parents already, we can wrap
     up dummies to look like dead bodies
     and put them on back of the sleds-

                    HELGA
              (interrupting)
     What happens if the villagers want
     to follow the procession to the
     burial site?

                    KAIL
     I'm way ahead of you. We have two
     mushers as the decoy, each one
     carrying the dummy bodies. If caught
     and questioned, they can honestly say
     they did the burial already, that,
     this is just a ceremonial gesture out
     of respect.

                    VERA
     Then, where are the fugitives?

                    KAIL
     They are both on my sled with flowers
     piled on top of them. The mushers go
     straight to the burial site, while I
     keep going with Sky on the back
     heading out of town.

                    HELGA
     Won't people wonder where you two are
     going?

                    KAIL
     You can say, Sky wanted to pick
     special flowers for the ceremony and
     we're heading to the meadow first.

                    VERA
     What do we say when you don't come
     back right away?

                    KAIL
     Just say Sky was upset and he probably
     got cold feet. The villagers will
     expect that from a little boy.

                    HELGA
You want Vera and I to travel behind
the mushers as decoys?

                    KAIL
Exactly, but, we must make sure we
don't tell Sky until last minute. I
was thinking we should do this
tomorrow morning to catch everyone off
guard.

                    HELGA
This sounds like the best plan we
have.

                    RODGER
If we're laying down on the sled,
isn't that gonna be a crazy bumpy ride
for the both of us?

                    KAIL
Yes, but it's only for five
kilometers. I'll put cushions on the
sled to make it an easier ride.

                    GRACE
What do you tell Sky? He's gonna
wonder why this is happening!

                    KAIL
In Sky's eyes, we did the ceremony
yesterday. We tell him it's an extra
bonus for his parents, and when we're
finally out of the village limits I'll
tell him the truth. He'll be cool with
it. On the way back, I'll let him
drive the dog bike in the open meadow,
that should keep him distracted.

                    HELGA
This sounds like a great plan.

                    RODGER
Sounds great, count me in.

                    GRACE
Me as well.

                    VERA
Whatever you're doing, Kail, I'm in
one hundred percent.

                    KAIL
             (to Vera)
     Great, when we're done with this
     stressful event, maybe you and I
     can spend the weekend at the hot
     springs camping?

                    VERA
     I think that's a wonderful idea. Count
     me in one hundred percent.

                    HELGA
     I'll stick around and keep an eye on
     Sky. I'm thinking since you're that
     deep in the forest, why don't you keep
     going straight to my house and pick up
     the military weapon?

                    KAIL
     I have a better idea. Let me talk to
     one of the mushers. He has family in
     your village. Maybe he'll take you by
     dog bike so you don't have to walk.
     After camping, we head to your house
     for a bit and enjoy the cave pools and
     some laughs with Adrian.

                    VERA
     That's a great idea, I can ask Lotus
     to keep an eye on Sky and the house.

                    HELGA
     Now you're thinking. God knows there's
     plenty of room at my house now that
     the girls are gone.

                    KAIL
     The girls are gone? Where did they go?

                    HELGA
     Didn't Vera tell you? My sister took
     them to the border, then the
     orphanage.

                    KAIL
     Wow, that's great! At least they'll
     have a chance. I did that trip, spent
     most of my time in Japan. What a
     wonderful experience. But, as you can
     see I came back, this will always be
     home.

                    GRACE
          Your trip sounds fun.. camping and the
          hot pools.. I wish we weren't
          fugitives, we would join you.

                    RODGER
          But unfortunately we have a date with
          our adventure reality.

                    KAIL
          Maybe next time. Ok, I have to run,
          I'm gonna get moving on prepping the
          dog bikes with the mushers for
          morning.
               (then, to Rodger)
          I know, extra cushion on the sled.

                    RODGER
          We'd appreciate it.

Sky walks in from the back door.

                    VERA
          I'll talk to Lotus about Sky.

                    SKY
          I heard my name! What about Sky?

                    VERA
          Sky come with me, we're gonna talk to
          Lotus about minding you and the house.

Sky gives two thumbs up.

                                        FADE OUT.

EXT. BACKYARD - MORNING

Kail and two mushers arrive with dog bikes. Rodger and Grace
enter the backyard.

                    RODGER
               (whispering)
          Good morning Kail, I see you have
          extra cushion on the sled, we
          appreciate that. The other two
          sleds really look like they have
          bodies, you are truly an artist.

                    KAIL
          No time to talk, both of you get in
          the sled and lay down, we're gonna put
          these wreaths on top of you.

Rodger and Grace put their packs at the back of sled and get in. Kail and the musher decorate the sled with flowers. Helga, Vera, and Sky enter the backyard.

                    HELGA
          Good morning guys, sled looks great.

                    VERA
          Good morning Kail. I'm gonna take a
          flower for my hair.

Vera plucks a flower from the sled.

                    SKY
          Thanks Kail, this is a nice thing
          you're doing for my parents. But I
          have no way to pay you. I'll have to
          get food for you next week.

                    KAIL
          Sky, you don't pay me. Remember, I'm
          your big brother.

                    SKY
          Ohh, that's right. Where's big brother
          Rodger and Grace?

                    HELGA
            (quickly)
          They're gonna catch up with us
          later.

                    SKY
          Oh, ok, great.

                    KAIL
          Ok we're good to go, let's do this.
          Sky you ride on the back with me as
          the guest of honor.

Sky gives two thumbs up and climbs on the back of the bike.

                    SKY
          Awesome. Kail, can we go to the
          meadow before the burial grounds? I
          want to pick some special flowers.

Everyone stares at each other.

                    KAIL
          Sure Sky, we'll do a steady gallop,
          while the mushers do a slow walk. Ok
          folks, let's do this.

Kail takes off with Sky on the back. The mushers do a slow walk through town with Vera and Helga following by foot. Lotus comes out to join, as well as a few villagers.

                                        FADE TO:

EXT. MEADOW - LATER

Kail and Sky pull over on the dog bike, Rodger and Grace still in the sled covered with flowers.

                    KAIL
          Ok, we're here, come on out.

Rodger and Grace emerge from under the flowers.

                    RODGER
          That wasn't as bad as I thought,
          pretty smooth ride.

                    GRACE
          That's cause every time we hit a bump
          you landed on me!

Sky, confused, jumps off the bike.

                    SKY
          What were you doing back there? I
          thought we were meeting at the
          burial grounds!

Rodger grabs his rucksack.

                    RODGER
          Sorry Sky, we won't be able to make
          it. We have to start walking
          towards the border today. We'll
          light a candle at church for your
          parents.

                    GRACE
               (motherly)
          I'm gonna miss you Sky.

                    SKY
          Please, take me with you. I need to go
          as well, I won't be a burden.

                    GRACE
          Sky, we would love to, but we can't.

Sky walks away, towards the border.

                    SKY
          I'm going anyway, I'll meet you
          down the trail.

Kail, Rodger, and Grace look at each other in shock. Kail runs
after Sky and grabs him. Rodger and Grace follow.

                    KAIL
          Where are you going? They said they
          can't take you with them! We have a
          burial to go to.

                    SKY
               (shouting)
          Leave me alone, let me go! I'm
          going to the orphanage.

                    KAIL
          Sky you're to young for the orphanage.
          It's not like it used to be, you can't
          go yet.

Sky struggles to free himself from Kail's grip.

                    SKY
          Leave me alone, let me go right now!
          If you don't let me go, I'll tell your
          dogs to go home and they'll drag your
          bike the whole way, destroying it. Now
          let me go.

Kail lets go of Sky.

                    KAIL
          I know my dogs will listen to you,
          they love you. That's a good reason
          to stay!
               (pause)
          I'll tell you what. If you don't
          go, I'll give you your very own dog
          bike team.

                    SKY
          Thanks for the offer, Kail, but I
          can't stay around anymore. I'm
          thinking, I wanna meet up with Prim
          and Zane at the orphanage and move on
          with life.

                    KAIL
          I can't let you go.

                    SKY
It's ok for them to go to the
orphanage, but not me?

                    KAIL
Helga's daughters are much older, they
have been groomed for their upcoming
experience at the orphanage. You
haven't. The orphanage isn't the same
anymore, you can't just walk in
without an understanding. Besides, you
don't even have money.

                    SKY
I don't need money, I can live off the
land.

                    KAIL
I got an idea, we can go to the secret
river you mentioned, gather yellow
stones, and when you get older we'll
prepare you for the orphanage and
you'll have money. I'll take you to
the border personally.

                    SKY
Now I'm definitely not going back.
That's a sacred river, those are
sacred stones, that's a blessed place.
We would bathe there and the animals
would come to the river edge and say
hello. It's magical, you can't just go
there and ruin it.

                    KAIL
I'm sorry Sky, I really can't let you
go.

                    SKY
        (almost crying)
I have to go! I have no life in
Border Village anymore. I need to
find something new, different. I
need your help, not your
disapproval. I lost everything. My
parents, my home, my belongings..
and I took it like a young man.
Please leave me alone, let me be,
let me go.

                    KAIL
Is this what you want to choose? Jump
the barder and go to the orphanage?
            (MORE)

                         KAIL (CONT'D)
          This is your decision? Then, I'm gonna
          miss you!

                         SKY
          I'll be back. I just want to get an
          education and I need to see the world
          after my schooling. I want to see
          Thailand, Vietnam, Indonesia, New
          York. I want to talk to the elephants,
          pet the orangutans, hug a skunk.

Everyone looks shocked.

                         SKY (CONT'D)
          Ok, maybe not hug a skunk. I want
          to meet all my animal friends I've
          seen in the magazines-

                         RODGER
              (interrupting)
          Kail, we'll take him to the border
          and the orphanage. We'll talk to
          him about life on the way. We have
          some gold to give him for a better
          life. We'll make sure he's set up
          before we part ways.

Sky gives two thumbs up and hugs Rodger.

                         SKY
          Thank you, Brother Rodger.

Rodger pulls out the survival satchel and gives it to Sky.

                         RODGER
          This is a survival kit given to us
          by the captain of the airplane. I
          want you to have it. When we get to
          the orphanage, we'll give you some
          clothes and a rucksack so you look
          prepared for the staff at the
          orphanage.

Kail gets on his bike.

                         KAIL
          Well if this is everyone's decision,
          I'm gonna take all of you closer to
          the border to quicken your journey.

Grace walks up to Kail.

                         GRACE
          Thank you Kail for everything. And
          thanks for understanding Sky's plea.

Kail violently grabs Grace, bends her over his motorcycle and
pulls down the back of her pants, exposing her bum with a crown
shaped birthmark.

                         GRACE (CONT'D)
               (screaming)
          What are you doing? Stop! Stop!

                         RODGER
               (angrily)
          What are you doing? That's my wife!
          Stop!

Kail sees the royal birthmark and pulls up her pants, stands
her up, gets off his bike and bows.

                         KAIL
          If you will forgive me your Royal
          Princess, I never meant to do you
          harm.

Kail still stands in bow position.

                         RODGER
               (to Grace)
          What the fuck is going on here?
          What's this all about?

Kail stands up.

                         KAIL
          I knew you were the great princess
          when I first met you the other day.
          I alway had a fond love and great
          respect as a child. I'm sorry for
          pulling down your pants and
          disrespecting you. I thought if I
          asked, you would say no and I'd
          never know for sure. At least now I
          have closure.

                         RODGER
          Will somebody please tell me what the
          fuck is going on!?

                         SKY
          I want to know as well. I never saw
          such skinny underwear before.. it
          looked like rope.

                    KAIL
               (to Rodger)
     When I was a young boy, I ran away
     from Border Village to seek a
     better life. I crossed the border
     by myself and went straight to the
     orphanage. There, I was treated
     better then the other children
     because I was half-Japanese.

                    GRACE
     You were in the orphanage?

                    KAIL
     Yes, and since I was almost a
     privileged child, I would get better
     treatment than the other children. One
     day, the Emperor came to the orphanage
     with his young daughter. He felt he
     wanted to humble her by letting her
     play with the less fortunate children.

                    GRACE
     Did I play with you?

                    KAIL
     You did. On many occasions. You even
     requested to your father to bring you
     back to the orphanage year after year
     because we were best friends. I was
     quite a few years older then you, but
     still a young boy. I remember it like
     it was yesterday, I think we fell in
     love.

                    GRACE
     I remember this.

                    KAIL
     Every time we went swimming your
     bathing suit would ride up your bum
     and expose your crown birthmark.
     That's how I knew you were Royalty at
     a young age.

                    GRACE
     Are you Bream?

                    KAIL
     The one and only. Bream, at your
     service. I really didn't like that
     name so I changed it back to my birth
     name.

                         GRACE
               I used to have the biggest crush on
               you.

Grace starts crying, they both hug in a long embrace.

                         KAIL
               When I left the orphanage, I was
               depressed for two years.

                         GRACE
               Me too. I always loved you, I missed
               you.

Grace starts kissing Kail passionately. Rodger, still wearing
his rucksack, faints and hits his head on a rock.

                         SKY
               Help, Rodger's bleeding.

Kail and Grace run over to Rodger.

                         GRACE
               Oh my god, Rodger are you ok?

Kail takes off his shirt and puts it on Rodger's head.

                         KAIL
               Rodger, are you ok? Get up, let me
               see.

Grace shakes Rodger.

                         GRACE
               Rodger, are you ok? Wake up, are
               you ok?

                                        DISSOLVE TO:

INT. HOSPITAL ROOM - MORNING

Rodger lays in a hospital bed. SKYLAR, the head nurse, wipes his
forehead with a wet towel. He shakes him.

                         SKYLAR
               Rodger, are you ok? Talk to me
               Rodger, are you ok? Wake up.

Rodger wakes up and grunts.

                         RODGER
               Yeah.

                    SKYLAR
          Wow, you're finally awake. How do you
          feel? You must have had some crazy
          dreams. You were constantly flailing,
          talking, and yelling in your sleep.

Rodger can barely open his eyes.

                    RODGER
               (groggily)
          Where am I? What happened?

Skylar preps a thermometer.

                    SKYLAR
          You are in the Bang Khong Hospital
          in North Thailand. You have been in
          and out of consciousness for three
          weeks! Where did you think you
          were?

                    RODGER
          I'm not sure. My head is throbbing
          Doc, three weeks?

                    SKYLAR
          I'm not a Doctor, I'm a nurse. I bet
          your head is throbbing, you fell down
          two flights of stairs at the airport.
          Let me give you some more medicine
          drip.

                    RODGER
          At the airport? Three weeks?

                    SKYLAR
          Mr. Ridgeway, you almost left us
          twice. I was very worried about you.
          We were getting no brain response at
          all the first week, and then your
          brain started swelling.

Rodger tries to sit up, in aches and pains.

                    RODGER
          Why am I handcuffed? What's going
          on? Nurse, please, explain.

                    SKYLAR
          From what I'm told, you were at the
          airport and the police arrested you
          for smuggling. With all the
          excitement, you fainted and fell down
          two flights of stairs.
                    (MORE)

SKYLAR (CONT'D)
What were you smuggling? Heroin, meth,
cocaine, ecstasy?

                RODGER
No.
      (pause)
It was gold.

                SKYLAR
I thought so. You didn't come across
as a drug dealer. Did you know that
gold and drugs are the same penalty
here, in Thailand? It doesn't make
sense, but it is.

                RODGER
Did they catch my buddy Skipper?

                SKYLAR
I don't know the answer to that
question, I only know who is brought
to my facility.

                RODGER
Can you help me? Please, I need to get
out of here, I need to go home.
Please, help me!

                SKYLAR
I have been helping you, since you got
here.

                RODGER
      (desperately)
Yeah I know, you're a nurse and you
help people, but I truly need to
get out of here. Please, can you
help me?

                SKYLAR
Like I said, I have been helping you,
since you got here. You see, all the
doctors gave up on you after the first
few days as you were nearing the brain
dead stages. They thought you were a
lost cause. I had hope, I had faith,
you became my personal care patient.

                RODGER
I'm not brain dead. My memory is
coming back to me. I'm remembering the
airport and everything else.

                    SKYLAR
I know, that's because I've been
giving you CBD oil eight times a day,
every day, since you arrived. You see,
my plan is to get you better, well
enough to travel, slip you out in the
dark of night and over the border to
Cambodia. My goal is to help you be a
free man again.

                    RODGER
Now, I'm really confused. Why would
you have preplanned my escape without
speaking with me? You don't even know
who I am. Why would you take that
risk? I have no money or gold to pay
you! The police took everything from
me at the airport.

                    SKYLAR
I don't want gold or money, I don't
want anything.

                    RODGER
Surely you must want something. People
don't take huge risks in life for no
apparent reason.

                    SKYLAR
Let me tell you a little story. When I
was a little boy, maybe six or seven
years old, I was mushroom picking in
the mountains with my parents. We were
maybe twenty, twenty-five kilometers
from home. My mother found a large
cluster of mushrooms on the side of a
ravine, but when she went to reach for
them, the rocks gave way and she met
her untimely demise.

                    RODGER
Ohh, I'm so sorry to hear.

                    SKYLAR
Thank you. So, my father went down the
ravine to get my mother, and he
slipped and fell to his death as well,
leaving me on the mountain all alone.

                    RODGER
Ohh my god, I'm really sorry. But, how
does this equate to trying to help me.

                    SKYLAR
Please, let me finish. So, I was left
all alone on this mountain, clueless
how to get home. After about a week,
roaming around the forest, eating
mushrooms, berries, and what the
forest had to offer, a strange thing
happened. All the animals came out of
the darkness of the forest, to guide
me home.

                    RODGER
Animals came out of the forest? Guided
you home?

                    SKYLAR
Yes, it started with a fox. I chased
him to pet him, then a squirrel, then
a deer, a chipmunk, even a bear.

                    RODGER
Even a bear?

                    SKYLAR
Yes, even a bear! You see, I was
unknowingly chasing these animals to
play and distract me from my
loneliness. All the while, these
animals were leading me in the
direction to my home. It's amazing how
nature helps one another.

                    RODGER
So, that's why you want to help me?
Because animals helped you get home in
your hour of darkness?

                    SKYLAR
Almost, but, not exactly. You see,
when I finally got back to my village,
all the villagers thought we were
dead, so they stole my family's
worldly possessions. A few villagers
felt sorry for me, so they all took
turns feeding and taking care of me.

                    RODGER
So, you want to help me, for what your
village people did to you.. or for
you? I'm confused.

                    SKYLAR
Yes and no. If my memory serves me
well.
                    (MORE)

                    SKYLAR (CONT'D)
About the same time I returned to my
village, a Western man and an Asian
woman walked into my village escorted
by a neighbor. I never saw a Caucasian
person before. I was so amazed by the
look of a Western person that I
followed him around. They were trying
to illegally get across the border.

                    RODGER
I almost feel like I was part of this
story. The Western man, reminded you
of me?

                    SKYLAR
Yes, he did! He was smuggling gold as
well.

                    RODGER
Okay... Western man, gold smuggling...
sounds like a trend.

                    SKYLAR
It could be. So I befriended these two
travelers and I kept begging them to
take me with them, but they wouldn't
have it. Bringing a little kid on
their travels with no documents would
have been a world of trouble.

                    RODGER
So, what did you do?

                    SKYLAR
So, as they were leaving my village, I
followed them and I wouldn't stop. I
figured any place is better than that
poor border village. Besides, I lost
everything - my parents, my
possessions, my house, everything! So,
every kilometer we walked, I got
closer to my new traveler friends,
until we were finally walking next to
each other.

                    RODGER
Were they still angry at you?

                    SKYLAR
No, they gave up yelling at me and let
me walk beside them.

                    RODGER
How long did you walk for?

                    SKYLAR
          Not sure. Maybe four, five days. In
          the end, they were happy I tagged
          along. I was the one who kept everyone
          well fed with what nature had to
          offer.

Skylar give two thumbs up.

                    RODGER
          That's a fascinating story... but,
          why, are you helping me?

                    SKYLAR
          I'm almost finished. So, like I said
          we followed the border for days, and
          when we found our chance to cross,
          they were hit with the reality of
          illegal gold smuggling. They weren't
          sure what to do, so, I grabbed the
          pack with the gold and slid through
          the border undetected.

                    RODGER
          No one noticed you? How did you get
          through the fence?

                    SKYLAR
          I was a tiny little thing. Besides, no
          one ever bothered the children at the
          borders. Children play between the
          borders all the time.

                    RODGER
          So, you're a gold smuggler as well,
          there's the connection!

                    SKYLAR
          I did it once. I was a kid that didn't
          know better, I was desperate. You on
          the other hand, knew what you were
          doing and knew the consequences and
          you got caught. You're stupid.

                    RODGER
          Well, there is some truth to that.

                    SKYLAR
          You see, when we finally reached
          Japan, my traveling friends and I
          parted ways. The Western man was very
          generous and gave me some gold pieces
          to help me with my future.

                    RODGER
          They just left you on the streets to
          fend for yourself?

                    SKYLAR
          No, they gave me cloths, an English
          dictionary and brought me to the
          orphanage. I knew how important those
          gold pieces were, I didn't know its
          worth. I knew it was important, so I
          buried them for safe keeping.

                    RODGER
          What was the weight of your gold
          chunks?

                    SKYLAR
          It was well over a kilo.

                    RODGER
          Wow, that was a good score. Very
          generous.

                    SKYLAR
          So you see, because of this Western
          man, I was able to move to another
          country, learn another language, start
          a new life, and have enough money for
          school to become a doctor.

                    RODGER
          You said you were a nurse!

                    SKYLAR
          Yes, I am a nurse, but that changes
          next month. So, this is the reason I
          want to help change your life around.
          Because a Westerner helped me change
          my life around.

                    RODGER
          You're a good man, sir. What is your
          name?

                    SKYLAR
          Skylar, but everyone calls me Sky.

Skylar puts two thumbs up.

                    RODGER
          It's almost like we met before.
          Pleased to meet you Sky, my name is
          Rodger.

                    SKYLAR
          Yes, I know who you are. I have all
          your documents, including your
          passport.

                    RODGER
               (excitedly)
          You have my passport?

Skylar gives two thumbs up.

                    SKYLAR
          I sure do. I told you, I've been
          helping you since you got in here.

                    RODGER
          You are a great man, Sky. So take off
          these handcuffs so I can get out of
          here.

                    SKYLAR
          It's not that easy Roger. The police
          stop in to check if you're awake from
          the coma. When you finally wake up,
          they will formally charge you with the
          smuggling crime and put you in the
          system.

                    RODGER
          So, technically, I haven't been
          charged with a crime?

                    SKYLAR
          Correct. You see, when you fell down
          the stairs, you must have been on your
          way to the interrogation. When you
          didn't enter that room to speak to the
          captain, you didn't get a formal
          charge.

                    RODGER
          So why am I cuffed to the bed, if I
          wasn't formally charged?

                    SKYLAR
          Because this is Thailand. The law
          works in mysterious ways here, unlike
          Japan or China.

                    RODGER
          So now what?

                    SKYLAR
You have been in a coma for three
weeks, we need the police to think
you're still in a coma. They've been
reducing their visits by half, I think
we can get you out of here within a
few days.

                    RODGER
So, I need to pretend I'm sleeping for
the next day or three.

                    SKYLAR
Precisely, they usually make their
last visit around seven thirty at
night and return around eight in the
morning. This means we would have
almost twelve hours to get you to the
border of Cambodia, thru Cambodia, and
into Vietnam.

                    RODGER
Don't I need a visa for Cambodia, as
well as Vietnam?

                    SKYLAR
Not the way I go. I've been doing this
trade route since I was a little boy.
But, if you do get caught, you'll have
a passport and some US dollars to
continue your journey. I looked in
your wallet, you should have enough.
When you finally get to Vietnam, go to
your embassy and tell them you've been
robbed. They'll get you home.

                    RODGER
Sounds like you've done this before!

                    SKYLAR
I may have smuggled gold before, but
this is the first time I'm human
trafficking.

Skylar gives a big smile and two thumbs up.

                    RODGER
What happens when the police find me
gone? Won't that get you in trouble?

                    SKYLAR
No, not at all. I'm one of many care
providers for the hospital, we're not
their security.
                    (MORE)

                              SKYLAR (CONT'D)
They want control of their prisoners,
they need to take control. Here is a
key for your handcuffs, don't ask me
where or how I got this. What's very
important, you need to take the
handcuffs with you, off the hospital
premises before you discard them.

                              RODGER
Why is that so important?

                              SKYLAR
Because, then, no one has a reason to
investigate the hospital, having
police equipment still in the hospital
would be a very serious penalty. Here
is a metal cutting blade as well.

                              RODGER
What's that for? I have a key.

                              SKYLAR
You need to cut your bed frame to make
it look like your still wearing the
handcuffs.

                              RODGER
But, won't they be suspicious how I
obtained the cutting blade?

                              SKYLAR
That's their problem. Let them do
their own investigation. The hospital
staff will ignore any questions they
might have. Like I said, we're care
providers, not security. Now, on the
right side of the mattress there's a
slit, do you feel it?

Rodger feels around on the mattress.

                              RODGER
Yep, got it, is this where I hide
the key and the blade?

                              SKYLAR
Correct. I have to go make my rounds.
Remember, if you want this to work,
you need to keep sleeping till further
notice. Also, don't do any cutting
until after the night nurse makes her
rounds.

                    RODGER
          Rodger that, no pun intended. And I
          guess I need to keep real quiet when
          cutting.

                    SKYLAR
          Like a mouse. Keep the cut low on the
          bed frame, so it's temporarily
          undetectable. Enjoy your sleep and no
          more crazy dreams. You look like
          you're in pain laying there.

                    RODGER
          I can't thank you enough Sky, I really
          appreciate all your troubles.

Skylar gives a two thumbs up and exits.

                                        FADE TO BLACK.

What What

What what - what can I say?
You were pretty frisky
When you're running my way
You're always starting fights
And that ain't nothing new
What what - what do you want
All you ever do to me is
Talk talk talk
What what - what do you write?
You're 20,000 volts and 50 megabyte
If I loved you, you would...
Never leave me
If I knew you, you would...
Never deceive me
I just thought that you would
Kindly spit in my face
What what - what do you hold?
There's really no hold
On a fist full of gold
What what - what do you drive?
I like to drink and drive
With a chance to survive
What what - what do you smoke?
Like a cut off engine
When you pull out the choke
What what - what do you love?
I really love to love
When it's push come to shove
Baby won't you take me home
Oh no I don't wanna go
Baby won't you take me home
I don't ever want to go home

One of my many poems turned into music.

NATIONAL FOUNDATION FOR FACIAL RECONSTRUCTION
PRESENTS

BROADWAY FOR MEDICINE

ONE NIGHT ONLY!
MONDAY, MARCH 12, 2007, 7:00PM

A GALA CONCERT FEATURING THE BEST OF BROADWAY COMING TOGETHER ON ONE STAGE TO BENEFIT CHILDREN

Charles Busch

Tyne Daly

Manoel Feliciano

Malcolm Gets

Deborah Gibson

Joanna Gleason

Debbie Gravitte

Julie Halston

Mimi Hines

Judy Kuhn

Michele Lee

Andrea McArdle

Howard McGillin

Donna McKechnie

Rosie's Broadway Kids

John McDaniel

Music Direction by John McDaniel
Directed by Carl Andress

The National Foundation for Facial Reconstruction is a nonprofit organization raising money for children with facial differences. All proceeds from this event will help to transform lives.

NYCITY CENTER
CATCH THE CURTAIN

CITYTIX® 212.581.1212
NYCITYCENTER.ORG
WEST 55TH STREET (BTWN 6TH & 7TH)
TICKETS $25 - $120

Broadway performers and program subject to change

With countless theater production gigs under my belt—from Ssummer stock to dinner theater, regional theatre to off-Broadway—
I was thrilled to be working on a Broadway stage as a Production Manager for an awesome children's charity.

A Rubber Baby gig somewhere in Fort Lee, NJ.

Me and my brother Dave (Potters Field) performing and producing one of many back to back gigs together.

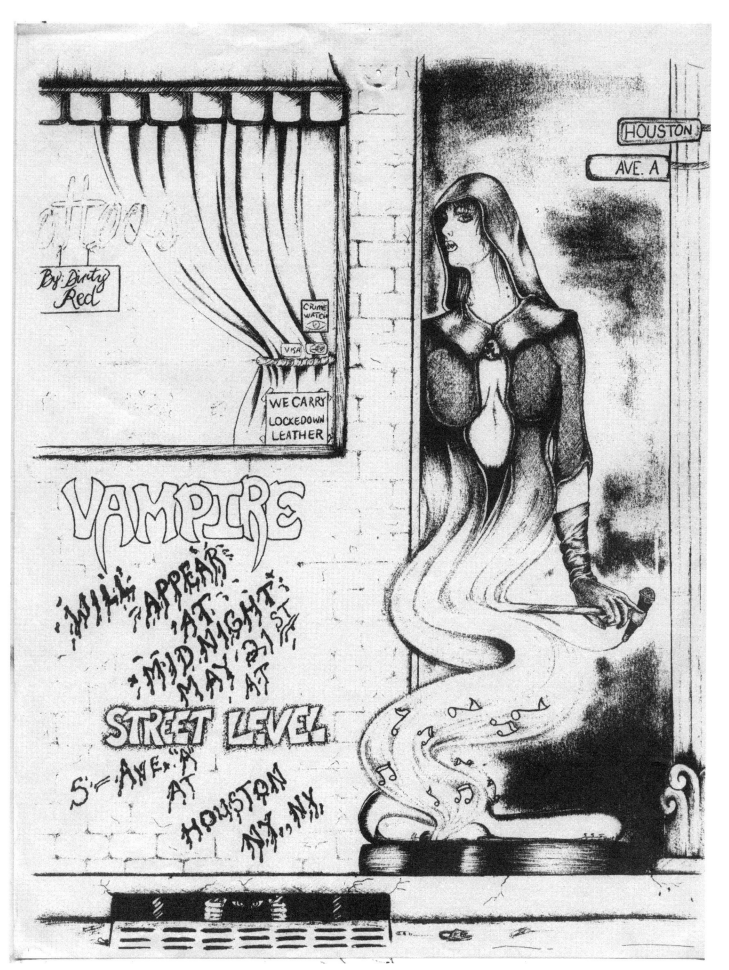

I joined a really cool Goth Band called Vampire for a spell in the 90s.

At one of the many CBGB gigs.

Made in the USA
Middletown, DE
01 September 2022

72691177R00243